The Ethics of Political
Resistance

The Ethics of Political Resistance

Althusser, Badiou, Deleuze

CHRIS HENRY

Edinburgh University Press is one of the leading university presses in the UK. We publish academic books and journals in our selected subject areas across the humanities and social sciences, combining cutting-edge scholarship with high editorial and production values to produce academic works of lasting importance. For more information visit our website: edinburghuniversitypress.com

© Chris Henry, 2019, 2020

Edinburgh University Press Ltd
The Tun – Holyrood Road, 12(2f) Jackson's Entry, Edinburgh EH8 8PJ

First published in hardback by Edinburgh University Press 2019

Typeset in 11/13 Adobe Sabon by
IDSUK (DataConnection) Ltd

A CIP record for this book is available from the British Library

ISBN 978 1 4744 4773 7 (hardback)
ISBN 978 1 4744 4774 4 (paperback)
ISBN 978 1 4744 4776 8 (webready PDF)
ISBN 978 1 4744 4775 1 (epub)

The right of Chris Henry to be identified as the author of this work has been asserted in accordance with the Copyright, Designs and Patents Act 1988, and the Copyright and Related Rights Regulations 2003 (SI No. 2498).

Contents

Introduction	1
A note on methodology	5
Notes	7
1 Badiou: Being and Failure	8
A question of dualities	8
Being resistant	11
Political ontology	15
Presuppositions	18
The truth of mathematics	24
Who resists? Just Some-One	28
The failure of being	41
Notes	49
2 Contra Axiomatics: The Persistence of Althusser, Badiou and Deleuze	64
An Althusserian conjuncture	64
Which Althusser?	68
Relative autonomy within unity	74
Philosophical dualisms	76
A very full void	81
Time and persistence	83
The subject as practice	91
Non-dogmatic philosophy?	102
Notes	110
3 A Time for Practice	123
Speculative or problematic?	123
Meillassoux's problem with Hume	127
The way the world really works	130

The hope of speculative resistance	134
Ideas and the social formation	141
Time and the syntheses of Ideas	146
An ontology proper to structuralism	158
Philosophy and idealism	160
Notes	162
4 Genius and Ethology	175
Deleuze, morality and ethics	175
Ethical mediation	183
The necessity of ethics	189
Genius and the art of life	192
The repetition of genius	196
Mediated genius	199
Notes	202
Conclusion: The Art of Practical Resistance	210
Note	213
Bibliography	214
Index	232

These three dimensions – knowledge, power and self – are irreducible, yet constantly imply one another. They are three 'ontologies'. Why does Foucault add that they are historical? Because they do not set universal conditions . . . they do vary with history. What in fact they present is the way in which the problem appears in a particular historical formation: what can I know or see and articulate in such and such a condition for light and language? What can I do, what power can I claim and what resistances may I counter? What can I be, with what folds can I surround myself or how can I produce myself as a subject? On these three questions, the I does not designate a universal but a set of particular positions occupied within a One speaks-One sees, One confronts, One lives. No single solution can be transposed from one age to another, but we can penetrate or encroach on certain problematic fields, which means that the 'givens' of an old problem are reactivated in another.

(Deleuze 1988: 114–15)

Introduction

What and how should individuals resist in political situations? Both the liberal and republican traditions of political theory, as expressed in contemporary literature by influential names such as Dahl (1973, 1989), Pateman (1970) and Warren (2007), maintain that representative democracy channels citizens' voices into political institutions which exercise legitimate authority. As such, legitimate political resistance is targeted towards the state, and must be pre-authorised by the institutions that are often being resisted: a monstrous grandchild of Locke's theory of toleration, where fidelity to the state is the pre-condition for resistance to it (Locke [1690] 1988). Rejecting this 'juridical model of sovereignty', Foucault (2003) reversed Clausewitz's dictum to claim that 'politics is the continuation of war by other means', and demonstrates both the superficiality of political elites' claims to legitimacy and the contingency of their authority. If Foucault is correct, it is clear that any attempts to prefigure the target and mode of resistance must be examined for the pre-conditions that accompany them.

These predominant schools of political theory are accompanied by a mode of analysis in Anglo/American political studies: comparative analysis. According to this analysis, individual actions are prefigured by the type of actor one happens to be within given situations; an empirical 'grid' is placed over a situation that classifies the situation as a set of dominant political actors, and analysis then attempts to predict the actions they may undertake (Althusser and Balibar 1970: 18). In assuming the stability of political institutions, as codified by the liberal and republican traditions, the best approach to resistance for comparativists can only be understood having ruled out all other available options.[1] De Vaus demonstrates the commitment to naive realism in such analysis, claiming that 'it is only through making *comparisons* that our observations take on much meaning and we are able to eliminate alternative explanations' (De Vaus 2001: 40). However, whereas comparative analysis may well be able to offer up logical political choices, having subtracted all other apparent options, it is unable (and often unwilling) to take into account the politics of that logic: 'one may applaud *différance* [. . .] in the humanities, but not in the social sciences' (Gerring 2008: 7). The idea that things may not be as they seem is an importance relegated from the study of politics to areas (presumably) less consequential, and questions of political ontology in contemporary political analysis are often superseded by the discussion of methodology (see Katznelson in Lichbach and Zuckerman 1997: 81–112).

The various schools of Marxism know very well however that things are not what they seem and, worse, things might be concealed by false images of ideology. Although developed by Engels and not Marx (Engels 1893), the idea of 'false class consciousness', has provided the Marxist tradition with a useful image by which to analyse situations and prescribe the relevant course of action. Whether it is expressed by the Frankfurt School of critical theorists, humanist Marxists such as Gramsci and Benjamin or Hegelian Marxists such as Lukács, Sayers and McLellan, the dialectic between (either true or false) thought and matter provides the means by which to understand historical change and articulate practices of resistance. Marx's third thesis of Feuerbach proves foundational with regard to understanding resistance against oppressive actors and structures, arguing that the materialist doctrine must 'divide society into two parts, one of which is superior to society. The coincidence of the changing of circumstances and of human activity or self-changing can be conceived and rationally understood only as *revolutionary practice*' (Marx [1845] 1969: 13). In support of revolutionary practice, the various schools of Marxist thought keep the current of ontology flowing, relying on an ontology of the dialectic to conceptualise the structure of practices of resistance. Whether in the form of contradictory ideas in Hegel's *Science of Logic* ([1830] 1969, 1991), consciousness and objects in his *Phenomenology of Spirit* (1998) or Marx's dialectic of history (Marx [1867] 1976), the relation of two into one as the motor of change underpins much contemporary political theory and accounts of political resistance.[2] And yet, rarefying the dialectic to such importance risks dogmatic idealism, defined by Kant as the use of an idea without prior understanding of its function

(Kant [1787] 1996: B xxxv, p. 34). The idea of what is false as opposed to either true or real, and the sublimation of two into one, begs investigation into the ontological nature of dualities and whether or not practices of resistance necessitate idealism in one form or another.

In contradistinction to commitment-orientated accounts of resistance and the return of classical ontological dyads, this book develops an ontology proper to structuralism that engenders non-idealist and non-dogmatic, yet ethical, practices of resistance. Chapter 1 discusses a prominent account of a philosophy that *does* rely on both commitment and dyads for its theory of political resistance. A prominent contemporary philosopher, an interlocutor with Althusser and Deleuze, and a figure of admiration by writers such as Žižek, Hallward, Douzinas and contemporary Marxists, Badiou writes with a strong polemical style which has garnered the attention of both authors and activists. The chapter examines what is at stake in the three dyads (truth/*doxa*; intelligible/sensible; is/is not) that Badiou maintains – alongside that of being and event – in order to support his 'metapolitical' criticism of contemporary political philosophy. In developing his neo-Maoist metapolitics, Badiou follows both the Marxist tradition of dialectics and Platonic ontology by claiming that political practice can only be carried out in truth by paying fidelity to an event which ruptures the presented order of things. It will be argued that Badiou's axiomatic decision to rarefy mathematics to the height of ontology furnishes him with the grounds upon which to clearly and powerfully criticise contemporary politics and political philosophy. However, his insistence that matter must be subtracted from thought for the purposes of thinking truthful resistance prohibits him from accounting for how his idea of resistance might engage empirically with events. In formally maintaining the distinction between ideas and matter, Badiou's meta-ontology maintains an idealist commitment to mathematics which cannot be explained on its own account, and which Badiou does not explain otherwise. Unable to account for the relation that sublates its neo-Platonic dialectic, his meta-ontological project cannot therefore adequately conceptualise the practice of resistance.

As a member of Althusser's reading group on Spinoza, and an attendee of his 'Philosophy Course for Scientists', Badiou drew inspiration from Althusser's appropriation and development of Spinoza's ontology. Deleuze also drew heavily on Spinoza, both in his books *Spinoza: Practical Philosophy* (1988) and *Expressionism and Philosophy* (1992) and a lecture series on the latter's concept of affect (1980). Nevertheless, whilst all three authors share a commitment to anti-humanism in their work, Deleuze's ontology differs significantly from Badiou's in that he accounts for the differential relations between dyads, as opposed to arguing that they are ruptural (Bowden 2011: 173–7). How though can two ontologies, so apparently at odds with each other, nevertheless claim the same inspiration? Chapter 2 examines the relationship between Althusser's thought with that of Badiou and Deleuze. The chapter begins by outlining Althusser's appropriation of Epicurean atomism to inform his ontology, upon which he builds his social and political theory. When he reads Althusser's ontology however, Badiou reads it through the grid of his own ruptural meta-ontology and thus forces his strict ontological differentiation upon Althusser's work. Having first outlined Althusser's ontology, the chapter substantiates Badiou's misreading of Althusser before foregrounding the differential relations that separate Althusser's categories and situate his work more comfortably in line with that of Deleuze. Althusser's aleatory materialism, however, will be shown still to suffer from an idealism in the form of the Epicurean void, which breaks the persistence of ideas in philosophical practice and, thus, an understanding of series. In order to overcome the idealisation of the void in the work of Althusser, the chapter proceeds to suture onto Althusser's materialism Hume's idea of human nature. Whilst bearing in mind the explicit anti-humanism of Althusser's philosophy, the suture of Hume's relational conception of human nature to Althusser's historical materialism furnishes the latter with a conceptualisation of persistence and overcomes the otherwise eliminative effect of a philosophical void.

However, there is still the danger of replacing one dogma for another: the idealism of Badiou's dyads for the dogma of the relations that constitute Hume's idea of human nature. Why should there be only one particular set of relations, as Hume argues, as opposed to others? What seems to be at stake here is either an ontological or a socio-historically specific account of the relationship between ideas and matter. Extending the argumentation from Chapter 1's criticism of Badiou, Chapter 3 argues that it is necessary for philosophy to be able to explain both. This is to say that philosophy must be able to explain the ontological account of social forms, as well as the social formation's account of ontology. Comparing Chambers's reading of Althusser to Meillassoux's criticism of Hume, Chapter 3 demonstrates that Althusser's ontology, with Hume's idea of human nature, can indeed account for both, yet that it is necessary to suture onto this conceptual assemblage Deleuze's theory of time (Deleuze [1994] 2011). The chapter argues that Deleuze appropriates and modifies Bergson's theory of time to account for how ideas, time and matter are related in a synthesis that avoids the criticism of idealism. Althusser's emphasis on political practice is then read through Deleuze's synthetic conceptualisation of the individual to form the foundations of a non-dogmatic practice of resistance developed in the final chapter.

This practice is developed in Chapter 4 with an unlikely turn to John Stuart Mill's idea of genius. Distinguishing the idea of genius from both Mill's moral philosophy, as well as utilitarian thought more generally, the chapter argues that the idea of genius provides the ethical imperative that motivates practices of resistance. As opposed to conceptualising political philosophy according to the juridical model of sovereign institutions as per the liberal and republican traditions, or the formal axiomatics of Badiou's militant politics, the political philosophy of Deleuze is, following the work of Patton, described as a 'structural normativity' (2011: 117). Whilst critics of post-structural philosophy have charged it with an inability to adequately account for normative concepts (see Habermas 2015: esp. 282–4), Chapter 4 argues that structural normativity provides in fact the key to conceptualising the relationship of the individual with (political) norms that are also accounted for as part of a structure. The chapter expands upon the benefits of conceptualising this relation as such: with Deleuze's ontology accounting for the individual's structural relation within situations, the idea of genius is the non-ideal function of practice that informs resistance both to and within situations. In sum, this book argues that the principle of genius impels the individual towards cautious, yet creative, practices of resistance, with an emphasis on experimental learning to inform the best course of action. In accordance with this principle, the individual must pragmatically experiment within presented situations, tactically choosing options that supplement and liberate the individual from that which attempts to homogenise and confine them.

A note on methodology

This book avoids, on the whole, sections that exhaustively define ideas. Where exegesis and explanation is needed for clarity, primary and secondary sources have been given. Occasionally, technical ideas are explained when necessary for argument's sake. The secondary literatures on all of the authors drawn upon herein are developed enough that full discussions of their ideas can be found in much more substantial form there than can be reproduced here. As Bryant avows, this methodology is wholly in line with Deleuze's own reading of the history of ideas, and focuses on addressing philosophical problems rather than simply listing the 'tools' with which one might address them (Bryant 2008: 4–5). So, in line with Deleuze and Guattari's argument that philosophy is the 'art of forming, inventing, and fabricating concepts' (Deleuze and Guattari [1991] 1994: 2), this book has been written with the aim of fabricating the idea of a non-dogmatic and non-idealist practice of resistance.

In this light, it is understood that the reading of Badiou that comes across in Chapter 1 may appear polemic, if not harsh in its conclusions. Unfortunately, given the vigour and commitment that Badiou infuses into his political arguments, it is difficult not to make similar gestures in response. However, as stated in the chapter's discussion, there is no desire to target Badiou himself, or to undermine the brilliance of his argumentation. Although the chapter is firm in its disagreement with Badiou's political statements, all attempts have been made to disagree on theoretical grounds and to fully elucidate the important conceptual differences. As Hughes clarifies of the critical methodology in *Difference and Repetition* ([1994] 2011), a 'radical critique demonstrates the genesis of that which it has criticised' (Hughes 2009: 3), and so the theoretical presuppositions underlying Badiou's meta-ontology have been excavated in order to level the criticism contained in Chapter 1. The purpose of the discussion of Badiou in Chapter 1 is, on the one hand, to highlight problems with an important, contemporary theory of resistance and, on the other hand, to introduce the key ideas which are thematised throughout the rest of the book: resistance, ontology, thought, being, practice, ethics. These ideas run as guiding threads throughout the argument, structuring the discussion of each author's ontological commitments, towards the conclusion.

With regard to writing conventions, terms (i.e. idea/Idea) are capitalised throughout the book according to the capitalisation found within authors' works. All instances of 'z' in a word (i.e. 'standardize') have been standardised to an 's', not out of a desire for correctness, but uniformity.

Notes

1. For accounts of the comparative method in political analysis, see Heywood (2007), Jones and Gray (2010) and Pollock (2012).
2. Influential examples include Freud's *Civilisation and its Discontents* ([1930] 2015), Lacan's conceptualisation of the mirror stage (1956, [1949] 1977), Agamben's conceptualisation of biopolitics in *Homo Sacer* (1998) and Žižek's resurrection of Hegel (2012a).

Chapter 1

Badiou: Being and Failure

A question of dualities

As Laruelle puts it, 'the spontaneous usage of philosophy involves an exaltation of force, of combat and of war that stems from certain of its origins, its axioms even' (Laruelle 2013: xvii) and, from this, two things can therefore be said of philosophy. Firstly, to the extent that philosophy is *used*, philosophy and the subject who engages with it exist within a milieu of signification, problematisation and power structures, which engender its application within a situation. Secondly, that which exists on paper, or in discussion, is actualised in accordance with a significant encounter between the subject and its target: a 'war' partly constituted within philosophy itself. For the biologist to develop philosophy might be to inscribe a vitalism within the conventions of a philosophical debate in which they are situated, or, were a social theorist to feel themselves not fitting in with a dominant psycho-sexual paradigm, they may then resist this trend with a method for the critique of its constitutive social norms. If then, as Laruelle puts it, philosophy presents an embodied fight against a particular target, what has Badiou got in his sights? Constituting a principle target of his oeuvre, according to Badiou, '[o]ne of the core demands of contemporary thought is to have done with "political philosophy"' (Badiou 2005d: 10). Yet, if philosophy is constituted in part by its placement within a particular milieu, what motivates Badiou's philosophical efforts to make such a demand? Are we to believe that his philosophy is not political? When Badiou declares that 'mathematics, throughout the entirety of its historical becoming, pronounces what is expressible of being *qua* being' (Badiou 2001: 25), or that there are four – and only four – truth procedures which condition the development of the subject (Badiou [1992] 2008, 2009: 9–33, 2011: 16), it is necessary to uncover the presuppositions in Badiou's use of these statements and assess the validity of his criticism of political philosophy.

The guiding thread of this chapter will therefore be to investigate how Badiou accounts for the veracity of the theoretical presuppositions in his work – not with regard to the intricacies of his materialist dialectics – but with regard to his claim that mathematics is the language of being *qua* being, conditioning a political truth procedure that is only unveiled through an impasse of being (Badiou [1982] 2013: 22–8). As mathematics plays a central part in Badiou's ontology, some of his usage of it (in particular his exposition of Hegel's dialectical method in *Theory of the Subject* ([1982] 2013) and a brief outline of his use of set theory) will be set out in what follows. However, this chapter will not analyse Badiou's understanding of mathematics; this is to say that, given that this chapter investigates the relationships between mathematics, ontology and ethics, there will be no questioning Badiou's mathematics *per se*, where it has been applied. Furthermore, in line with Fraser's argument that a 'disproportionate amount of ink has already been spilled' over it, neither will this chapter dwell on Badiou's concept of the event (Badiou [1966] 2007: xvi).[1] What will be investigated are both the rationale conditioning Badiou's adoption of mathematics as his meta-ontology, grounding his political philosophy, and its resultant implications.[2] In doing so, this chapter will develop a symptomatic[3] reading of Badiou's work in order to, firstly, advance an understanding of what Badiou is arguing when he develops a philosophy of politics upon a metapolitics of mathematics[4] and, secondly, explain what decisions it has been based upon, without reducing his work to a philosophical autobiography. In this regard, the chapter will 'divulge [. . .] the undivulged event in the text it reads, and in the same movement relate it to *a different text*, present as a necessary absence in the first' (Althusser and Balibar 1970: 28).

Unlike other works more polemically addressed at Badiou, the purpose of this investigation is not intended as an *ad hominem* attack on Badiou's attempt to 're-educate', 'eviscerate', or, as Gironi puts it, to 'Badiolise' philosophy (see Laruelle 2013: xviii–xxi, Gironi 2014: 5). The temptation to place Badiou's decision to ground philosophy within the rigorous confines of mathematics (or, more accurately, to position philosophy as the capturing of a political truth procedure illuminated by the expression of mathematics) upon a penchant for technical obfuscation would be a grossly reductive misattribution and it would ignore the rigorous and innovative power of his work. Yet there is nevertheless a necessity to elaborate on its positioning as such, in part, due to the specific nature of the politics that, for Badiou, mathematics authorises to be thought. As Livingston argues, there is a tension in formal systems (of which the more mathematised expressions of Badiou's meta-ontology are an example) between their coherence and their totality (Livingston 2011: 15–16). In order for a system to remain internally coherent (and its properties to make sense) it must be totalised to the extent that this totalisation generalises and legitimises the system's rules according to all possible situations that might present themselves to the system. However, as Livingston argues, a system's internal coherency cannot account for its totalisation by itself;[5] a system's rules cannot legitimise themselves and, rather, the rules of a system have to be legitimised by a 'higher' power.[6] In order to avoid an infinite regress of systems legitimising themselves with another, Livingston invokes Gödel's first incompleteness theorem to argue that a formalist is obliged to settle for a system that is either internally consistent (i.e. containing meaning) or totalising, creating what he terms a 'metalogical duality' (Gödel 1931, Livingston 2008: 20, 34, 53). As will be shown, Badiou's entire meta-ontological construction amounts to nothing without the subjective intervention in a situation which co-constitutes the subject as such and authorises the coherency of Badiou's meta-political schema. Well aware of the problematic raised by Russell's paradox and the Gödel sentence (a later development along the same lines of the Russell paradox, albeit with different implications (Livingston 2008: 21–5)),[7] Badiou addresses Livingston's problematic duality by positing the subject as the totalising element in his otherwise consistent theory.[8] It is the engagement of a subject (a subject, in Badiou's terms, of 'infinite thought' (Badiou 2005c), and not an anthropomorphised human) that totalises an otherwise internally coherent mathematical system, preventing an infinite regress of sets, the rules of which must be accounted for (Trott 2011: 87). The intervention of the subject therefore, seemingly, pulls the rug from under Livingston's feet, yet: can Badiou have his cake and eat it?

It is this claim – that the subject totalises an otherwise coherent system – that will be put under investigation whilst looking at the motivation for Badiou's system. Clearly, as a key part of his mathematical, meta-ontological system, the subject's relationship to the formalist aspects of Badiou's system forms a determining part in its overall consistency as a generic (or axiomatic) system. Nevertheless, it must not be forgotten that Badiou is writing against the background of a particular conception of politics. He was a 'committed Maoist in the 1970s', currently 'retains an assertive voice in radical politics' and is 'directly involved in a number of campaigns concerning immigration, labour issues, and political justice in the broadest sense' (Hallward 2003: xxii). Indeed, Badiou made his political presuppositions clear when he wrote in 1982 that 'today's political subject [is] that of the Cultural Revolution, the Maoists' (Badiou [1982] 2013: 247). Even though his involvement in the *Organisation Politique* (which he ran with Sylvain Lazarus, amongst others, between 1983 and 2007) did not echo the same explicitly militant tones of his writing in *Theory of the Subject*, Badiou nevertheless struggles with one particular question, asking '[h]ow we are to move from the aggressively fraternal "we" of the warlike epic to the peaceful "we" of the disparate collectivity, without compromising the principle that "we" must remain *truly we*?' (Hallward 2003: 47). If Badiou's subject is political in the first instance, that is before its meta-ontological position has been fully worked out in his oeuvre, what role does it then fill as part of his meta-ontology? The answer to this question is the 'second text', 'present as a necessary absence in the first', that this chapter will suggest.

Being resistant

Alain Badiou's oeuvre provides a strong argument as to why liberal politics, representative politics and political philosophy based upon poetic sophistry are to be rejected in favour of a militant communism.[9] According to Badiou, commonplace understandings of politics primarily conceive individuals as existing within, and interacting with, an external world that conditions the subject as a 'world spectator' (Badiou 2005: 12). World spectators exist as an audience in front of a stage on which the political acts and with which they have no real interaction. A discussion of politics, i.e. 'political philosophy', is, in this case, 'nothing more than the erudite servant of capito-parliamentarism', which claims to '"found" politics, or even "the political", and to impose upon it norms that are, ultimately, moral norms: "good" power, the "good" state, "good" democracy and so on' (Badiou *et al.* 2010: 38). A politics that is instantiated by philosophy, for Badiou, 'concerns, and only concerns, *public opinion*' (Badiou 2005d: 13), that is, the mere discussion of current affairs that results from the bifurcation of individuals into two separate groups: the political and the civil. Badiou crusades, as Sacilotto puts it, against the 'new sophists' who 'propose a relativisation of Truth to the contingent historicity of cultures, thereby deflating the universality of the former in favour of the transient plurality of opinions circulating in the latter' (2013: 65) and, as a former student of Badiou, Meillassoux expands his teacher's argument to claim that politics, following the post-modern stripping of its metaphysical recourse to either theological or Enlightenment rationalist authority, now relies upon a purely nihilistic and personal belief system.[10]

Highlighting the dogmatic faith towards what is, in fact, a lack of any truthful underpinning of contemporary political thought, he argues that 'faith is pitched against faith, since what determines our fundamental choices cannot be rationally proved' (Meillassoux 2008: 46). According to both, then, the political realm is constituted by the prevailing freedom for individuals to think whatever they want to, given that there is no basis upon, or definite recourse to, truth. The two writers agree that parliamentary politics is 'sophistry in the modern sense of the word, that is to say a sophistry dedicated to the promotion of an entirely particular politics' (Badiou 2005d: 14).[11] This, particular, parliamentary politics is that which happens in the sphere of the Other, and is effected and commentated upon by the individual; it is a separate realm in which the individual is afforded no meaningful engagement, but of which the individual is encouraged to develop opinions, in the belief that this is all that has any real meaning.

Badiou's critique of what counts as meaningful political engagement in the world – and corresponding forms of political resistance – centres around liberal individualism, whereby individuals must have a say in the given parliamentary structure which then sets out what is legitimate in terms of political activity. In turn, democratic theorists and parliamentary proceedings set out the conditions within which it is acceptable to resist. Both Hobbes and Locke can be seen as keystone figures within liberal and democratic theory, discussing the key notions of natural rights and sovereignty which still underpin contemporary liberal thought today. Yet, either in the case of wilful harm of the individual by Hobbes' Leviathan,[12] or against the turn to tyranny or deficiency of Locke's republic to enforce contracts,[13] the legitimate conditions for resistance against the state are prefigured and conditioned by the political and moral arenas within which individuals are placed. In other words, the prescriptions of Hobbes and Locke both place individuals within their positions in society *and* tell them how they are to resist. According to Badiou's argument, both of these political philosophies prefigure a manner by which to understand the individual and consequently construct an illegitimate political order upon a foundation constructed from their opinions. In contrast to this dogmatic mode of institution-centred politics, Badiou argues that '"politics" is the name of what concerns, not determinant judgement, but reflexive judgement' (Badiou 2005d: 16). Politics cannot constitute a prefigurative framework for judgement because this would foreclose both the possibility for the individual to identify with other communities than that within which they are placed as well as 'the place for debating *genuinely* alternative options, which at best are subject to dispute' (Badiou 2005d: 17). It is in this way that political philosophy, for Badiou, is inherently dogmatic.[14] With respect to the individual, Badiou argues that contemporary '[p]olitics is to be found in a public judgement which states whether *this* – which is not an object, but an appearing, a taking-place – pleases or displeases me, and is exercised in the debate of such judgements' (Badiou 2005d: 16). In other words, Badiou rejects any distinction between a public realm where politics applies and a private realm in which it doesn't, as well as any philosophy that conceives of politics as the process of pluralist debate.[15] Indeed he takes his criticism yet further, strongly criticising philosophers 'such as John Rawls who are persuaded by the central importance to thought of human rights and individual liberties' (Hewlett 2010: 24). For Badiou, even fundamental protections, such as laws prohibiting murder, would constitute the illegitimate pre-structuring of politics by the state which forecloses the potential for genuine politics.

It is as a result of his analysis, Badiou argues, that '[o]ne of the core demands of contemporary thought is to have done with "political philosophy"' (Badiou 2005d: 10). If such thought is to think the possibility of genuine political change, for Badiou, it must not only provide arguments against political philosophy, it must completely ignore the possibility of the latter setting the terms of what constitutes legitimate politics. Political philosophy, being a form of thought complicit with the state, must be revoked entirely, constraining as it does the possibility of thinking the pure 'event of the multiple' – or the possibility of the subject becoming other than what is predetermined in the possibilities that are laid out for him or her by a *particular* philosophy (Badiou 2010: 7). A politics that is to enable activity which is not simply an extension of anything condoned by the state needs to escape the 'sophistry' of public debate and political philosophy (Badiou 2005d: 14–15). Indeed, although his earlier work in *Theory of the Subject* tended to emphasise the destructive nature of politics as an operation *against* the state (see Hallward 2003: 37, Badiou [1982] 2013: 146–7), in his latter work Badiou concentrates more on the creative potentiality imbued within revolutionary situations. He argues resolutely that it is impossible to form a truly revolutionary political movement from any position that is connected to forms of knowledge that are themselves connected to the state; the task instead is to negate the *placement* of the proletariat itself.[16]

To explain this position, Badiou invokes Hegelian dialectical movement in order to show how a proletariat fighting against the bourgeoisie will never end up doing anything but repeating the same structural formation it sets out with: 'it is the bourgeoise world, imperialist society, of which the proletariat, let this be noted, *is a notorious element*, as the principal productive force and as the antagonistic political pole' ([1982] 2013: 7, emphasis added). In other words, if the proletariat allows itself to be described, or 'placed', by the bourgeoisie as a proletariat, it can never escape its relationship with the bourgeoisie – even in a negative form. The 'placing' of the proletariat in its position within the bourgeois world – i.e. in a class relation to the bourgeoisie – is an operation of the bourgeoisie itself, and not an essential part of the relationship between the two classes. An analysis that takes as its base '[t]he famous contradiction of bourgeoisie/proletariat is a limited, structural scheme that loses track of the torsion of the Whole of which the proletariat *qua* subject traces the force' (Badiou [1982] 2013: 7). In other words, there is an ontological nuance that is ignored when essentialising the identity of the two groups in a pluralist (i.e. comparative, agonistic or liberal) conceptualisation of politics, namely that of their placing; the bourgeoisie quite literally puts the proletariat in their place. Revolutionary politics is, for Badiou, not the eternal struggle of the proletariat over the bourgeoisie, because this would imply that the proletariat accepts its place *vis-à-vis* their bourgeois masters. Instead, 'the project of the proletariat, its internal being, is not to contradict the bourgeoisie, or to cut its feet from under it. [Its] project is communism, and nothing else' (Badiou [1982] 2013: 7). The objective of proletarian politics is, as a result, 'the abolition of any place in which something like a proletariat can be installed. The political project of the proletariat is the disappearance of the space of the placement of classes and an ignorance of the prefigurative structure that forms the legitimate sphere of the political for the bourgeoisie' ([1982] 2013: 7). It is 'the loss, for this historical something, of every index of class', where 'something' is the unnameable proletariat removed from its placement ([1982] 2013: 7). However, if an understanding based upon philosophical sophistry and a reduction of what constitutes politics to a Schmittian notion of 'the political' is the problem for Badiou's idea of politics, then how does he avoid a similar recourse in his argument?[17] His answer lies in foregrounding an understanding of politics within an ontological schema, after which politics manifests as a series of truth claims based upon this ontology. For Badiou, '[p]hilosophy is the general theory of being and the event as tied together by truth' (Badiou 2005b: 26), and it is this claim to truth that legitimates the faithful militant in their actions. This *meta*-ontological position (i.e. that ontology can be formally presented to condition a philosophical prescription) will be developed, before showing how this affords Badiou the ability to claim that politics is routed in the truth of the void of non-being.

Political ontology

Badiou bases his ontological position in *Theory of the Subject*, his first major work in the realm of philosophy, upon the Parmenidean duality of being and nothing (Badiou 2011: 23, Laruelle 2013: 70). In the poem *On Nature*, Parmenides argues that there are two states, that of 'being' and 'not being', stating that, '[i]t needs must be that what can be spoken and thought is; for it is possible for it to be, and it is not possible for what is nothing to be' (Parmenides 1920: §6). Using the declarative 'It' – as opposed to a named subject or 'the *something*' – to signify the object of being, Parmenides' strict duality of being and non-being involves a non-signifying unity of being ('it is') which is contrasted against that of which nothing possible is sayable ('it is not').[18] Because, for Parmenides, it is only possible to talk of what is, rather than what is not, we must presume that there is being to express: Parmenides' monist ontology of being is therefore expressed in a language which 'teaches us about what *must* be said concerning what *is*, not about what is *permissible* to say concerning what we think there is' (Badiou 2010c: 16, original emphasis). For Badiou, this is mathematics in its particular formation in ZFC set theory and is what he means by a language of 'being *qua* being'. Because there can be nothing outside that which 'is' to define what is included in the subject and object of being, in the terms used by Livingston, the whole of Badiou's meta-ontology is non-totalisable and non-representative because epistemological concerns are immanently wrapped up in the initial ontological and axiomatic dual postulate of being and non-being. In other words, being is not representable by anything that might be in excess of it and is not the result of an *a priori* state of being, *qua* Heidegger's idea of *es gibt* (Badiou 2011: 9–10, 123–9). For Badiou, it is mathematics that thinks being (and its negating inconsistent multiplicity of non-being) and is that which must be harnessed. As Sacilotto puts it, '[a]gainst the primacy and transparency of experience avowed in Aristotle's "intuitive induction" (*epagoge*), modern empiricisms, as well as all forms of vitalism and phenomenology, Badiou avows the Platonic separation of being from appearance, and identifies mathematics as the medium that accesses being *intrinsically* rather than *representationally* or *hermeneutically*' (2013: 64, original emphasis). Yet how can Badiou leverage mathematics as a language that does not fall foul of the same epistemological concerns as natural language does and, therefore, the same politics of truth? In attempting to construct the idea of a truthful political procedure according to what Badiou calls the 'rational ontology' of numbers (Badiou 2004: 71), how can he prescribe the status of truth to an ontology without also having to validate precisely the truth of this prescription?[19] Badiou's answer to this question would seem to determine whether or not the political prescriptions of his oeuvre contain the kernel of truth – in its procedural form – that he wishes them to, or whether they remain tainted by the *doxa* he recoils from. Badiou's answer to this question will be developed following a necessary detour to show how he employs the two Platonic dyads of truth/*doxa* and reality/appearance in his own schema. This is important for Badiou and the ability for his idea of the subject to access the true reality of a situation, yet it is also where he faces a problem when conjoining mathematics to his understanding of being in the world.

In his 1981 lectures at the Catholic University of Louvain, Foucault stated that, 'if critical philosophy is the philosophy that starts not from wonderment that there is being, but from the surprise that there is truth, then we can clearly see that there are two forms of critical philosophy. On the one hand, there is that which asks under what conditions – formal or transcendental – there can be true statements. And on the other, there is that which investigates the forms of veridiction, the different forms of truth-telling' (Foucault 2014: 20). Badiou's conception of truth takes the first form, and then comes down on the side of formalism. For Badiou, transcendental truth conditions would rely on the counting operation for their legitimacy, an operation which truth in fact negates.[20] Indeed, Badiou's answer to the problematic of truth's justification is to claim that truth is revealed, not as a process of verification or veridiction, but as a subtraction from what is commonly presented as sensible.

Whilst, for both Parmenides and Badiou, the only thing that can be said to exist is that which is presented (by itself) as being, Badiou defines this as only the 'state' of being which dominates and confines the infinite potential of being different. It is the fact that there is a dominant discourse – that which is affixed in a position of authority within parliamentary government and which defines all that is sayable about life – that is the political problem with contemporary thought for Badiou. In contrast to Parmenides, for whom that which 'is not' is entirely unimportant and merits no further discussion, that which 'is not' is, for Badiou, as important as that which can be said to be, because it (in-)consists the ground for the possibility of becoming different than what is stipulated by the state.[21] Nothingness does not consist in any knowable way, yet its existence remains sayable in its non-consistence purely through its formal opposition to consistent being. As Barker puts it, 'the event cannot be, its non-being is unthinkable'; '[b]etween the void and its mark, ∅, there is nothing, not even the void. But this "nothing" is still part of the void' (2002: 67–8). It remains, as Parmenides states, 'unthinkable and nameless (for it is no true way)' (1920: §8). Badiou thereby places ontology in the seemingly paradoxical position whereby it must present being on 'the other path [which] is real and true' (Parmenides 1920: §8), present it through a mathematical rupture of the presented, yet also point it towards the being of nothingness.

What sense is to be made of the being of nothingness and, if it 'is not', how can anything be said of it at all? For Badiou, the other path of 'real truth' can only be what Badiou calls the 'language of being *qua* being' because, taking his influence again from Parmenides, 'it is the same to think and to be' (Parmenides 1920: §5, Badiou 2010c: 49, Sacilotto 2013: 64). It is this call to thought's immanent existence with being that Badiou uses to ground his claim that we can think being as a form of revealing the truth of it. In other words (and in a strong connection to Spinozist Pantheism),[22] being speaks to us through its own language which is intelligible to us because we are also a part of being.²³ Badiou states that 'the determination of the One (this multiple, such that it can unequivocally receive a proper name) is strictly immanent, because a set is identified by its elements, i.e. by the sets that belong to it. Such is the foundational character of the sign of belonging, ∈, which is the veritable index of being *qua* being' (Badiou 2014: 55). It is therefore the language of being *qua* being that, because it expresses the being of itself (and therefore illuminates the site of the void in which being is not) and does not represent being in the mind of the subject, provides Badiou with the ability to make claims about both what is, but also what is not (which still has an unnameable name in its non-being).²⁴

Presuppositions

In order to ground a philosophy of politics (which, in Badiou's language, would certainly not be a political philosophy), on a soil cleansed of *doxa*,²⁵ Badiou reverses the lexical priority of philosophy and politics and argues that politics forms the condition of philosophical thought – not the other way round. Badiou's topology, therefore, is one whereby ontology provides the *logos* of philosophy, grounding thought on the basis of the truth of what being says about itself. Being, expressing itself through a language that tells of its own void, opens a ruptural door for a political subject to realise the possibility of it becoming other than what has been specified by a dominant order. As a modification of the example Badiou himself uses: a family might fill out a census to the best of their ability, tracing the family line back as far as they know. However, a knock at the door might reveal an adopted family member that, by blood, could be included within the family set, but had not been presented as such before. This 'evental site' would highlight an excess of being (in this case, the existence of a non-counted family member) through the inability of the state's census to capture the set of the family. In turn, this allows a new understanding of the family, in lieu of a fidelity to the initial event (Badiou 2011: 174). Badiou's system is therefore aptly capable of dissecting a presented situation, highlighting the errancy of the constricting and coercive dominant state (the 'count-as-one' in Badiou's terms) in certain events that happen to highlight the state's presentation of the situation. It is for this reason, given an event (whereby 'true' being expresses itself alongside a rupture of the political order – which is itself made sensible by the rupture), that Badiou turns to mathematics in place of traditional political philosophy, or 'bourgeois epistemology' (Sacilotto 2013: 83).[26]

How does Badiou show that the counting operation reveals itself through an event? To clarify, Badiou's concept of the event is a subtraction from ontological determination, or the revelation of the possibility for infinite thought brought about, not as a miracle, but as extracted from a particular situation (Badiou 2004: 98). It is this process of revelation that highlights the errancy of the void and reveals the operation of the count-as-one.[27] As Badiou informs the reader in the 'dictionary' at the end of *Being and Event*, '[g]iven the non-being of the One, any one-effect is the result of an operation, the count-as-one. Every situation (+) is structured by such a count' (Badiou 2011: 504). In other words, a census constitutes a 'one-effect', that is something which takes the form of a totalising gesture or a claim to hegemonic classification, but does not in fact legitimately totalise it because '[t]he one [. . .] is not' (Badiou 2011: 90, original emphasis). As Heidegger puts it, highlighting the illegitimacy of an operation of understanding, 'it is not knowable because it simply cannot become a possible object of knowing, i.e., the possession of a knowledge of beings. It can never become such because it is a Nothing' (1997: 86). There is thus the potential for viewing the 'excess' of the state over the situation albeit, due to the fact that Being is unknowable in itself, this is an indeterminate excess which is only borne out by the violence in the event's rupture with what is presented.[28] It is this rupture, sensible yet not measurable by the subject, that constitutes the eventual site and in which the event can be located. In contrast to Badiou, Lacan, who became increasingly influential for Badiou as the editor of the journal *Cahiers pour l'Analyse* (Hallward 2003: x), consistently argued that there is in fact 'such a thing as (the) One' (Lacan [1973] 1999: 5).[29] This 'One' was developed from Saussure's linguistics, itself influenced by 'Lévi-Strauss and Benveniste', who, following Saussure, 'insist upon a dimension of total structure that is present in language as such and prior to any individual action or occurrence' (Livingston 2011: 73). This linguistic structure of signifiers (which signifies the coherence of being, or 'that which is signified') led Lacan to argue that the 'Freudian unconscious is "structured like a language" and thus can be read and interpreted in the terms provided by Saussure's structuralist picture and its subsequent refinements' (Livingston 2011: 73). Lacanian psychoanalysis was therefore constituted as the project of uncovering the errancy and excess of the subject's being in the world through the unfolding of formal signifiers as the latent presentation of being within the subject itself. Indeed, Lacanian desire is only meaningful when it is placed within the structure of the signifying chain that constitutes the totality of the subject's understanding of the signified world, despite the fact that '[t]he subject is nothing other than what slides in a chain of signifiers, whether he knows which signifier he is the effect of or not' (Lacan [1973] 1999: 29). Badiou modifies the Lacanian statement that, '[t]he real can only be inscribed on the basis of an impasse of formalisation' (Lacan [1973] 1999: 73), arguing that '[t]he real is the impasse of formalisation; formalisation is the place of the forced pass of the real' (Badiou [1982] 2013: 22). In declaring this, Badiou reverses Lacan's reliance on formalism to present the constituted subject 'being towards death' in favour of the subject emerging from a rupture with what is presented formally.[30]

However, there is another component to Badiou's ontological schema – a *meta*-ontology – that imbues his system with the necessary consistency for him to ground a revolutionary political standpoint based on truth. This meta-ontology takes the form of a decision by an individual who completes the ontological schema, as well as the justification for his use of mathematics. Because, for Badiou, non-being, or in his terminology 'inconsistent multiplicity', is not actually presented as such – since all that can be said of being in its sensibility is done under the law of the count – inconsistency, as pure multiplicity, is solely the presupposition that, prior to the count of a state, the one is not (Badiou 2011: 52). In other words, inconsistent multiplicity (the possibility that being can be radically different from what is presented) can never be properly within what is presented because, by virtue of the Parmenidean duality of is/is-not, it is nothing.[31] To lay out the stakes clearly then: Badiou needs a way of accessing being in itself that both removes any contamination of *doxa* or ideology from within the expression of being and, perhaps more importantly for his project, does not do so from within the realm of ideology itself. As Sacilotto puts it, 'the sophist begins by denying the philosophical use of dialectical rationality in its power of *exclusion* in refusing the primitive separation between Truth and *doxa*, what is and what is not, reality and appearance' (2013: 65). Furthermore,

> [a]gainst both the irrationalist hijacking of the negative which pushes the Real too far from thought, and the affirmationist annihilation of the negative which annuls the separation between Truth

and Opinion in the name of life's affirmative potency, the rationalist dialectician insists on thought's capacity to access being and on the difficult, but possible, participation in Truths. The implication is that philosophy's dialectical task is at once *analytic* and *synoptic*: it brings together the autonomous procedures than condition it at a given time by way of the concept of Truth, but to do so must render explicit the protocols of discernment between the space of mere opinions and the exceptional form of Truth. To stave off the sophist, the dialectical philosopher must distinguish reality from appearance, being *qua* being from mere semblances, and finally the exceptional character of Truth from being itself. It must recognize order if only to admit of the possibility of its disruption. (Sacilotto 2013: 66)

This is the crux of Badiou's efforts to legitimise his ontological schema and avoid the charge of dogmatism: in other words, Badiou's materialist dialectic must 'render explicit' that which determines truth as truth in terms that are not self-referential. Mere recourse to rationalism, i.e. upholding thought in order to separate truth from the pollution of sensible *doxa*, would beg the question 'what, in comparison to sense, is non-ideological about thought?'; and yet it is within thought that Badiou locates the grounds of the truth procedure. What, then, is truthful about thought that distinguishes it from the realm of sense perception?

The first characteristic of thought that cements its role in capturing truth is precisely its ability to distinguish through the negative. In this sense, it is only within the realm of thought that distinctions can be made between what is true and false, new and the same, and so on. Sacilotto defines Badiou's philosophy as assuming an inherently revolutionary role 'accomplished by aligning the concept of Truth with the production of novelty across the different conditions of its time in politics, art, love and science' (2013: 61). As has been shown, Badiou is not interested in the minor discussions governing day-to-day political manoeuvring. Rather, he is concerned with the development of an immanent logic of novelty which can be harnessed by political militants to guide their activities.[32] In this sense, logic is to be 'understood in the Hegelian sense in terms of which one articulates a transparent discourse that adjudicates on rational grounds between what is and what is not' (Sacilotto 2013: 62). The crux of Badiou's anti-sophistic argumentation – his ability to say what really is (or at least how this might be grasped) – is an adherence to the decision of the negative, or to say what is not. Badiou's problem, or as he puts it, 'our problem is the problem of negativity' (2013a: 1).³³ Indeed, for Badiou and his followers, the negative is important as 'it is the negative that empowers thought to differentiate itself, to bring itself forth or to make itself explicit in the rule-governed transparency of a discourse' (Sacilotto 2013: 62). This is one of Badiou's *a priori* conditions of any possible ontology, arguing that 'we find ourselves on the brink of a decision, a decision to break with the arcana of the one and the multiple [. . .]. This decision can take no other form than the following: the one is not' (Badiou 2011: 23).³⁴ Where Sacilotto identifies two dyads in Badiou's thought, the first Platonic dyad of truth/*doxa* or Philosophy/Sophistry and the second Platonic dyad of the intelligible/sensible or reality/appearance, there is, in fact, a third dyad which conditions the coherency of the first: the Parmenidean dyad of is/is not.³⁵ This dyad can distinguish the Parmenidean/Platonic intellectual heritage of the one, the many and the multiple, as opposed to the Hericlatean passage of becoming; as Sacilotto argues, it is precisely in opposition to the 'affirmationist annihilation of the negative which annuls the separation between Truth and Opinion in the name of life's affirmative potency, [that] the rationalist dialectician insists on thought's capacity to access being and on the difficult, but possible, participation in Truths' (2013: 66). In other words – and in comparison to sense – it is thought's capacity to think the negative that prioritises it over sense within the realm of truth. Because sense cannot speak of the negative and thereby either affirm or, in Badiou's case, productively negate that which is, it is left to the attribute of thought to tell the truth of being.³⁶

Thought having been identified as the realm wherein truths can be known, Badiou makes a distinction between philosophies that he labels 'poetic' – those that maintain the sophistic penchant for fudging important distinctions within thought, such as true and false or good and evil – and those of the Platonic line which do not (see for example Badiou 2011: 9–10). As Norris puts it, that which sets poetic philosophers out ('though some more than others') is, for Badiou, 'a sheer dereliction of philosophy's proper role' and 'their way of falling back on an appeal to language, discourse or representation as the ultimate horizon of intelligibility or the end point of ontological enquiry' (2012: 21). If it is thought which rids the individual of the obfuscating haze of the sensible that blurs the boundaries of what is or isn't, then poetic philosophy, for Badiou, reinserts the sensible into thought through the back door. As it does not attempt a recourse to the authority of being to express itself, poetic philosophy 'draws authority only from itself, abhors argument, and states *what is*, in the sensory form of what imposes itself without having to share this imposition' (Badiou and Toscano 2006: 40). Resultantly, if thought is to not reinstate the authority of presentation back onto itself or is, in other words, to escape ideology, then it must do so through the authority of being presenting *itself* through thought and negating any mediation by representation or *mimesis*. It is therefore to mathematics that Badiou turns as the 'guardian' or 'language' of 'being *qua* being', going so far as to say that 'mathematics is ontology' (Badiou 2011: 15). As Brassier puts it, reflecting Badiou's uptake of the Althusserian quest to rid dialectical materialism of ideology, 'for Badiou axiomatic set-theory is the science of being as sheer multiplicity, the science of the presentation of presentation (rather than of what is presented); in other words, the science that guarantees access to presented reality' (2005: 135–6). Where science constitutes the purification of representation from historical analysis for Althusser, Badiou's utilisation of mathematics, as the science of being, is intended to rid analysis from the semantic and poetic illusions of ideology.[37]

Badiou here seems stuck at an impasse himself. Having stated that '[t]he real is the impasse of formalisation; formalisation is the place of the forced pass of the real', yet also that all hitherto presentation consists under a count-as-one operation, thereby affixing it within the realm of statist ideology, does this not also put axiomatics within the same camp as ideology? If mathematics (even in its formalist variants) consists of statements that prescribe a structure onto being, then this would resemble precisely the same mode of thought that operates within Badiou's understanding of political philosophy. To the extent that this philosophy must be 'done with', would this not also be entirely appropriate for the prescriptions of mathematics? As Sacilotto asks then: 'how is this *intrinsic* access that formalisation achieves *vis-a-vis* the world to be conceived, if not by a relation of *identity* between the forms and the real, one which would however render the world inherently "mathematised", and thus preemptively *idealise* it' (2013: 72)? In having subtracted the sensible from the possible criteria by which to know being, Badiou risks idealising his meta-ontological gesture that prescribes mathematics as that which adequately presents being. Moreover, following the revealing of being through an event, would not the militant be forced to negate precisely the mathematical structure that expresses the eventurupture in the first place? If Badiou is to avoid the charge of dogmatism, he must therefore also avoid both an essentialist recourse to the Platonic formation of the real, and the reproduction of an evental rupture alongside a truth procedure whilst, at the same time, maintaining a veracity to the truth of it.[38]

The truth of mathematics

In order to address this question, i.e. 'is mathematics non-ideological under Badiou's own conception of ideology?', a brief summation of Badiou's position would be helpful. Refuting contemporary politics as a sophistic world external to the subject, Badiou upholds the necessity to reveal the truth of politics and constitute the subject according to this revelatory truth procedure. This dyad – opposing truth to opinion (synonymous with *doxa* in Badiou's usage) – constitutes the first of two Platonic dyads that compose his thought, the second being that of the distinction between the sensible and the intelligible. Because the sensible cannot provide the grounds for telling the truth of what is, it is the intelligible – subtracted from the thought of the sensible – which provides the only method for doing so. Both of these dyads are premised upon the Parmenidean dyad of is/is not which, for Badiou, conditions the ground upon which to make truthful decisions. This being the stage set, it is clear that any conception of mathematics which bases its operative power within its propositions will not suffice for Badiou, who terms this 'formalism'. Whilst semantic language is needed to mathematise in an active sense, the subject itself remains in the ideal position of authoritatively setting out that which it will then organise and manipulate. In forming matter with mathematics, the subject would take on the role of governing the state as did the philosopher kings of Plato.

Instead of this reversion to blatant dogmatism, Badiou addresses the position of mathematics containing its own expressive authority in *The Concept of Model* ([1966] 2007). Reformulating the dogmatism inherent within semantics, Badiou argues that 'nothing is more indistinct, and more empiricist, than the notion of a collection of objects, to the point that if it maintains this notion, semantics will have no chance of articulating itself scientifically' ([1966] 2007: 29). Instead, Badiou attempts to demonstrate how 'the intrasyntactic difference between logical and mathematical axioms is fully thinkable only with reference to the models in which such axioms are "true"' ([1966] 2007: 28). It is not the case that mathematics exists in the empirical sense by which language formalises a model that captures a particular instance, but rather, as what Brassier calls 'scriptural materiality' (Brassier 2005), mathematics constitutes its own productive sense by virtue of its inherent rules which are then inscribed by an individual. Badiou argues that mathematical models consist of three elements: individual constants (a, b, c), predicates (P, Q, R) and variables (x, y, z . . .) and that, because not all sequences in mathematics will be correct, the governance of 'syntactic sense' is performed by punctuation to achieve the '*rules of formation*' ([1966] 2007: 23–4, original emphasis). From this collection of variables ('in respect of which it is implicitly agreed that they denote pure multiples' (Badiou 2011: 60)), it is possible to write well-formed expressions, which present particular operations, whereby 'a rule of formations authorises an inscription of each mark' (Badiou [1966] 2007: 24). In this sense, Badiou can talk of mathematics existing as a language of 'being *qua* being' because he views mathematics' rules of formation as contained within the progressive development of its own model, and not as the result of a semantic *discussion* of what may/may not, or should/should not, be.[39] For him, it is the axiomatic and syntactical operation of mathematics itself, *a priori* of its inscription by a mark, that accords it productive capability and an independence from semantics. Yet the mark is important to Badiou's use of mathematics because it differentiates the agency of mathematics in its operation from the agency of an active subject who 'mathematises'.

In *Theoretical Writings*, Badiou distinguishes between the little and grand style of mathematics, whereby little mathematics 'strives to dissolve the ontological sovereignty of mathematics, its aristocratic self-sufficiency, its unrivalled mastery, by confining its dramatic, almost baffling existence to a stale compartment of academic specialisation' (2010c: 3). Accordingly, versions of either empirical or formalist mathematics are subservient to philosophy and take their stage under the watchful eye of a scholarly director who can correct them when they are wrong. As the proper alternative to the little style, Badiou prescribes the grand style: 'arithmetic as an instance of stellar and warlike inhumanity!' because 'there is no essential harmony between mathematics and the human intellect' (2010c: 12–13). The grand style of mathematics is, for Badiou, a separate pre-constitutive part of the world (ontology) that exceeds intellect, yet a part that can nevertheless be harnessed and expressed. It is because of the *a priori* validity of its axioms to itself that mathematics constitutes the language of being *qua* being before it is expressed by humans semantically. Badiou demonstrates that '[e]very measurement can therefore be expressed in a formal language (the system of reals), where the rationals are effectively *marked*; and the forms of calculation, the operations, would essentially be conserved, thanks to a certain invariance of the 'species of structure' [*l'espèce de structure*]' ([1966] 2007: 21) and, correspondingly, this allows him to state that 'it is impossible to be lazy in mathematics' ([1992] 2008: 96).[40]

As a way of illustrating his argument (that science cannot incorporate semantic or empiricist arguments and is based upon those of syntax) he states that, '[i]n these expressions the quantified variable x cannot be replaced by a constant. This is clear enough: the statement $(x)P(x)$ does not tell us *which* particular constant is marked by P, but only that some such constant exists' ([1966] 2007: 24–5). The truth of the statement $(x)P(x)$ is not predicated upon its deduction from the sensible, leading to an infinite series of asking 'are we sure?' (where truth would imply the semantic use of either induction or inference), but from the conditions demarcated by the axioms of mathematics itself.[41] Put generally: given Badiou's argument that sense cannot be trusted to present being, that the attribute of thought is the only realm in which being can truly be known, and that poetry roots thought in sophistry, it is only by holding onto the axiomatic integrity of mathematics that the subject can know what is possible to exist.

In a statement that sums up the later development between his two major works, *Being and Event* and *Logics of Worlds*, Badiou's position from this point is telling. Having demonstrated that it is only via the syntactic operations of mathematics that being can be thought, yet acknowledging that philosophy must also account for the sensible, Badiou states that '[i]t would indeed seem legitimate to found an epistemology of models on the systematic study of correspondences between syntactic and semantic concepts' (Badiou [1966] 2007: 21). It is necessary for Badiou to account for the connection between mathematical and poetic thought – and yet two problems emerge as a result of this necessity. On the one hand, why does Badiou assume that there is in fact a correspondence between syntactic and semantic concepts, having gone to such lengths to repudiate the latter? There is hitherto no reason to assume that there is any meaningful correspondence between the two to study (given Badiou's own reasons to rid ontology of poetic thought). Furthermore, even supposing there were some correspondence, what would the truth of this correspondence be grounded in given that, hitherto, it is only the mathematical logic of models (also referred to as set theory in Badiou's other works) that contains access to truth? On the other hand, even if there were a correspondence between the two, why should it be that either of the two kinds of statements make any meaningful contribution to understanding the sensible? Whilst the axiomatic integrity of mathematics enables the subject to know what is possible to exist, this has been accomplished through the subtraction of the sensible from thought to the extent that it is assumed that the translation of thought back into the sensible makes sense. There are philosophical grounds to presume a connection between thought and the sensible, for example either in Spinoza's parallelism or Hume's positivist associationism. Yet, whilst he does not subscribe to either philosophy, and having argued that the presentation of being itself cannot be trusted to show what truly is (hence the resort to an axiomatic model in its place), Badiou must account for *why* the prescriptions of mathematics should be taken as structuring political activity. Does he simply rely on a negative argument akin to saying that, 'it can't be anything else *other* than mathematics that creates the rupture of political truth'? This would seem too weak an argument upon which to ground his otherwise tightly presented system, and so Badiou must provide the imperative to condition politics upon the logic of set theory in a more substantial manner. It is not sufficient to simply claim that mathematics, in its axiomatic purity, *should* condition 'some-one's' (Badiou 2001: 40–57) politics without accounting for the legitimacy or authority of the claim itself.

Both problems place Badiou into the position of what Meillassoux terms a 'weak correlationist', whose argument proscribes 'any knowledge of the thing-in-itself (any application of the categories to the supersensible), but maintains the thinkability of the in-itself ' (Meillassoux 2008: 35).[42] Given that, for Badiou, the 'one is not' and that being's very existence is only knowable by its mark, he precludes the knowledge of the thing-in-itself other than through mediation of mathematics.[43] As Meillassoux invites, 'let us call "speculative" every type of thinking that claims to be able to access some form of the absolute' (i.e. Badiou's being), 'and let us call "metaphysics" every type of thinking that claims to be able to access some form of absolute being' (Badiou's truth procedure, albeit in a negative/subtractive form) (Meillassoux 2008: 34). This being the case, and if 'all metaphysics is "speculative" by definition', it must be demonstrated that 'it is possible to envisage an *absolutising* thought that would not be *absolutist*' (2008: 34). Put in the terminology of Livingston, the correlationist faces the problem of accounting for the authority of a totalising element in a system that does not gain its authority from itself, lest it succumb to dogmatism. Both Meillassoux and Livingston constitute a challenge for Badiou: account for why mathematics should be held up as that which presents the in-itself, as opposed to anything else.[44] Put directly in terms of political resistance: what does Badiou say of the activist, or the refugee; why should they take heed of the bafflingly complex political rallying call of set theory to put them in the place of a militant? Do they not already know that they are resisting and do they need mathematics to tell them how? Indeed, knowledge of the in-itself, evacuated by sense, seems to lead to what Ryder calls an 'impersonal subject', constituted only by the fact that it is part of an axiomatic system that prescribes its places as part of it (2013: 38). The resistance of activists only becomes authorised if it conforms to the mathematical prescriptions of the void set, whilst the individual is mere '"generic human stuff" that is ontologically indistinguishable from pure mathematical multiplicity' (Hallward in Badiou 2001: xxxii). As part of the axiomatic mechanics of set theory, and following the originary Parmenidean postulate of is/is not, it could very well be that this is the role of the subject that Badiou has in mind. Yet the lack of connection between the syntactic and semantic, as well as the axiomatic and sensible, hint at the fact that Badiou offers, as Osborne puts it, 'a full-blown idealism struggling with the limitations of its grasp on actuality, which *redefines reality* in terms of the gap that structures the limitation (Osborne 2013: 22, original emphasis). Whilst Badiou has attempted to avoid this criticism (by collapsing the distinction between sense and the transcendental logic of mathematics), the following will show that, first, Badiou does not in fact escape this criticism and, secondly, that Badiou's subject can only be seen as a supplement to an originary decision-making individual.

Who resists? Just Some-One

Although Kant's project may seem far removed from Badiou's, Kant being a 'philosopher of relation, of the linkages between phenomena, and [as] this constitutive primacy of relation forbids all access to the being of the thing as such' (Badiou 2010c: 135),

Badiou relies on 'Kant's subtractive ontology' for his conception of the subject. Indeed a chapter, dedicated to Kant, is named as such in *Theoretical Writings* (2004) and is used to draw out the distinction between the synthesis of the manifold of phenomena (*binding*) and the originary basis for this (*unity*). For Badiou's reading of Kant, the synthesis of the manifold is the transcendental aesthetic which is experienced by intuition. Unity is then that which conditions the possibility of the transcendental being held as such, giving it the ability to be intuited. This unity is precisely what Badiou uses himself in order to answer 'the problem of how the inconsistent manifold comes to be counted-as-one', a unity which 'must have been decided in advance in order for relational synthesis to be possible' (2004: 135). Badiou agrees with Kant's claim that 'the consistency of multiple-presentation is originary, and that the relations whereby phenomena arise out of that multiple-presentation are merely derivative realities of experience' (2004: 135). In other words, for both Kant and Badiou, the mechanism by which phenomena appear and combine within the realm of the sensible must be governed by a realm that originates before the phenomena themselves: this is the role of Kant's unity and Badiou's real/undifferentiated multiplicity (Badiou 2011: 283–4, 298).[45] Badiou points out another similarity in his conception of the subject with Kant's showing that, '[i]f we set aside the subjective connotation in the notion of originary apperception, which is conceived of by Kant as the "*transcendental* unity of self-consciousness", and focus strictly on its functioning, we should have no difficulty recognising in it what I call the counting-as-one, which Kant applies to representation in general, conceived as a universal abstract situation' (2010c: 136, original emphasis). Kant therefore has in place both a non-presentational conception of the real (in the correlationist sense that the subject cannot grasp the thing-in-itself), as well as the claim that what is sensible by the subject is in fact a *re*presentation of 'multiple-presentation' (or the ability of being to express itself). Both of these claims are shared by Badiou, with Badiou using the Kantian terminology of the 'function of synthetic binding' and his own nomenclature 'systems of categories' synonymously, to express the transcendental category of logic that structures the appearance of phenomena.[46] However, Badiou claims that Kant's problematic was not the radicality of his conclusions, but the necessity to think a unitary subject that was induced upon his work to the extent that his conclusions 'do not always clearly deliver the full extent of their significance' (2010c: 137). Badiou claims that, unlike Kant, his subject does not maintain a relation of understanding in order to weakly separate the potential of it developing separately to the hypothesised object = x (Ryder 2013: 47). So, if Badiou conflates the emergence of the subject with the unified presentation of the multiple under the political form authorised by set theory, what is it that makes the decision to claim fidelity to the event in the first instance?

Badiou shows that, for Kant, both the subject and object are split into empirical and transcendental forms. Whereas the empirical subject 'exists according to the determinations of our state in inner sense', is changeable and 'has as its correlate represented phenomena' (Badiou 2010c: 138–9), the transcendental subject, 'as given in originary apperception' is 'the supreme guarantor of objective unity' relative to which 'representations of objects is alone possible' (Badiou 2003: 139). As a correlate to the transcendental subject there is an 'object which cannot itself be intuited by us because it is the form of objectivity in general', i.e. the transcendental object = x (Badiou 2010c: 139). In other words, Kant's transcendental logic provides both the grounding to condition the existence of the sensible subject ('given the synthesis of the manifold to experience, the subject exists to make judgements upon it') and the existence of the transcendental subject ('the transcendental subject exists in order to be able to make determinations of x in the first place'). It is only on the basis of having a transcendental subject as a placeholder in his system that Kant can make statements about the cohesion of the rest of his system (including those pertaining to the empirical subject).[47] As Badiou argues, this is because, without the transcendental subject existing in a separate ontological category to the object, the subject's empirical side would have no consistent ontological grounding on which to make epistemological claims. In this sense, the minimal form of the subject for Kant acts as the same prerequisite for systemic cohesion as it does within Badiou's ontological configuration. Like Kant's transcendental subject, for Badiou, a 'subject is not a substance' and, rather, the 'intrinsic indiscernability in which a generic procedure is resolved rules out any substantiality of the subject' (Badiou 2011: 391). As has been shown, however, the axiomatic prescriptions of mathematics for Badiou exist *a priori* of their inscription within a mark; mathematics, as the language of being *qua* being, does not necessitate a subject – transcendental or not – for the ontological to be sensed. Because Kant 'posits that his originary and empty "transcendental object = X" guarantees that any given content will enter into a realm governed by relational, logical, and categorial limitations', as Ryder explains, 'an ontological question is glimpsed through eyes open wide just enough to admit a guarantee for the certainty of logical judgments' (Ryder 2013: 44). For Badiou, however, the subject cannot be understood as 'the empty centre of a transcendental realm but rather as the operational unity of a multiplicity of effectuations of identity' (Badiou 2010c: 142). In other words, the subject is not 'a result' of any operation (including that of mathematics), but is the '*local* status of a procedure, a configuration in excess of the situation' (Badiou 2011: 392); Badiou's subject is a subject within the structure of a truth procedure (not given as a product of it, but as an intrinsic component of it), and is only revealed as part of a given situation. Were there no situation to contain an eventual site, through which the subject is made knowable, then the subject would act as an empty category within Badiou's ontology.

The crucial difference, for Badiou, with regard to Kant's subject, is that there is no necessity for a form of subjective consistency (even in the sense of Kant's originary apperception) to condition the consistency of Badiou's ontology as a separate "kind" of ontology to the subject itself. The subject is simply another part of the ontological framework structured and described by mathematical set theory. Kant provides (in Badiou's reading of him at least) an ontological basis for the epistemological category of originary apperception and, therefore, can argue that 'the conditions of the *possibility of experience* in general are likewise conditions of the *possibility of the objects of experience*' (Kant [1787] 1996: A157/B197, p. 228). Badiou stops short of claiming that Kant places the transcendental subject within the count-as-one (and thereby within the realm of ideology), yet does argue that 'Kant's powerful ontological intuitions remain tethered to a starting point restricted to the form of judgement [. . .], while in the order of localisation, they remain tied to a conception of the subject which makes of the latter a protocol of constitution, whereas it can, at best, only be a result' (Badiou 2004: 141). The necessity that Kant felt to account for judgement in the first place conditioned his theory to separate the subjective form of originary apperception from the transcendental object = x. Yet the dual nature of Kant's subject (as both transcendental pre-supposition and empirical) *can* therefore account for the problematic laid out above, i.e. that Badiou must account for the connection between synthetic and analytic statements. The Kantian subject exists transcendentally because it conditions the unification of the manifold of phenomena with regard to itself, and empirically because it judges concepts based on these phenomena. Badiou, on the other hand, does not see the need to account for judgement because any form of semantic discussion – the use of concepts involving analytic and synthetic propositions – is rooted within the epistemological realm of the sensible. His subject is purely one of ontology, within the truth procedure (Badiou) or multiple-presentation of unity (Kant), and, as a result, Badiou does not specify either the transcendental conditions of a subject or its empirical features.

Instead of constituting either a transcendental prerequisite of consistency, or a purely empirical phenomenon for analysis, the subject for Badiou is therefore neither more nor less than a part of his ontological framework: it is constituent of the prescriptive axiomatisation of mathematics. The ideological covers of a political situation are thrown off to reveal the subject of the event as an operant and essential element of the mathematical structure – but only within its mathematical construction. Badiou's *Ethics* is the most revealing in this regard, demonstrating Badiou's claim that, 'Man thinks, Man is a tissue of truths' (2001: 12). If there is a subject in any way connected to the human animal, it is due only to the ability of humans to effect the truthful logic of mathematics. Indeed, appropriating the Aristotelian distinction between man and animal as delineated by the capacity of the former to think politically, Badiou argues that it is the 'enormous effort' on the part of human beings, who have been subjected to torture or imprisonment, to stubbornly 'remain what he is – that is to say, precisely something other than a victim, other than a being-for-death, and thus: *something other than a moral being*' (Badiou 2001: 11–12). Furthermore, Badiou claims that, when the individual is not political, i.e. 'the status of victim, of suffering beast, of emaciated, dying body, equates man with his animal substructure, it reduces him to the level of a living organism pure and simple', and that 'humanity is an animal species. It is mortal and predatory. But neither of these attributes can distinguish humanity within the world of the living' (2001: 11). The distinction between man as an animal and something to be rarefied as more than simply one species amongst others is that humans have the ability to re-affirm what they are, or were, before that which attempted to reduce them to animality: thought.[48] This thought must, of course, be purified of *doxa* which, for Badiou, is only the realm of sophistry and statist communication (see Badiou 2001: 50–2). How then does mankind relate to the truth procedure itself? Ryder is not entirely correct when he argues that 'Badiou's conception of a political subject relies on a chance encounter with a truth-process' (Ryder 2013: 55), because this implies a Kantian distinction between the transcendental subject of unity and the empirical subject of the truth procedure-become-sensible. The chance that the subject relies upon is actually the chance that an event emerges from an evental site, making it possible for the subject to be thought by its human tissue. If 'true (rare) politics [. . .] is the coming to light of an indiscernible of the times' (Badiou 2011: 17) or, in other words, is the revelation of undifferentiated being within a particular situation, then the subject does not rely on an encounter with a truth-process so much as is uncovered by it.[49]

Yet what does this say about the human animal, the animal engaged in political situations, amorous encounters, scientific exploration and artistic creativity? If man (and woman?) thinks, though it is only *through* man that the truth procedure can construct a real political sequence, does Badiou value anything else that constitutes the activist? It cannot be, of course, that the activist 'is' in any way, because anything that is remains within the realm of representative ideology. Yet does that mean that everything else that constitutes the human, bar thought, is to be discounted alongside ideology? What then of Marx's valorisation of the struggle he argued was at the heart of human life? Badiou argues that every truth 'deposes constituted knowledges, and thus opposes opinions. For what we call *opinions* are representations without truth, the anarchic debris of circulating knowledge' Badiou (2001: 50, original emphasis). His portrayal of the militant subject is complicated somewhat when, despite his praise of the truth procedure, Badiou argues that 'opinions are the cement of sociality. They are what sustain all human animals, without exception, and we cannot function otherwise' (2001: 50). So, on the one hand, Badiou upholds the purity of truth as opposed to mere opinion yet, on the other, claims that opinions provide vital sustenance for the individual: Badiou's attitude to the human condition itself must surely be called into question.

With his earlier work in *Metapolitics* (2005) lamenting the march forward of political philosophy, as well as what he calls the 'anarchic debris' of opinions in *Ethics* (2001: 50), Badiou's disdain for everything that is not ordained by the truth procedure can also be seen to include the animality of the human itself. Badiou disavows everything that enables the human to think mathematically, praising only that they happen to do so. Humanity's ability to think mathematically is entirely contingent, however, because there is nothing within Badiou's ontological schema that separates the individual human from any other presented being whatsoever. For Badiou, everything that constitutes human individuality that has not yet reached the status of being synonymous with the ontological prescription of the truthful subject – activists, the subaltern, the polyamorous, refugees, indeed anyone at all – is no more worthy of consideration than the parliamentary politics he derides. What a shame, it seems for Badiou, that humans have so much human baggage to carry with them. *If only* they could see what truly is, rather than toil away at their erstwhile naive needs and desires.

The condescension of Badiou's reference to those who have not been ordained by the aleatory encounter with a truth procedure is shown in his reference to such individuals as a 'some-one' (Badiou 2001: 44). Although the neologism neatly captures Badiou's portrayal of the individual as only existing within the count-as-one operation of a state, as well as the non-specific nature of their existence in the realm of *doxa*, it nevertheless entirely discounts the effort of every human that does not live up to Badiou's prescription of political success. As he says, the subject 'in no way pre-exists the process. He is absolutely nonexistent in the situation "before" the event. We might say that the process of truth induces a subject' (2001: 43, original emphasis). The subjectification of some-one is therefore the process by which he (or she) makes a decision to relate 'henceforth to the situation *from the perspective of its eventual supplement*' (Badiou 2001: 41, original emphasis). The subject exists as the supplement to some-one, sutured onto the biological excess of the truth that is inferior to the purity of truth, but a contingent prerequisite for its revelation. Indeed, Badiou is very clear about the insufficiency of the individual to reach the status of a subject: stating that 'the subject of a revolutionary politics is not the individual militant' but rather, for him, it is a 'singular production, which has taken different names (sometimes "Party", sometimes not)'.[50] Badiou gives three examples of the subject whereby the individual is insufficient to reach the adequate status of subject. Firstly, and almost at pains to acknowledge the individual's efforts in a political process, he accepts that, '[t]o be sure, the militant enters into the composition of this subject'. However, because both the sensible and *doxa* must be purged from the truth of the political truth procedure, the truth procedure 'exceeds him' (Badiou 2001: 43). For his second and third examples, those of two lovers and the artist (what is wrong with polyamory and why not an artistic collective?), the individuals again occupy an entirely separate ontological register to that of truth. This is the result of Badiou's prescription that the sensible needs to be subtracted from mathematical thought yet, again, a result that negates the lover and the artist who is not faithful to an event. According to Badiou, some-one then is the passive recipient of a truth procedure who 'enters into composition' of an assumed 'point of truth' (2001: 44) and any endeavour on the part of the individual to affect political, amorous, scientific or artistic change that does not involve an aleatory event is cast aside as unworthy of being named under one of the categories.

Yet what is it that makes the decision to act in either a political, amorous, scientific or artistic manner? Against Kant's presupposition of the transcendental subject, that which allowed for the consistency needed to think in time and space separately from the manifold of phenomena, Badiou argued that the subject was 'the operational unity of a multiplicity of effectuations of identity' (2004: 142). Badiou's subject is not the decision-making actor to initiate fidelity to a truth procedure because it is not a separate ontological component from the structure itself; it was shown above that Badiou's most significant criticism of Kant was precisely the rarefication of the transcendental category of the subject due to the perceived necessity to account for judgement in the first place. As such, and existing only as it does within the matheme, it cannot be that the subject decides to pay fidelity to the truth procedure, for the subject is always-already part of the truth procedure. Rather, for Badiou, it is the 'some-one' that makes the decision to put into motion their fidelity to a truth procedure. It is *'this* body, and everything that it is capable of, which enters into the composition of a "point of truth" – always assuming that an event has occurred, along with an *immanent* break taking the *sustained* form of a faithful process' (Badiou 2001: 44–5, original emphasis). Taking for granted that an event has taken place – for there is no possibility to pay fidelity to a truth procedure if there has not been an event – it is the animality of the individual, complete with *doxa*, weakness and its lack of rarefication with regard to animals, that submits to the truth procedure.

As the term for ordinary human behaviour, or 'the law that governs some-one in so far as he knows himself', Badiou appropriates Spinoza's concept of 'perseverance in being'. However – and crucially for Badiou's conception of the subject – he argues that this law does not constitute the 'test of truth' (given that the void cannot be known) (2001: 46). Badiou's account of perseverance is therefore the knowledge that some-one has of them-self but, as knowledge is opposed to truth for Badiou, perseverance is without the subtracted realm of truth. Following a truth-event, the individual's perseverance leads to 'consistency', or the 'manner in which our devotee of mathematics will engage his perseverance in that which breaks or opposes this perseverance, which is his belonging to a truth-process' (2001: 46–7). Consistency then describes the combination of the individual's perseverance through life (characterised by knowledge, sense and *doxa*), the subject of truth *and* the two things combined. Consistency is a new 'thing', a politicised individual (within a 'Party' for example) or the loving couple, but only in the knowledge that the someone must constantly reaffirm their animality by their attempts at fidelity to the truth prescriptions of mathematical ontology, whilst always knowing that they aren't themselves sufficient to the task of *being* political or amorous. However, Badiou's use of perseverance is not the same as Spinoza's, leading to a misappropriated understanding of consistency.

In *Ethics* ([1677] 1992), Spinoza describes the being of the conatus, or the inherent tendency in a thing towards its self-preservation. According to Spinoza, '[e]ach thing, in so far as it is in itself, endeavours to persist in its own being' ([1677] 1992: IIIP6). Given Spinoza's univocal world with its parallel attributes, perseverance is not delimited from any ontological truth that might exist as a supplement to the thing in itself. As Nadler puts it, '[b]ecause ultimately everything is an expression of the power of one and the same substance, a substance from which "there must follow infinitely many things in infinitely many modes," there is, [Spinoza] is saying, really only one order of things. This order of things that has its source in substance must express itself within each of the substance's attributes' (2006: 128). In other words, the single 'order of things' is expressed by each of the attributes in a method particular to that attribute. It is not the case that, *qua* Meillassoux's portrayal of Kant's and Badiou's epistemologies, there is only a *correlation* between the thought and the existence of being in Spinoza. Instead, 'Spinoza is making the stronger claim that there are ordered series of ideas in Thought each of which *corresponds* in its order to the ordering of modes in one of the other attributes. More particularly, the order and connection of the modes in Thought that are ideas of extended bodies is the same as the order and connection of the modes in Extension that are those bodies' (Nadler 2006: 127, emphasis added). To couch this in Badiou's terminology, it is not the case, for Spinoza, that the truth of mathematics has any greater ontological priority over the sense of the phenomenal because they correspond as different expressions of the same substance. As a result of this correspondence, Spinoza metaphysically conflates the radical distinction between the (non-)being of truth and the realm of the sensible found in Badiou, stating first that, '[e]very substance is necessarily infinite' (Spinoza [1677] 1992: IP8) and then that, '[t]he more reality or being a thing has, the more attributes it has' ([1677] 1992: IP9). Because substance contains an infinite number of attributes, substance is necessarily the only real that there is and mathematics cannot constitute a subtracted real that takes any greater priority than substance.

Given, then, the lack of any ontological hierarchy between Spinoza's conception of thought and extension, Badiou's use of perseverance without the realm of truth is a partial misuse of the concept. According to Spinoza, an individual can persevere in life without recourse to any underlying authoritative truth claim because no attribute has any greater authority to truth than any other. The lack of a mathematical language of truth in Spinoza's ontology therefore highlights a corresponding lack of any imperative in Badiou's work for fidelity to the truth: why is it that some-one *should* pay fidelity to a particular (in this case, mathematic) truth procedure, rather than not? Recalling the challenge posed above, and given Badiou's conception of some-one persevering (without truth), why should some-one pay fidelity to an event in accordance with Badiou's highly complex and schematic prescriptions? What might constitute the individual to become a militant: is there an imperative for them to do so? More importantly, were such an imperative to exist, whilst Badiou maintains his revocation of opinion, what is the ontological status of this imperative? Given Badiou's dismissal of opinions and in order to substantiate his ethical framework, he stands at his own impasse, whereby he must account for why some-one should pay fidelity to the truth as prescribed by his mathematics. Indeed, the lack of an imperative underpinning fidelity highlights Osborne's charge that Badiou has set up a 'full-blown idealism', unable to justify some-one's adherence to an event aside from Badiou's own prescription that they should. Unless he provides such an imperative, Badiou's 'subject to truth' will remain forever an abstract dialectic category, unreachable by anyone not worthy of Badiou's naming.

As Žižek explains it, Badiou's 'Truth is contingent; it hinges on a concrete historical situation; it is the truth of this situation, but in every concrete and contingent historical situation there is one and only one Truth which, once articulated, spoken out, functions as the index of itself and of the falsity of the field subverted by it' (2000: 131). Žižek recognises the contingent nature of the truth of a situation and the fact that, for Badiou, there is only a singular 'ethics' of each particular situation (Badiou 2001: 40–41). Yet he also identifies the necessity for Badiou to be able to identify the event from what is not an event, i.e. the standard operation of life from within the count-as-one. Despite the necessity to account for a militant's decision to pay fidelity to a truth procedure however, Žižek points out that, in order for this decision to bear any ontological weight, it has to be part of ontology itself. He argues that, 'there is no neutral gaze of knowledge that could discern the Event in its effects: a Decision is always-already here – that is, one can discern the signs of an Event in the Situation only from a previous Decision for Truth, just as in Jansenist theology, in which divine miracles are legible as such only to those who have already decided for Faith' (2000: 136).

So why should a subject decide to pay fidelity to a truth procedure? Because it has already discerned the emergence of a truth from a situation, as a result of having previously belonged to a truth procedure. Žižek shows an entirely circular argument in Badiou's concept of fidelity, going so far as to say that an 'Event is thus circular in the sense that its identification is possible only from the standpoint of what Badiou calls "an interpreting intervention" – if, that is, one speaks from a subjectively engaged position, or – to put it more formally – if one includes in the designated situation the act of naming itself ' (2000: 135). Badiou does not object to the argument that his concept of the subject is circular, given that (as has been shown) it is a necessary and prerequisite part of his ontological system.[51] Yet Žižek clarifies the fact that the decision to become a militant does not exist in the language of the sensible and *doxa* and, therefore, not within the world of someone. It is precisely because the potential consistency of the subject is subtracted from the sensible that the subject can only be induced as a supplement onto the human animal by the subject itself. Given that this happens only as part of a situation, the 'intuitive power of Badiou's notion of the subject [. . .] effectively describes the experience each of us has when he or she is subjectively fully engaged in some Cause which is "his or her own": in those precious moments, am I not "fully a subject"?' (Žižek 2000: 141). In accordance with a truth-event, some-one might ask themselves whether they are or are not a subject. Of course, this individual will already know Badiou's answer that they are not – and that they can only ever attempt subjectification – yet the individual can nevertheless never know whether they have achieved the status of militant correspondent, or not. Bearing in mind that this question is motivated by the event itself, rupturing at the order of things at the evental site, as Žižek then asks, 'does not this very feature [of the event] make it ideological?'. It seems in fact that the 'Truth-Event is uncannily close to Althusser's notion of ideological interpellation' (2000: 141).

In *Ideology and Ideological State Apparatuses* (1971a), Althusser clarifies Marx's revision of the social topology in the latter's early work, arguing that the legal and ideological superstructure does not merely derive from the economic infrastructure (or 'base'), but in fact reproduces it (1971a: 136). For Althusser, a plurality of 'distinct and specialised institutions' exist within the private realm (as opposed to state apparatuses which exist within the public realm), which seek to symbolically educate, discipline and censor the individual (1971a: 144). Defining ideology as 'the imaginary relationship of individuals to their real conditions of existence' (1971a: 162), Althusser argues that it is not 'their real conditions of existence, their real world, that "men" "represent to themselves" in ideology, but above all it is their relation to those conditions of existence which is represented to them there' (1971a: 164). As a result of this representation of their existence to themselves, and because 'an ideology always exists in an apparatus, and its practice, or practices', Althusser argues that the distinct institutions that make up private life impress upon individuals the ideas that constitute them (1971a: 166).[52] Badiou agrees with Althusser that 'ideology is characterised by the notion of subject, whose matrix is legal and which subjects the individual to ideological State apparatuses' (ISAs), and clarifies that this process is what Althusser called 'subjective interpellation' (Badiou 2004: 63). A subject, for Althusser, is thus an individual infused by an identity that is itself created by their relationship with both the repressive and ideological apparatuses of the state. As, for Althusser, all 'ideological State apparatuses, whatever they are, contribute to the same result: the reproduction of the relations of production, i.e. of capitalist relations of exploitation', Badiou's individual occupies the same ideological position as Althusser's subject. As shown above, Badiou's proletariat is conditioned by its placement within its dialectic with the bourgeois class; the identity of the proletariat is determined not by the bourgeoisie itself, but by the relationship it has with it, in the same manner as Althusser's subject is interpellated by its relationship to ISAs (Althusser 1971a: 165). Yet Althusser's subject always becomes subjectified by a greater subject (which he capitalises, 'Subject'), in what set theory describes simply as a larger set that counts the subject within it. The structure of all ideology interpellates subjects as part of a greater Subject (Althusser uses the example here of God) who then, in reference to Freud's mirror stage, recognise themselves as subjects (Althusser 1971a: 181). Importantly, because, for Althusser, *'individuals are always-already subjects'*, this is an immanent and non-historicist process of constitution that the individual can never escape from (Althusser 1971a: 176, original emphasis); although Althusser proposes a form of scientific method to analyse society from outside of bourgeois class relations, he does not hold Badiou's position that the subject exists separately from any development of ideology.[53]

Žižek describes the process of ideological interpellation, which he ascribes to Badiou as well as Althusser, as circular. He asks, is not 'the circular relationship between the Event and the subject (the subject serves the Event in his fidelity, but the Event itself is visible as such only to an already engaged subject) the very circle of ideology?' (2000: 145). If, as has been shown, the individual (or 'someone') must already be implicated within a truth procedure, even as the excess of its subjective capacity for truth, then the individual has been interpellated to understand the eventally site as what it is: the capacity for the production of truth. As Žižek summarises,

> when Badiou dismisses the topic of human finitude, from Heideggerian 'being-towards death' to Freudian 'death drive', as the morbid obsession with what makes man equal to and thus reduced to a mere animal [. . .] his theoretical gesture involves a 'regression' to 'non thought', to a naive traditional (pre-critical, pre-Kantian) opposition of two orders (the finitude of positive Being; the immortality of the Truth Event) that remains blind to how the very space for the specific 'immortality' in which human beings can participate in the Truth-Event is opened up by man's unique relationship to his finitude and the possibility of death. (2000: 163)[54]

These two orders and, more importantly, the gap between the two, are then the same two orders – and the same gap – that Badiou criticised Kant for instantiating in his transcendental and empirical subject. Indeed it is only from within the 'finitude of positive Being' that some-one can align themselves with the truth procedure, yet only ever as an alignment, or a correlation, never as the Spinozist correspondence that Badiou strives to reach. Whilst the subject consistently remains within the three-part attachment to the individual (some-one, subject and consistency), the would-be activist's constant affirmation of their status as a militant (and correction of their activities if they are not one), keeps consistency within the ideological (and Kantian) realm of recognition.[55] To put it simply: a militant knows that something was an event because it appeared to be so, as consistent with their interpellated understanding of what an event is. Yet this understanding is based upon the knowledge, indeed an homage, to a prior Subject who defines the characteristics of the event. Even if it cannot point out an event were it to happen (because it can only determine what its characteristics and name might be), 'Badiou elevates the figure of the Master: the Master is the one who *names the Event* – who, by producing a new *point de capiton*, Master-Signifier', and reconfigures the symbolic field via the reference to the new Event (Žižek 2000: 164). Yet, again, if Badiou is to maintain his correlationist position against the sensible world, then the fact that this naming can only be justified from within the sensible prevents it from being a truthful ethical imperative. Indeed, Badiou's ethical imperative is tautological in his formation: in order for the subject to maintain a fidelity to the truth, Badiou's consistent individual must already have been interpellated by the ideological knowledge that there is an event, and that it has certain characteristics to look out for, and it will then look for another event with the same characteristics. Following interpellation, the truth that the event brings forth a truth procedure is only the truth for the subject (as always-already a component of the truth procedure itself). For the animal-individual, it can never be true that an event is a pure 'truth-event', dwelling as the animal does within sense and *doxa*, devoid of the thought of truth, and always-already ideologically interpellated. When asked: '*Why is that name the name of the Event?*' (Žižek 2000: 164), Badiou's slavish individual can only answer, 'Because my Master told me so.'

The failure of being

Badiou's conception of truth must be able to explain the truth of its own position in order to avoid the charge of dogmatic idealism, and, as has been demonstrated (and, indeed, as Badiou himself admits), it cannot.[56] A result of its own auto-authorisation and, as Žižek has demonstrated, because Badiou's account of truth in fact actualises a particular form of ideological interpellation, it is not as devoid of epistemic conditions as Badiou might like his readers to believe. Instead, because Badiou's truth is conditioned on *a priori* assumptions, a question to be asked is, 'what is the truth of the truth that Badiou describes?'[57] However, to ask 'what is?' idealises a presupposition that there is something to be revealed and, as has been shown, Badiou's truth condition (the matheme) axiomatically authorises itself, creating precisely this presupposition. To ask 'what is?' would therefore play Badiou's own game and take his conception of truth as is, without critique of its formation. This empirical question can only be answered by comparison with the requirements of an alternative model of truth, a comparison that would rely on an (ultimately infinite) recourse to ever-deeper justifications for truth. In order to rescue Badiou's ontology from Osborne's charge of idealism then – i.e. to understand under what conditions Badiou's idea of truth is true – it must be placed back within its own relations of production. At the risk of removing the transcendental authority of Badiou's ontology, and therefore negating the categorical structuring of the sensible in *Logics of Worlds* (2009), the question to be asked is: 'how is Badiou's ontology truthful?' Whilst a similar question was asked above regarding Badiou's conception of thought, positing this question of ontology allows Badiou's four truth procedures to be seen as concepts constructed by, and bound within, a very particular set of propositions. In removing the presumption that there is a truth to be investigated, its differentiated contours left to be determined, any conception of truth that has been built up can be seen as a result of its constitution and nothing more. This chapter will conclude by arguing that Badiou's truth procedures (and his resultant ethical position) can only ensue from the failure of revolutionary moments, resulting from the three dyads of thought presented above, as well as an always-already interpellated subject who looks for an answer to the question, "why didn't this revolution work?".

The first of the three dyads that were discussed above was, as identified by Sacilotto, the Platonic dyad of truth/*doxa*. Although this distinction has been used uncritically throughout this chapter, Badiou's use of it is nevertheless not without its baggage and does not conform to the standard conceptions of truth. Hallward outlines three conventional conceptions of truth that define the conception 'in terms of coherence, correspondence, or confirmation'

(2003: 153) and yet, he states, 'Badiou's conception of truth is not only not reducible to any one of these three alternatives; it undercuts the basis for their distinction *tout court*' (2003: 154). As has been shown, for Badiou, an axiomatic truth procedure does not need any form of external condition in order to legitimise its claims and, indeed, anything that is legitimised as such is under the illegitimate authority of the count-as-one. Hallward clarifies Badiou's truth procedure as that which 'links its assertion with the method of its verification' (2003: 154), and this is due to the now familiar reason that any form of verification not contained within Badiou's axiomatic system exists in the realm of *doxa*, from which truth must be subtracted. Put simply, for Badiou, the truth procedure is true because it determines itself as true and it cannot be otherwise because this would make the procedure's truth conditional. Yet Badiou's conception of truth *does* have a pre-condition that is belied by his statement that it cannot be what is *doxa*, because the negative distinction of the truth as 'not being *doxa*' is not obvious; why is a statement about the world that is not routed in Badiou's particular conceptualisation of the expression of being not truthful in itself? If, as Hallward argues, verification in Badiou's system of truth is linked with its own assertion, how is this any different with any other truth condition, all of which anchor the conditions for their veracity in their own systems? In distinguishing between truth and opinion, yet declaring that truth is true purely by virtue of it being so according to its own prescription, Badiou does not account for why his particular conceptualisation of truth should be taken as any more truthful than any other conceptualisation.

Badiou's rejoinder to this criticism is that ontology's role is that which understands what is (not), hence the association of the event with a truth procedure as an expression of the void. Yet this association artificially limits the scope of truth's remit, given that it involves an *a priori* procedure of subtraction and a concomitant isolation of what it is (not) that the truth procedure pertains to (i.e., non-being). Hallward argues that 'the subtractive approach understands that the operations that consolidate "reality" – representation, appearing, semblance: the state of the situation – are not simply external to the real as a cover that might be removed, but are organised as its ontologically irreducible repression' (2003: 163). And yet, if the state of the situation (and therefore also *doxa*) plays such an active part in repressing "reality", how can the state not also be part of reality and, consequently, also fall within the realm of truth?

The second dyad employed by Badiou is the second Platonic dyad, that of the intelligible/sensible. This is based upon a precondition, namely that the argument as to why truth cannot be borne out of the ontic realm is not immediately obvious. Badiou announces his starting point for a conceptualisation of truth in *Infinite Thought* as the Heideggerian passage, '[i]n becoming a property of the proposition, not only does truth displace its locus; it transforms its essence', clarifying that this 'must be understood as stating that the entire effect of the decline of thought, which is also the decline of being, is manifested in the fact that truth is presented, after Plato, as localisable in the proposition' (Badiou 2005c: 59). Continuing, Badiou argues that this 'localisation is also a de-naturing. Nothing of the truth, in its authentic sense, remains accessible if we allow that the phenomenon of truth occurs in the proposition' (2005c: 59). The virtue of the axiomatic for Badiou is that it does not contain its truth localised in a proposition, but rather takes the form of a procedure whose ramifications are *verified* by the militant. Invoking the axiomatic allows Badiou to avoid a number of metaphysical issues that plague other non-immanent systems of truth (such as those that Hallward outlines).[58] However, in negating the truth of propositions, Badiou replaces this with mathematical thought which reductively takes on the role of another vehicle for truth. Although he justifies thought as the proper vehicle for truth and the only way of distinguishing between that which is and that which isn't, this only maintains Heidegger's propositional character of truth in its inverse form: as opposed to propositions containing truth, mathematics expresses truth in a particularly anthropomorphic manner. Yet Badiou does not account for why it is thought that has the glorious position of presenting being in the first place; why does dance not present the being of the world as truthfully as any mathematical articulation, or the struggle of refugees against arbitrary immigration targets? As with the first dyad, Badiou's conception of truth sets out its own declarations of what it will tell (i.e. the four truth procedures) and does not attempt to address the truth of the sensible at all (for reasons he is, of course, very clear about). If the first dyad stipulates an inability to account for the truth of *doxa*, then the second dyad likewise stipulates a condition of truth which can only tell of the noetic and not the sensible. Yet what is a truth that denegates an entire attribute of the world as a way of expressing this same world? As Bergson argues, preempting Badiou's account of the matheme, '[i]t is of no use to hold up before our eyes the dazzling prospect of a universal mathematic; we cannot sacrifice experience to the requirements of a system. That is why we reject radical mechanism' (Bergson 1911: 39).

The third dyad at work in Badiou's ontology is the Parmenidean dyad of is/is not. The biunivocal distinction elaborated in *On Nature* governs, for Parmenides, the presentation of reality as that which is, and which is necessarily thought by the subject.[59] Badiou's modification of the dyad, as is set out in the first meditation of *Being and Event*, reverses the priority of what is in favour of what is not in order to escape an infinitely unfolding, yet preconditioned, universe. Although interpretations of Parmenides differ with regard to his status as an idealist or not, in his introduction to the *Dialogues of Plato*, Benjamin Jowett credits Parmenides as 'the founder of idealism, and also of dialectics, or, in modern phraseology, of metaphysics and logic' (Plato 1892: 13). For Jowett, the distinction between being and non-being is itself a dialectic operation of thought which, as a similar operation to the Kantian position discussed above, relies on a transcendental judgement of thought. It is from this Parmenidean duality that Plato, and then later Aristotle, developed the three laws of thought: the law of identity, the law of contradiction (or non-contradiction) and the law of excluded middle (see Hamilton 1860: lec. 5). However, Badiou's distinction between is/is not – even after Badiou's reversal of their priorities – remains an idealist differentiation, necessitating thought to distinguish one from the other. Badiou's reliance on this grand distinction is never discussed in any greater depth than discussions of the one, multiple and the void (which all presuppose this distinction), and so this third dyad remains an idealist presupposition on which Badiou's truth procedures are conditioned.[60]

Badiou's conceptualisation of truth is therefore tautological: employing a procedure that allows the identification of 'is not' from 'is', Badiou creates the very conditions of his ontological system of truth (the three dyads) which can only tell the truth of his own presuppositions. How is Badiou's ontology truthful? That which is truthful is any subjective (and therefore purely logical) position that emerges as the prescription of an unsayable event (again, a purely logical category), and that can be verified as having similitude with an empirical situation. This truthfulness casts aside any ongoing struggle for resistance, as well as any material political, artistic, scientific or amorous practice, in favour of a logical analysis from someone already interpellated with the schema of what to look for. So why does Badiou, given his significant involvement in theatre and literature, a lifetime of active political resistance and his previous Maoist identification, hold on to such a limited account of truth? The answer to this question lies in *The Communist Hypothesis* (2010a), a small collection of previously written essays, bound in red, with a cover written in the gold leaf of a hotel bible. As David Morgan writes in his review of it, 'the great strength of this book, and of Badiou's work in general, is in its commitment to defending and carrying forward the achievements and lessons of the last two centuries of revolution' (2011: n.p.). Although Badiou declares that *The Communist Hypothesis* is not a book of politics or political philosophy (2010a: 37),[61] he nevertheless discusses series of significant political failures which he then expands on throughout the work. The three failures (May '68, the Cultural Revolution and the Paris Commune) all constitute political events which have (according to Badiou) failed in their goals, although Badiou's purpose is to explain that '"failing" is always very close to "winning"' (2010a: 31). In Badiou's terms, each event failed because a moment within each truth procedure was badly handled or, in other words, because a 'tactical decision' correlated with a 'strategic impasse' (2010a: 39). Because Badiou's truth procedure is veridical (i.e., it relies on the militant to ensure that their actions conform to the prescriptions of the truth procedure), there is always the possibility that the militant fails in their fidelity to the event and strays off course. Yet this does not mean that each event was an entire failure, because lessons from each event, for Badiou, can continue to be learned even after the event has come off its tracks. Badiou writes that, 'we must accept that there was an element of universality in the terrible failure of the Cultural Revolution. And let us remember in this context that the fact that something ends in bloody failure is not the only thing that can be said of it. Once again, you use the failure of the Cultural Revolution as a facile argument in order to deny its importance and contemporary relevance' (2010a: 273). As Morgan puts it, the 'core of [Badiou's] philosophical project (and of his activism) has been an attempt to understand what it means to be faithful to the great revolutionary events of the previous two centuries' (Morgan 2011). Indeed, this is Badiou's conception of subjectivity: fidelity to an event and consistency brought about by acting in accordance with its prescriptions. So Badiou can count on himself to be a militant of each event because it is his ontology that defines the event, interpellated as he is by knowledge of each historical situation.

Yet Badiou's project is plagued by one significant impasse, highlighted by Žižek: each event is called an event *a posteriori* of its occurrence, only within the knowledge of the fact that it is not a part of the state. In other words, Badiou's post-evental philosophy will forever be condemned to tell the truth only of failed events, for the militant must verify his actions as true or not against those of the state. Whilst being cannot be accessed by a mortal someone in any way other than through a rupture in presentation, the mortal must rely on this rupture failing in order to tell its truth as a consistent militant. So, as Žižek argues,

> against Badiou, one should insist that only to a finite/mortal being does the act (or Event) appear as a traumatic intrusion of the Real, as something that cannot be named directly: it is the very fact that man is split between mortality (a finite being destined to perish) and the capacity to participate in the Eternity of the Truth-Event which bears witness to the fact that we are dealing with a finite/mortal being. To a truly infinite/immortal being, the act would be transparent, directly symbolized, the Real would coincide with the Symbolic. (Žižek 2000: 164)

It is therefore Badiou's specificity in determining the event according to the three dyads (truth/*doxa*; sense/intelligibility; is/is not), and a mathematical modelling of ontology as that which is not, that means he can only bring to bear truths of the failure of being. The success of being, i.e. an entirely militant population alongside the dissolution of the state with all its capito-parliamentary representatives, would be unsayable given the lack of internal elements within the event by which to specify truthful actions. Just as when God made Saul blind before entering Damascus and he was helped into the city by those accompanying him (Acts 9:8–16), the militant, guided by Badiou's idea of the event, still needs the state in order to guarantee that their faith is to the event and that they haven't slipped into the heresy of obedience to the state (in Badiou's terms: a 'slip to the right'). Badiou's political truth procedure can therefore only remain a hypothesis and lacks any possibility to manifest itself outside of a dialectic relationship with the realm of sensible *doxa*. When Badiou asks of a historical sequence that had 'experimented with one or another form of the communist hypothesis' if it was 'a failure that simply proves that it was not the right way to resolve the initial problem' (2010a: 6), his question is undermined by the impossibility of there being any way to know the correct way of resolving the initial problem, this knowledge only being knowable in relation to the state.

What then is the second text that this symptomatic reading of Badiou can relate to? When Kropotkin (1989) laments the situation in Russia that he saw under Alexander II, his finger is pointed not at the serfs and peasant population as the source of their own misery, but at the rule of the emperor. Kropotkin writes that, when the people of Chitá sent estimates to St Petersburg for permission to build a new watchtower for their fire brigade, it took the government two years to sign off on the plans. By this stage however, prices for raw materials had gone up and the estimates were now out of date. This happened for twenty-five years, until the population of Chitá sent requests for twice what was necessary to build the watchtower, an amount which was enough to finally build it once the standard delay in replying had passed. This, for Kropotkin was the situation of all throughout Russia under Alexander II, who,

> [y]ielding for a moment to the current of public opinion around him, [. . .] induced men all over Russia to set to work, to issue from the domain of mere hopes and dreams, and to touch with the finger the reforms that were required. He made them realise what could be done immediately, and how easy it was to do it; he induced them to sacrifice whatever of their ideals could not be immediately realised, and to demand only what was practically possible at the time. And when they had framed their ideas, and had shaped them into laws which merely required his signature to become realities, then he refused that signature. No reactionist could raise, or ever has raised, his voice to assert that what was left – the unreformed tribunals, the absence of municipal self-government, or the system of exile – was good and was worth maintaining: no one has dared to say that. And yet, owing to the fear of doing anything, all was left as it was; for thirty-five years those who ventured to mention the necessity of a change were treated as suspects; and institutions unanimously recognised as bad were permitted to continue in existence only that nothing more might be heard of that abhorred word 'reform'. (Kropotkin 1989: 183)

Kropotkin celebrates the will, ingenuity and energy of the Russian people, whilst highlighting the stultifying effects of the state governance which dampened the people's development and fulfilment. It is this lamentation, and the work of other revolutionaries who write of the failure of popular movements, that must be read into

Badiou's work, as he attempts to find answers to why political resistance so often fails, despite the energy of the struggling people. A reading of Badiou's work that focuses solely on its mathematical/ontological components will fail to understand the important efforts that Badiou has gone to in attempting to understand the failure of radical leftist politics.[62] On the other hand, read separately, Badiou's polemics (for example, *Manifesto for Philosophy* (1992), *The Communist Hypothesis* (2010) and *The Idea of Communism* (2010)) are overly triumphant in their assumption that communism will ultimately emerge victorious against the oppressing forces of neocapitalism and parliament. His work can only be fully appreciated if seen as a programmatic understanding of the failure of revolutionary politics, supported by a rigorous onto-mathematical base. However, it is ultimately the specificity of what Badiou is indeed attempting to explain – a select number of eruptions in the everyday mundanity of governmental politics – which undermines his ability to account for an ethical practice of resistance, limited as he is by the idealised contours of the event.

Notes

1. For discussion of Badiou's theory of the event, see Hallward (2003: 107–30).
2. Rather than 'grounding', 'authorising' is technically the correct term to use in this context as it is developed by Badiou. Its meaning is developed towards the end of the chapter, but requires an amount of exposition in order to make sense beforehand. See note 57 to this chapter and the discussion to which it relates.
3. According to Montag, a symptomatic reading 'presupposes the coexistence of two texts, one of which becomes visible only when we note the lapses and gaps that normally function to make certain parts of the text illegible' (2003: 49).
4. This is not, of course, for Badiou, a 'political philosophy'.
5. As Wittgenstein put it, no 'course of action could be determined by a rule, because every course of action can be made out to accord with the rule' (Wittgenstein [1953] 2001: 201). Deleuze was well aware of this, and developed the relationship between totalisation and coherency in *What is Grounding?*, albeit not in these terms, in this light ([1956–7] 2015).
6. Cantor, a leading architect in the development of set theory, 'showed the strict excess of the size of the *power set* of any set – that is, the set of all possible sets recombining its elements – over the original set itself. By means of this operation, the vast Cantorian hierarchy

of "transfinite" sets, each an infinity strictly larger than the last, is born' (Livingston 2011: 21).
7. Published by Bertrand Russell in a 1908 paper, Russell's paradox demonstrates that a formal system cannot be both consistent and totalising at the same time and can be understood in terms of the Cretan liar: Epimenides (himself a Cretan) says that all Cretans are liars. This statement is paradoxical to the extent that it cannot be true whilst Epimenides himself forms part of the set of Cretans to which the statement pertains. Epimenides' statement is therefore logically consistent but non-totalising (in that it cannot include Epimenides himself in the statement) and is thus an example of Russell's paradox. As Livingston puts it, in combination with the Gödel sentence, 'both results were often taken together as demonstrating the fundamental untenability of the earlier formal projects of *logicism*, which had sought to reduce mathematical truths and objects to truths and laws of pure logic, and *formalism*, which had sought to reduce mathematical reasoning and inference to purely mechanical procedures' (Livingston 2008: 25).
8. Hallward clarifies the coherency of Badiou's ontological system, arguing that 'Badiou's truth coheres, in the sense that a generic procedure must group an internally consistent set of investigations or conditions; it is expressly founded on the real of the situation and implies the unrestricted application of bivalence; and it is effectively self-verifying, composed over time in a laborious series of incremental steps' (Hallward 2003: 154).
9. Badiou's portrayal of sophistry comes from Plato's portrayal of doxosophia. In the *Sophist*, Plato's Stranger describes the sophist as having come 'to light for us with a certain opinionative science (knowledge) about everything, but he's without truth' (Plato 2006: 233D). For Plato, the sophist is a rhetorician who, akin to a hunter preying on its target, targets wealthy young men with promises of knowledge. Lacking a basis to question arguments from a position of truth, Sophists 'question thoroughly about whatever anyone believes he's saying something while saying nothing (sic.). And then, because those questioned wander, they examine their opinions with ease, and once they bring the opinions together into the same place by their speeches, they put them side by side one another, and in so putting them they show that the opinions are simultaneously contrary to themselves about the same things in regard to the same things in the same respects' (Plato 2006: 230B). Badiou's position runs counter to this and, as Hallward neatly summarises, his philosophy 'provides some resources for thinking the "situated" character of a universal truth, for instance its localisation in an "evental site", or its incorporation in a "body" shaped by regional norms of appearing or existence' (2009: 114). Badiou intersperses his writing with reasons as to why sophistic philosophy should be rejected, but specifically addresses

the issue in two places: for arguments in favour of why liberal and representative philosophies should be rejected, see 'Against "Political Philosophy"' in Badiou (2005d) and for why poetic philosophy must be rejected more generally, see 'Conditions' in Badiou (1992).
10. Neither Badiou nor Meillassoux make any distinction between the organisation of political institutions, political philosophy and the discussion of politics in terms of their separation from capito-parliamentary dogma. All (anti-)philosophies that do not cement themselves on a foundation of truth, as well as any discussion that a group of people may have about politics in a pub, are grouped together under the category of sophistry.
11. Deleuze also argues in similar fashion that 'many people have an interest in saying that everybody knows "this", that everybody recognises this, or that nobody can deny it. (They triumph easily so long as no surly interlocutor appears to reply that he does not wish to be so represented, and that he denies or does not recognise those who speak in his name)' (Deleuze 2004b: 166–7). Deleuze does not recourse to the same formal, mathematised ontology for his conception of politics as Badiou, but does interrogate political notions of 'good' and 'common' sense that pervade political debate. See Deleuze (2004b: 164–70).
12. Hobbes argues that, 'if the Soveraign command a man (though justly condemned,) to kill, wound, or mayme himselfe; or not to resist those that assault him; or to abstain from the use of food, ayre, medicine, or any other thing without which he cannot live; yet hath that man the Liberty to disobey' (Hobbes [1651] 1996: 268–9). For a full discussion of Hobbes' arguments with regard to resistance, see Steinberger (2002).
13. Resistance against the sovereign, for Locke, becomes permissible because, '[w]herever law ends, tyranny begins, if the law be transgressed to another's harm; and whosoever in authority exceeds the power given him by the law, and makes use of the force he has under his command, to compass that upon the subject which the law allows not, ceases in that to be a magistrate; and, acting without authority, may be opposed as any other man who by force invades the right of another' (Locke [1690] 1988: §202). Locke provides arguments for resistance against tyranny in §214–17 and against a sovereign unable or neglecting to carry out their charge in §219.
14. As Kant defined it, dogmatism is the 'procedure . . . [of] reason, without prior critique of its own ability' (Kant [1787] 1996: B xxxv, p. 34). In Badiou's eyes, political philosophy cannot condition a critique of its own foundations, being based on sophistic judgement. The argument in this chapter however is that Badiou remains dogmatic because his condition for truth (i.e. his meta-ontology) likewise cannot condition a support for itself within its own framework.

15. In *Metapolitics* (2005d), Badiou develops his criticism of political philosophy using the work of Arendt, who uses Kantian distinctions to justify parliamentarianism, and the work of Revault d'Allonnes. He summarises his disavowal of political debate, arguing that 'debate is only political when it crystallises in decision' and that it turns '"politics" into mere passive commentary on current affairs, a kind of collective extension of reading newspapers' (Badiou 2005d: 15). A philosophy which underpins such a conceptualisation can therefore, for Badiou, 'do no more than oscillate between an intolerable mutism – that of Heidegger faced with Paul Celan – and the almost desperate search for a prose of thought that would prepare thought's leave for the poem' (Badiou [1992] 2008: 147).
16. Badiou uses the term 'state' meaning both the system of political and economic institutions that comprise a state and its government, as well as its meaning in the phrase, 'state of the situation'. He writes that the state is 'the system of constraints that limit the possibility of possibilities' and that 'the State is that which prescribes what, in a given situation, is the impossibility specific to that situation, from the perspective of the formal prescription of what is possible' (Badiou 2010a: 7). A small 's' is used to denote the state in a 'global' sense, i.e. a formal designation of the confines of a system – that which is the case in set theory – and a capital 'S' is used for a 'local' state, such as a census or legislation created by a national government.
17. See Schmitt's *The Concept of the Political*, where he calls for the support of 'the all-embracing political unit, the state' (1996: 32).
18. Parmenides' ontological position can be usefully contrasted against Heidegger's to establish where Badiou's loyalties lie. Heidegger states that, 'Beings are [. . .] interrogated with regard to their being. But if they are to exhibit the characteristics of their being without falsification, they must for their part have become accessible in advance as they are themselves' (Heidegger [1953] 2010: 5). In other words, Heidegger argues that 'the being of being "is" not a being' and thereby distinguishes the 'beingness' of that which 'is' with the fact that it is given as being. He argues this by stating that, 'Being [*Sein*] is found in thatness and whatness, reality. The objective presence of things [*Vorhandenheit*], subsistence, validity, existence [*Dasein*], and in the "there is" ["*es gibt*"]' (Heidegger [1953] 2010: 10–11). For Heidegger then, it is a question of exploring the relationship between that which is given as being and the process of being given as an existence in itself. Parmenides's position is different from Heidegger's in that, for him, there is only the existence of that which 'is' (i.e. Heidegger's '*Dasein*'), arguing that, 'it is complete, immovable, and without end. Nor was it ever, nor will it be; for now it is, all at once, a continuous one [. . .]. I shall not let thee say nor think that

it came from what is not; for it can neither be thought nor uttered that anything is not. And, if it came from nothing, what need could have made it arise later rather than sooner? Therefore must it either be altogether or be not at all' (Parmenides 1920: 8). For Parmenides, Heidegger's position would be unfounded in the sense that it names two conditions of being, one of which (*es gibt*) cannot be known within the formula 'there is'. Badiou uses Zermelo–Fraenkel set theory to develop the Parmenidean orientation and show how, although things can only be said about constituted being, certain events within constituted being can highlight the (necessarily unsayable) non-being of nothingness (or, "no-thingness"). As unstructured by an authoritative count (i.e. an authoritative operation that constitutes being), it is this no-thingness that is the site of pure becoming and militant subjectivity (see 'The Void: Proper name of being' in Badiou 2011: 52–60). In contrast to Parmenides, for Badiou, although he maintains the biunivocal relationship of being and non-being ('nothing' in Badiou's lexicon) and appears to approach the Heideggerian duality (*Sein/Dasein*), nevertheless '[n]ature is not a region of being, a register of being-in-totality. It is the appearing, the bursting forth of being itself, the coming-to of its presence, or rather, the "stance of being"' (Badiou 2011: 123). If Parmenides remains with either a state of 'is' (a position similar to Heidegger's *Dasein*) and an unsayable 'is not', and Heidegger invokes two modes of 'is', Badiou modifies the Parmenidean duality into 'is being' and 'is not'.

19. In the same passage as he defends the use of numbers as the multiple having been 'given to thought' (Badiou 2004: 71), Badiou takes issue with Deleuze and Guattari's disagreement on this point in *What is Philosophy?* (Deleuze and Guattari [1991] 1994: 151–3). Badiou accuses the two authors of a dogmatic insistence to 'filter' number theory through the duality of the closed and the open, which are for him are non-ontological ideas due to their partiality (Badiou 2004: 71). For Badiou's rationalist ontology and as with the truth procedure, ontological ideas must be undecidable or, in other words, they must not be determined by the empirical and instead will determine what might be (2004: 49–58). Deleuze and Guattari's emphasis on openness and closure however is in service of their argument that set theory attempts both consistency (the perfection of axiomatic coherence) and totality (the 'extrinsic determination' of multiples by thought) (Deleuze and Guattari [1991] 1994: 121). As this chapter argues, Badiou cannot adequately account for the consistency and totality of his ontology because he subtracts both *doxa* and the sensible away from the world in attempts to explain it. The 'decision' that accounts for ontology's consistency and totality is, for Badiou, made from the realm of *doxa*, undermining its ontological status by his own account (Badiou 2004: 51).

20. Although Badiou's subject does rely on the technique of verifying a 'forced' truth within situations subsequent to an event in order to guide his behaviour, this is not what Foucault had in mind for his classification. Foucault states that in the 'case of a critical philosophy that investigates veridiction, the problem is that of knowing not under what conditions a statement is true, but rather what are the different games of truth and falsehood that are established, and according to what forms they are established' (2014: 20). Different games of truth are precisely what Badiou criticises as all belonging to the realm of opinion-trading and, consequently, he does not fit within this model of philosophy.
21. The insignificance of that which is not is clear when Parmenides argues, '[f]or this shall never be proved, that the things that are not are; and do thou restrain thy thought from this way of inquiry' (Parmenides 1920: §7).
22. The interpretation of Spinoza was one of the battlegrounds over which Badiou and Deleuze fought during their at first hesitant and then later tumultuous correspondence (see 'Deleuze's Vitalist Ontology' in Badiou 1998: 63–71). In *The Clamour of Being*, Badiou criticises Deleuze for his 'fundamental problem [that] is most certainly not to liberate the multiple but to submit thinking to a renewed concept of the One' (2000: 10). Taking quotes such as one found in the final paragraph of *Difference and Repetition*, where Deleuze hails a 'single and same voice for the whole thousand-voiced multiple, a single and same Ocean for all the drops, a single clamour of Being for all beings' (2004b: 378), he argues that Deleuze remains a theorist of the One-All, or a single event from which all of history has unfolded. Because, for Deleuze, 'the One is sovereign', Badiou argues, the ontological work within *Difference and Repetition* can only be regarded as a '"dogmatic" treatise', wholly in line with that of 'classical philosophy', as can be seen in conjunction with Deleuze's book on Spinoza, *Expressionism in Philosophy* (Deleuze 1992a, Badiou 2000: 13). This problem, he argues, stems from their mutual reading of Spinoza (yet a reading that, in Deleuze's work, Badiou does not recognise (Badiou 2000: 1)). In both Spinoza and Deleuze, Badiou sees a 'circular doctrine', whereby the 'legibility [that] distinguishes individuals, whose multiple, supposed inconsistent, receives the seal of consistency once the unity of their effect is registered. The inconsistency, or disjunction of individuals is then received as the consistency of the singular thing, one and the same' (Badiou 2011: 112). 'Multiples' (or, in common parlance, 'objects') are, for Spinoza and Deleuze, given their singular existence by the *effect* that they have as multiples, having emanated from an originary unknowable multiplicity. For Badiou, this is a tautological proposition, in that both the singular multiple and its effect are born from the same originary multiple but are only knowable in their mutual coexistence, one emanating from the other. As he

writes, 'insofar as the operator of the count which articulates them, causality, can only be vouched for, in turn, by the count of the effect' (Badiou 2011: 113). In other words, the power that articulates being (and concordantly its consistency) is, in Spinoza, articulated only by that which it presents. Badiou addresses this tautology, arguing that a single state of being can account for the adequacy of its own presentation of itself only by signalling the existence of an underlying void of inconsistent non-being. This inexistent non-being is not a One (in the sense that it is itself totalisable), but rather it is a 'multiple of multiples' which underpins ontogenesis and the consistency of presented multiples (see Badiou 2011: 45). Because this multiple of multiples must necessarily not be presented, Badiou states that the 'great lesson of Spinoza' (and, by implication, that which Deleuze also did not learn), is that 'you will not be able to avoid the errancy of the void; you will have to name its place' (Badiou 2011: 120).

23. In Badiou's work following *Theory of the Subject*, the truth of politics is thought through a subjective decision and implication with the event (being itself revealing its underpinning nothingness). The transition from the early Badiou, who conflated 'the subjective process of becoming confident in oneself with the global process of historical struggle itself, as aspects of a single logic' (Hallward 2003: 39) to his later thought, in which the subject is a pre-ontological supposition in the consistency of his ontological model, will be developed below.

24. For Livingston, it is the fact that Badiou can make a claim about what is not that causes him to reject 'the legacy of Parmenides and, indeed, [. . .] the entire ontological tradition he founded' (Livingston 2008: 44). However, although Badiou does indeed reject the totalising operation of Parmenides One-All (the state of being that results from a properly singular form of 'to be'), Badiou nevertheless remains within the Parmenidean tradition in the sense that he maintains a radical duality between the presentation of being (for Badiou, that which is accessible through set theory) and the no-thingness of the void.

25. Hallward claims that, 'Badiou presents his enterprise as another step taken in the ancient struggle of philosophy against dogmatic prejudice or *doxa*' (2003: 3). Badiou clarifies the grounds of his enterprise, stating that 'mathematics is a condition for thinking or theorising in general because it constitutes a break with *doxa* or opinion. This much is familiar. But what needs to be emphasised is that mathematics *is the only point of rupture with* doxa *that is given as existing, or constituted*' (2010c: 30).

26. Badiou accounts for three other 'truth procedures': artistic, scientific or amorous, although it is predominantly that of the political which will be examined in this chapter because it is most relevant for Badiou's idea of resistance.

27. See Badiou (1997) for Badiou's discussion of Saint Paul and the revelation of the event.

28. This excess over Being is not measurable because, in order for it to be so, the void of Being would have to be another constructible set. Were this the case, the excessive cardinality of the state could then be measured against the constructed set of Being. However, because Being is not constructed – but subtracted – from presentation, it remains immeasurable, yet present. As Badiou puts it, '[i]t is because the void is the point of being that it is also the almost-being which haunts the situation in which being consists' (2011: 77). In fact, constructionism (a position which Badiou is ardently opposed to) is described by Plato in the *Sophist*, where the Stranger portrays the sophist as 'just one of the genus of conjurors' (2006: 235C). It is the imitative art of conjuring reality in opinions, which are then set against each other in an ongoing creation of ever more *doxa*, that subtractive ontology attempts to eliminate. For a further discussion of why excess is immeasurable from the perspective of set theory, see Livingston (2011: 192–7).
29. Lacan's translator has since argued that the elusive French 'Y a d'l'Un' could also be translated as 'There's such a thing as One'; 'There's something like One'; and 'The One happens', giving some doubt as to the formalist consistency of what is signified by 'One' (Livingston 2008: 331).
30. Barlett, Clemens and Roffe develop what they rightly call some of the 'crucial – and reciprocal – points of influence' between the titular theorists of *Lacan Deleuze Badiou* (2014). With regard to the relationship between formalisation and the real, the authors foreground Deleuze and Guattari's reversal of Lacan's position in *Anti-Oedipus*, where the authors accept the Lacanian statement above, but treat the real as primary (and not as the consequence of signification) (2014: 66–7). Formalisation, for Deleuze and Guattari, is thus secondary to both desire and individuation with the consequence that there is always an element of experimentation and creativity to both. Barlett, Clemens and Roffe go on to demonstrate that, rather than ignoring or disparaging Deleuze and Guattari's criticism, Lacan in fact responds to it in his 1975–6 seminar series through the inclusion of an element of materialist signification. *Lacan Deleuze Badiou* is highly interesting for its contribution to the secondary literature on all three authors, demonstrating the relationship between the thought of all three, and that of the authors' with their theoretical predecessors.
31. The terminology here is important for Badiou. He states that 'once the entirety of a situation is subject to the law of the one and consistency' (i.e. once a state has been imposed upon any particular situation), 'it is necessary, from the standpoint of immanence to the situation, that the pure multiple, absolutely unpresentable according to the count, be *nothing*. But being-nothing is as distinct from

non-being as the "there is" is distinct from being' (Badiou 2011: 53, original emphasis). The distinction Badiou makes is that of something that does not exist in any expressible manner, yet which still has a trace or a name associated with its place of being, with that of something that simply does not exist at all. The pure multiple is nothing, yet 'is' to the extent that it is there as an ontological excess of the state of being. It is for this reason that, elsewhere, Badiou names 'being' *consistent* multiplicity and 'non-being' *inconsistent* multiplicity (see 'The Question of Being Today' in Badiou 2010c: 39–48).

32. See, in particular, 'Meditation Thirty-Five: Theory of the Subject' in Badiou (2011: 391–409).

33. Badiou further declares that he thinks 'the problem today is to find a way of reversing the classical dialectical logic inside itself so that the affirmation, or the positive proposition, comes before the negation instead of after it'. He claims that, '[i]n some sense, my attempt is to find a dialectical framework where something of the future comes before the negative present. I'm not suggesting the suppression of the relation between affirmation and negation – certainly revolt and class struggle remain essential – and I'm not suggesting a pacifistic direction or anything like that. The question is not whether we need to struggle or oppose, but concerns more precisely the relation between negation and affirmation' (2013a: 3). Whilst he is significantly less focused on the priority of the negative than in earlier works, Badiou nevertheless relies on the negative, in dialectical relation to affirmation, in stipulation of what is or is not as an unproblematic category.

34. Badiou's decision to align himself with the non-being of the One reflects the axiom of choice in his appropriation of ZFC set theory. According to Cantor's 'diagonal' argument, when a set, T is the set of an infinite sequence of binary digits, a second set, s can be constructed where each of its elements correspond to the digit n in the set T, i.e. $s1, s2 . . ., s_n . . . .$ Set T therefore cannot be counted because the second set, s would always differ from the sequence of T s_n and thereby consist of another set which would have to be included *post hoc* by sequence T. Cantor's diagonal argument has led to several conclusions in mathematical encampments leading constructivists, for example, to conclude that there is an infinite series of constructible sets (the set s must now be counted by a new set, and so on). More pertinent for Badiou however, given that constructivism is, for him, akin to sophistry, was the argument drawn up by Ernst Zermelo in 1908. Zermelo concluded that, because the set s is uncountable (it exists in excess of all countable sets), yet itself contains non-empty sets, there is an element common to all the non-empty sets within it. Given an infinite number of different pairs of shoes, one would be able to pick out an infinite number of left shoes (this being a common property of the infinite number of pairs of shoes according to

the axiom of choice). It is the axiom of choice therefore that Badiou employs as his 'decision', subjectively denying the encapsulation of presentation by a superior set (or 'power set' in his nomenclature), whilst enabling the subject to pay fidelity to an eventual rupture of presentation, to 'choose' what to take from this new-found and non-totalisable revelation of being. This is what Badiou refers to as fidelity to a truth procedure.

35. The claim that something is or is not is itself grounded upon an *a priori* conditional idea that distinguishes between the statuses 'what is' and 'what is not'. In one discussion of this dyad, Meillassoux (2008) discusses this 'facticity' of an object, arguing that the principle of sufficient reason in its negative form ('x is not true') carries with it truth conditions that cannot be justified. This results in a world of infinitely possible situations that may or may not happen because we cannot know for certain that they will not. Whilst Meillassoux disparages Deleuze by, alongside Kant, putting him into the category of 'correlationist', fruitful research could be carried out by combining Meillassoux's work on facticity with Deleuze's concept of significance in understanding the consistency of becoming-new.

36. Badiou's argument here stems from a contentious reading of Parmenides' poem On *Nature*. Cordero (2004) has written a full and nuanced discussion on the poem which discusses, amongst other important issues, the sensibility of nothing. Badiou's claim here is that, if sense senses, there must be something to sense. Even if one senses what they think is nothingness, that nothingness is nevertheless a thing they have simply termed 'nothingness'.

37. Excellent portrayals of Badiou's critical uptake of Althusser's 'epistemological break' from ideology can be found in Fraser's introduction to Badiou ([1966] 2007: i–lxv) and in Bosteels (2001). Althusser's distinction between scientific knowledge and ideology will be developed in the next chapter as a point of unity between Badiou and Deleuze.

38. Badiou recognises this problem early on in his writing, taking on the latter issue as the task left by Althusser. He develops the problematic in *Theory of the Subject*, where he discusses the placement (or 'splace'), P of pure being, A. As has been shown, for Badiou, the task of the proletariat is to negate the placing operation of the bourgeoisie to the extent that society becomes truly classless, otherwise it remains a set of the proletariat counting operation. The reproduction of the eventual rupture throughout a social upheaval would be written, with the language of the Hegelian dialectic, $Ap(Ap) = P$ where Ap is being-placed. This algorithm represents a deviation '"to the right", which leads back to the objective brutality of the place P in order to deny the possibility of the new inherent in the old' (Badiou [1982] 2013: 12). In other words, given a process of determination, the placement of being will not have disappeared, 'nothing will have

taken place but the place' and being will remain represented through the situation it intended to rupture (Badiou [1982] 2013: 10).
39. Badiou provides a rigorous defence of mathematics as the language of being *qua* being, as opposed to sophistry and superstition in 'Mathematics and Philosophy' in *Theoretical Writings* (2004). He declares that mathematics 'is "older than the sun,"' that it will remain intact 'on the ruins of time', and that mathematics 'is the discipline and the severity, the immutability and the image of "that supreme truth"' (2004: 12).
40. For further discussion of the little and grand styles of mathematics, see Badiou (2010c: 3–38).
41. Badiou pre-empts the criticism of inference, arguing that, rather than inferential, 'every universalising procedure is implicative. It verifies the consequences that follow from the evental statement to which the vanished event is indexed' (2004: 149). Badiou takes for granted the pre-subjective constituency of mathematics and, in his formation of his work at least (see below), does not rely on any synthesis (such as Kant's synthetic unity of the manifold) to reproduce and take active agency in applying its authoritative power. Mathematics acts through the subject it constitutes and is not constituted by an *a priori* subject.
42. Meillassoux's conception of correlationism will be developed further in Chapter 3.
43. It is unclear whether or not the mark as discussed in *The Concept of Model* and within *Being and Event* are the same for Badiou. In *The Concept of Model*, Badiou uses the term to refer to the inscriptions of mathematical terminology in a much more general sense than in *Being and Event*; in the latter book, the mark represents only the being-as-nothing prior to the count-as-one.
44. Laruelle puts this forcefully; of Badiou's ontological position, he claims that '[e]ither it is an "intricated" unity, philosophically self-intricated, that claims to found itself and to operate the act of subtraction – an act that conceals another, more pure, philosophical-style auto-foundation, but which does not know itself as such or is not announced explicitly; or else it requires a relatively detached meta-ontological act of being-posited, an explicit intervention of positing. Badiou as materialist tries to flatten one onto the other the object posited and the idealist act of positing. The difference in the two cases is the difference between the implicit and the explicit, but that makes no difference to the decisionist or arbitrary structure at work here' (Laruelle 2013: 82).
45. Kant states that '[t]his unity – speaking generally – is called pure concept of understanding. Hence the same understanding – and indeed through the same acts whereby it brought about, in concepts, the logical form of a judgment by means of analytic unity – also brings into its presentations a transcendental content, by means of

the synthetic unity of the manifold in intuition as such.' The 'pure concept of understanding' crucially is not understanding itself, but that which allows understanding as such. Kant uses this 'pure concept' of understanding in his argument against Hume to demonstrate how, despite the lack of our ability to access the thing-in-itself directly, there must be an in-itself in order to allows us the possibility of knowing.

46. The inner workings of Badiou's theory of categories, most fully developed in *Logics of Worlds* (2009), will not be discussed here because the purpose of this chapter is not to see how well Badiou accounts for the presentation of the transcendental. Instead, it is more important to account for whether or not Badiou's ontology can be connected back to the semantic, having previously extradited it, and the status of the political actor within the Badiouian system.

47. A full examination of Kant's philosophy is beyond the purview of this book. It is worth noting however that Deleuze complicates this preliminary exposition of Kant through his reading of the *Critique of Judgement* in (Deleuze [1963] 2008). According to Hughes, what fascinated Deleuze about Kant's project was that the third *Critique* examined the Kantian concepts of synthesis and schematism from the point of view of each other, in order to uncover the 'transcendental genesis' of each faculty (Hughes 2009: 5). In this way, for Deleuze, Kant goes some way to avoiding the dogmatic idealism of the first two *Critiques*.

48. Badiou offers no evidence that non-humans do not have a sense of self-identification and always uses the masculine pronoun (in both *Ethics* and his book on love (2012)). This leaves his anthropological reliability open to question, as well as the gendered and heterocentric logic of his philosophy.

49. Barker neatly summarises Badiou's concept of the situations as 'the set of circumstances, infinitely multiple, which is interrupted and named "after the event"' (2002: 134). To explain the evental site, Badiou turns to a strangely banal example of family composition. A family who have have all registered with the registry office and possess French nationality, yet who harbour a secret member of the family at home who has not been registered is a 'singular' multiplicity. This is because the presentation of the family itself has not been represented by the state. A family who has been entirely counted by the state is a 'normal' multiplicity in the sense that the count-as-one of the state functions here normally. This family has been presented (by itself) and represented (by the state). For Badiou, an evental site would be a family '*all* of whose members were clandestine or non-declared, and which presents itself (manifests itself publicly) uniquely in the group form of family outings' (Badiou 2011: 175). Because none of the terms of the family are counted as one and only the multiple 'family' forms a one,

this family is 'on the edge of the void', to the extent that it borders singular presentation and the count-as-one of the state. The eventual site belongs to the situation, although its contents do not. It is from here that there is a chance, under certain circumstances particular to each situation, for being to spring from the confines of representation and rupture into an event. See Badiou (2011: 173–7).
50. Badiou clarifies that, for him, it is 'important to understand that the "subject", thus conceived, does not overlap with the psychological subject, nor even with the reflexive subject (in Descartes' sense) or the transcendental subject (in Kant's sense)' (Badiou 2001: 43).
51. For an excellent discussion of why this is so from the formalist perspective, see Livingston's chapter on Badiou's paradoxico-criticism in *The Politics of Logic* (2011: 107–208).
52. For Althusser, ideology is not a positivist set of purely imagined dreams that has no bearing on reality, but rather an order of knowledge by which the individual can think their relationship with the objects of the world in which they live. As such, Ideological State Apparatuses constitute an image of the individual's relationship with themselves which is understood by the individual as reality. Althusser argues that this conceptualisation of ideology gives it a material basis, in the sense that ideology is routed in the performative practices that make up the individual's engagement with social institutions.
53. Althusser's claim that this is possible and the difference between scientific and ideological knowledge will be developed in the next chapter.
54. Badiou makes several references to his desire for immortality. For examples, see the title of *Infinite Thought* and *Ethics* (2001: 10–13).
55. For Badiou's account of how the subject relates to a situation, see Badiou (2011: 406–9).
56. Badiou often claims that mathematics is beholden to no justification and carries its own authority within its own presentation. His discussion in *Conditions* makes this argument particularly clearly, drawing his argument from Book VI of Plato's *Republic*, and stating that, in the 'form of the already-there, mathematics and it alone constitutes the only point of external support for breaking with *doxa*' ([1992] 2008: 102). One upshot of removing any necessity for mathematics to legitimise itself with external support is that, as Gironi (2014) argues, Badiou's conception of science becomes aleatory. As matter comes immediately after Being, rather than as a part of it, and because it is only through an event that scientific truth becomes knowable through its mathematical inscription, Badiou's scientific progress is constituted by a series of revelatory moments. However, in his attempt to naturalise Badiou's ontology within an account of structural realism, Gironi demonstrates that the progression from Galilean mathematisation (starting with observation and measurement of phenomena)

towards Dirac's 'methodological revolution' (where mathematics itself became an inductive tool for new phenomenic aspects) could only come about *via* Newton's initial success at conceptualising general mathematical laws (such as the law of universal gravitation). As he concludes, 'it is simply *not true* that the mathematised concepts employed by contemporary physics retain "a relation to the world which means that they cannot be deduced from any mathematical corpus whatsoever"' (Gironi 2014: 40). Not to mention the mystic/theological undertones of his revelatory conceptualisation of science, discussions of which can be found in Phelps (2013) and Frederiek (2009), Badiou's inability to account for the connection between the ontological and the sensible removes any possibility for understanding scientific continuity.

57. 'Authorisation' is the term Badiou uses to describe the statist process (i.e., the count-as-one) that formalises inconsistent Being into consistent multiplicities. It is because authorisation is a formalism that brings together that which is otherwise inconsistent into something that can be engaged with in practice that it is also appropriate to attribute it to Badiou's mathematics. Yet, Badiou's mathematics carries with it its own authorisation in the form of the axiomatic, hence the prefix 'auto-' attached here. For Badiou's discussion of authorisation, see Badiou (2011: 24–5).

58. For a discussion of Badiou's mathematical ontology and how Badiou avoids these issues, see 'The Ontological and the Empirical: Naturalist Objections' in Gironi (2014: 34–62).

59. Of being, Parmenides states that 'it is impossible for it not to be, [it] is the way of belief, for truth is its companion' (Parmenides 1920: §4–5).

60. For Parmenides, *doxa* is not simply the appearance of being, as it is for Badiou, because, in a similar position to Badiou's stance on the non-truthfulness of *doxa*, Parmenides 'knows that on that subject it would be possible to say something and also say the opposite' (Cordero 2004: 153). For Cordero, the important distinction in *On Nature* is between 'appearances' and 'presentations': whereby philosophers truthfully understand that being appears before a classification into an ontic object ('*tà ónta*'), mortals believe that they must name certain presentations of being in order to recognise them, though 'this has nothing to do with "appearances"' (Cordero 2004: 153). Although Parmenides' description of presentations is similar to Badiou's description of a counting operation, to the extent that sets are named by a power set which represents them to the state, Parmenides' solution is not simply that knowledge of that which is *not* presentation must be truthful. As Cordero puts it, challenging Badiou's conception of the evental site, 'if nothing existed, there would be nothing to think about' (Cordero 2004: 83). Rather,

Parmenides rejects the ability of humans to know the truth as they are only able to 'create opinions', i.e. to name and consequently understand presentations of being (Cordero 2004: 154). For Cordero, in a contrasting reading to Jowett, being in Parmenides' account *is* prior to thought (which is a necessary result of being being all that there is). As a result of his position that 'there is not and there will not be anything apart from that which is being' (Parmenides 1920: §8.36–7), and the priority of being over thought, thought in Parmenides prohibits the positing of any negative ontological void that contains a truth that presentation does not, although human thought of appearances is nevertheless insufficient to bear the truth of being. It is this problematic that Badiou attempts to unravel in the first meditation of *Being and Event*, suggesting that it can only be the void that unfolds in a truth procedure. Yet, Badiou's answer, that ontology can only present the void, is immediately undermined by the Parmenidean stipulation that all that is is. On the other hand, however, Parmenides' position seems to offer no way of articulating a truth of the world at all, given that thought does exist within being, yet only presides over presentation. This is the problematic that Althusser attempts to solve with his structuralist account of a science of being, and this will be discussed in the next chapter.

61. Instead, it is 'an attempt to define the generic form taken by all truth processes when they come up against obstacles that are inherent in the world in which they operate' (Badiou 2010a: 38).
62. See Gironi (2014) for one example of an exceptionally detailed discussion of Badiou's mathematical ontology which is left wanting for an appreciation of his contribution to politics.

Chapter 2

Contra Axiomatics: The Persistence of Althusser, Badiou and Deleuze

An Althusserian conjuncture

As Hallward says, the 'evolution of [Badiou's] relations to both Althusser and Deleuze certainly gives a colourful measurement of how far his position has shifted from the days when he labelled the former 'arrogant, idealist, irresponsible, hypocritical and metaphysical' and the latter a *'petit professeur de l'embuscade désirante'* (Barker 2002: 2, Hallward 2003: 29). Following on from the discussion of Badiou's ontology in the previous chapter, it is to the relation of his work to that of Althusser and Deleuze that this chapter will turn in the attempt to identify certain continuities and divergences between the three authors' ontologies. Discussion will centre around the particular importance of the role that time plays within their works, particularly in regard to the concept of the void. Badiou's subtractive ontology features an emergent void from the realm of the sensible. This is the void of the radically new, and creates ruptural times consistent with each event's rupture with representation. Deleuze (both by himself and in his writing with Guattari) emphatically rejected any reliance on the void at all (Deleuze [1969] 2004: 137), and his conception of time is not ruptural, but (akin to his appropriation of Bergson) immanent. Importantly, however, with respect to both Deleuze's and Badiou's inheritance from him, Althusser's stance on the void is not as clear as theirs, and his conceptualisation of time is underdeveloped in that it lacks an account of persistence. Whilst

Morfino's *An Althusserian Lexicon* (2005: §8–23) demonstrates several instances across Althusser's texts that do indeed discuss the void, this chapter will stray from a purely comparative reading of the three authors in order to evince a reading of Althusser that differs significantly from that which Badiou's and Morfino's neo-classical inferences develop. True to Althusser's own method of 'symptomatic reading', this chapter will show that his work – and particularly his seminal texts *Ideology and Ideological State Apparatuses* (1971) and *Essays in Self-Criticism* (1976) – indicate a void which is filled, not with 'nothing' as Morfino and Althusser argue (Morfino 2005), but a multiplicity that can be understood in relation to Bergson's concept of duration. In this context, Badiou's allegiance to Althusser's ontology seems misplaced, as Althusser's concept of the void more closely resembles the concept of the virtual in Bergson and Deleuze.

Althusser's thought is not in a spurious relationship to that of Badiou or Deleuze and the connections made in this chapter are not drawn of fancy. Badiou's references to Althusser are many (Badiou 1998: 58, Badiou 2005a, Badiou 2005c: 10, 70, Badiou 2005d: xix, xxxvi, 44–66, Badiou [1997] 2006, Badiou 2008: 647, Badiou 2013a, Badiou [1982] 2013: 23, 187, 224), he was taught by Althusser at the École Normale Supérieure, attended a research group on Spinoza organised by Althusser in 1967 and the same year was invited to join Althusser's 'Philosophy Course for Scientists' (Barker 2002: 1–2). Althusser's initial influence over Badiou brought the two in line in the latter's earlier work with their conception of science as a 'purely formal logic whose self-regulating rigour is maintained in the absence of any reference to an external object' (Hallward 2003: 32).[1] Yet Althusser's unrelenting flirtation with the French Communist Party (PCF) drew the ire of Badiou, who scorned its 'legal, reformist institutions' and its 'trade unions, along with the "false working-class left, the inheritor of anarchosyndicalism"' (Hallward 2003: 35–7).[2] Alongside Rancière, who accused Althusser of advocating a petty bourgeoisie of professors and scientists in place of party leaders (Rancière [1974] 2011), Badiou dismissed Althusser's revisionist pretensions (Bosteels 2005: 597, 602). Althusser's position was intolerable for any Maoist, and indeed it was 'exactly the opposite' of those taken by a number of prominent Marxist thinkers (for example Kautsky, Plekhanov, Lenin, Labriola, Gramsci, Luckács and Sartre) (Balibar 1993: 8). Althusser rejected 'any "dialectic" of Being and Consciousness, whether in its mechanistic or its speculative forms, and, instead of *adding* a theory of the "superstructure" to the existing theory of the "structure," he [aimed] at *transforming* the concept of the structure itself by showing that its process of "production" and "reproduction" *originally* [depended] on unconscious ideological conditions' (Balibar 1993: 8, original italics).

As was shown in the previous chapter, Badiou staunchly rejects any determination of being by consciousness under the first Platonic dyad of truth/*doxa* and, given that ideology and the production of the unconscious occur within the realm of *doxa* for Althusser, Badiou rejects Althusserianism as (mathematically) subjectless (Badiou 2005d: 58–67).[3] How then can Badiou be the Althusserian (as well as Satrean and Lacanian) that both he and others characterise himself as (for example, see Bosteels 2011: 612)? Put differently: what is Althusserian in Badiou's writing? Although Badiou praises his former teacher as the one who obliged philosophers to 'reject the humanist vision of the bond, or the being-together, which binds an abstract and ultimately enslaved vision of politics to the theological ethics of rights' (2005d: 66), Badiou's work is in direct contrast to Althusser's, given its reliance on a formal theory of the subject. Other than a shared revulsion of humanist politics, and their placement within the post-Marxist cannon, is there really much that unites teacher and student? The status of this purported unity will be explored in this chapter.

In comparison to the primary and secondary literature on Badiou in connection to Althusser, there is very little to connect Althusser with Deleuze.[4] Stolze's revealing article on Deleuze, Althusser and structuralism notes but two passing references to 'Louis Althusser' in over seventeen hundred pages of anthology dedicated to Deleuze (Stolze 1998: 52). The only other substantive and specific engagement with their work is Diefenbach's chapter 'Althusser with Deleuze: how to think Spinoza's immanent cause' (Diefenbach *et al.* 2013: 165–80). Yet what elucidation there is shows a significant compatibility between their work (for brief references to the two authors, see also Rancière [1974] 2011, Montag 2013b: 152). As Stolze points out, Althusser 'and his circle seem to have been quite favourably disposed toward certain of Deleuze's early works (such as a 1961 essay on Lucretius and the already classic book on Nietzsche published in 1962)' (Stolze 1998: 51). In an attempt to rectify what Stolze terms an 'astonishing silence' (Stolze 1998: 52), his article outlines the contributions that Althusser and Pierre Macherey made to the first draft of what would become Deleuze's essay 'How do we Recognise Structuralism?' (Deleuze 2004a: 170–92) and these contributions will be discussed below. This chapter will continue Stolze's efforts to fill the silence, or rather to amplify its deadened whisper, with the voice of Hume.

Despite Deleuze's inclusion of Althusser within the band of structuralists, and Choat's characterisation of 'Althusser's later work' as offering 'evidence that he was [. . .] influenced by post-structuralism' (Choat 2010: 5), Althusser refused this classification, declaring in fact that '[w]e were guilty of an equally powerful and uncompromising passion: *we were Spinozists*' (Althusser 1976: 132). Deleuze's own oeuvre is full of references to Spinoza, as is Badiou's; there is therefore something of a spectre of Spinoza haunting a conjuncture of all three philosophers' works.[5] Yet, whilst there is already a significant body of work that relates Badiou, Althusser and Deleuze to Spinoza, the influence of Hume on both Badiou and Althusser is relatively understudied.[6] This chapter will therefore explore Hume's attempt to reconcile the affective qualities of materialism with mental impressions in order to account for the ideational. This is, as was mentioned in the previous chapter, an important challenge for Badiou (in particular) to account for in his own work. Hume raises the question for both Althusser and Badiou: 'how is it that our ideas about ontology are constituted from our impressions of the world?', and this question also motivates Deleuze's development of Hume's work in *The Logic of Sense*. As will be shown, it is Hume's idea of human nature which constitutes the framework within which time is understood as part of the creation of ideas in the mind. Thus, it will be argued that Hume's idea of human nature is the key idea within a symptomatic reading of Althusser that constitutes the idea of persistence of objectivity within Althusser's aleatory void.

Before developing any work on Althusser, it seems necessary within his secondary literature to nod towards the events of his life as a generic preamble. In fact, much of the literature on Althusser (both in support or criticism of it) starts off with autobiographical details which the author will then determine either did or did not condition Althusser's theoretical work (Morfino 2005: §1). This chapter will however not dwell on any of Althusser's biographical details with the exception of those pertaining to his relationship to the PCF and, thus, to Badiou. In line with Deleuze's statements in the *Abecedaire* regarding biography being the worst kind of philosophical literature (Boutang 1988), and Montag's bitter disappointment at Althusser's theoretical contradiction in having written an autobiography (2003: 126), this chapter will focus solely on the philosophy (defined in Deleuze and Guattari's terms as the 'creation of concepts' (Deleuze and Guattari [1991] 1994)) within his work.

So, whilst the previous chapter demonstrated Badiou's mathematical ontology that sidelined the 'animal human', this chapter will develop Althusser's theoretical anti-humanism, and the following two chapters will develop Deleuze's focus upon immanent haecceity. This chapter will argue that all three philosophers have at least one thing in common: an anti-humanism/anti-rationalism that criticises humanism as a myopic ideology. Indeed, Althusser himself put it well when he wrote that the 'golden rule of materialism is *do not judge being by its self-consciousness*, for every being is other than its self-consciousness' (1996: 115). In particular, and in agreement with Protevi's characterisation of a rationalist explanation of behaviour 'as abstracting from its concrete practical ground and breaking free to posit itself as self-sufficient so that it pretends to ground that which in fact grounds it', this chapter will not therefore re-inject the personal back into a sterile discussion of its contribution to Althusser's thought, but will trace the contribution his thought made to both Badiou and Deleuze (Protevi 2010: 419).[7]

Which Althusser?

At a conference in 1988 on the work of Althusser, Balibar commented that '[f]or almost twenty years, Althusser was *the* controversial Marxist in France [. . .] controversial among "Marxists" (who would discuss his formulations and react to his positions in a passionate manner), but also one who forced other intellectuals to take Marxism seriously' (Balibar 1993: 1, original italics).[8] Balibar then noted that 'Italy is the one country where Althusser is still publicly discussed in militant and intellectual circles on the Left', and – paradoxically – the 'remarkable persistence of some expressions that have been either coined by Althusser or transferred by him out of their specialised initial field into common culture: "epistemological break," "overdetermination," "ideological state apparatuses," "Process without a Subject"' (Balibar 1993: 1–2). Montag has also noted that both Rancière and Foucault used parts of Althusser's work without acknowledging their influence and Althusser's influence thus stretches far into critical theory and post-structuralist thought (2013b: 151). If, as Jameson puts it, 'the current post-structural celebration of discontinuity and heterogeneity is [. . .] only a moment in Althusserian exegesis' (1981: 51), then Althusserian philosophy offers much more to contemporary thought than his near-disappearance from discussion seems to demonstrate. And yet, as Montag argues, to 'pose the question, "Why read Althusser today?" is to admit at the outset that his status as a philosopher remains unclear in a way that is not true of his contemporaries and friends, Foucault and Derrida' (Montag 2013a: 1). Althusser's detractors might indeed have wished his excommunication from the ranks of Marxists and 'real' philosophers; however, his contribution towards Badiou and Deleuze's work provides defence enough against this denigration.[9]

One particular issue that prohibits an easy discussion of Althusser's work is that 'there is more than one identifiable Althusserianism' and, further, that 'these divergent readings vary according to discipline' (Montag 2003: 3). Whereas Balibar identifies two kinds of Althusserianism, '"Althusserians of the Conjuncture and Althusserians of the Structure," precisely because this antagonism traverses his entire corpus' (Balibar 1993: 94), Williams and Montag show a third 'materialism of the encounter' at work in Althusser's later work (Williams 2002: 39, Montag 2010: 157). Such diversity in the work of Althusser was explained by Althusser himself however when he argued the history of philosophy is not a 'succession of closed systems, each of which could be identified with an author who would serve as its centre and principle of unity, of which Marxism or materialism would be one among others' (Montag 2013a: 5). Instead, and in a manner not dissimilar to Deleuze's interpretive methodology of 'buggery', Althusser's 'symptomatic reading' involved inserting oneself into a literary text and its 'theoretical conjuncture' in order to take up a position which will then be transformed by the process of philosophy.[10] It is for this reason – Althusser's refusal to dialectically oppose philosophers *ad hominem* – that he 'would appear to embody the opposition between postmodernism and modernism, between rationalism and irrationalism, and can be summoned in defence of either of the opposing sides' (Montag 2003: 133). Perhaps Althusser's most significant contribution to Marxism, however, lay in his criticism *in spite of* (or even because of) a lack of opposition; for example, despite entirely refuting the dialectic method in his later work in favour of 'aleatory materialism', Althusser's philosophy was far from quietist (contrary to Choat's accusation; see Choat 2010: 27–9). In fact, Althusser accordingly adopted both Napoleon's maxim '"*on s'engage et puis on voit*," (meaning, first we engage the enemy and then see what does and doesn't work)' to characterise the strategy with which he approached philosophy (Montag 2013a: 4) and Marx's 'famous "little phrase," [. . .] [m]en make their own history, but they do not make it out of freely chosen elements (*aus freien Stücken*), under circumstances chosen by themselves, but under circumstances (*Umstände*) directly encountered (*vorgefundene*), given by and transmitted from the past' (Althusser 1976: 98–9). Wholly in line with his theoretical anti-humanism (but not, as discussed above, in line with his autobiography), history, for Althusser, 'does not have a Subject, in the philosophical sense of the term, but a *motor*: that very class struggle' (Althusser 1976: 99, see also Althusser and Matheron 2003: 232–6). Althusser's concept of the motor, separately formulated as the unconscious, will be returned to at the end of the chapter in his account of how thought is synthesised in order to think the new.

Three 'different' Althussers contributing to one oeuvre and 'a network of mutually supporting arguments' means that 'it is difficult to assess his work except in its entirety and after taking at least one turn around it' (Resch 1992: 41). Balibar acknowledged this difficulty, pointing out that 'there is nothing in fact like a systematic work of Althusser, with a beginning, an end, a structural unity' (1993: 2). However, as stated at the beginning of *For Marx*, one of Althusser's tasks was 'to draw a line of demarcation between Marxist theory and the forms of philosophical (and political) subjectivism which have compromised or threatened it' (Althusser [1965] 2005: 12), and Althusser's works can be seen as a developing effort to delineate this Marxist theory.

One of the reasons that Althusser's work became the target of such personalised contempt was that his crusade to purify Marxism involved the dismissal of all elements that aimed to ground analysis upon a sedimented layer of ideology.[11] Althusser did not dismiss ideology entirely, sharing as he did Badiou's later position that human thought could not exist outside of terms (in part) constituted by ideology. As Ricœur puts it, although Althusser succeeds in calling out ideology as theoretically non-existent, that 'is not to abolish it' (1994: 50). Althusser's task was thus to develop a scientific theory which could account for the production of ideology itself, despite the inability of the subject to ever escape from ideological thought. This theory was thus 'concerned *not* with an investigation of what particular subjects may think, or even *how*, by what means, they carry out the act of thinking, rather he is concerned with the *ideological mechanism* according to which thought, perception and subjectivity are produced' (Williams 2002: 35–6, original italics). In order to carry out his task, Althusser's 'theory of theoretical practice' rejected the distinction between object and subject (due to the transcendentalism involved with a subject 'investigating' an object), and thus removed the distinction between ideology and traditional science. For Althusser, traditional science (which Althusser termed 'empiricism') produced an imaginary, ideological 'form of knowledge because it takes the subject's experience and perception of objects as the basis for knowledge' (Williams 2002: 32).[12] Empirical science thus cannot form the basis of a theory of theoretical practice because the abstraction of essence from a real object comes from the operation of a presupposed subject. For Althusser, the division between 'fiction and truth, between ideology and the real [and, thus, subject and object], *are wholly internal to ideology*' (Williams 2002: 34) and any *a priori* specification of the two would constitute the same abstract differentiation of subject from the empirical world that Badiou was shown to criticise in the previous chapter. Whereas Badiou looked to mathematics in order to formally differentiate a subject from the empirical world of presentation and ideology, Althusser sought to remove the subject/object distinction entirely, looking instead to develop a theory which understood their production.[13] The difficulty of reading Althusser is, for some readers, compounded by a theoretical problem that undermines the coherence of his work. When Althusser disregarded the subject of philosophy, assuming 'that philosophical texts presented the dissimulation of coherence and consistency', he argued that ideas had 'a material existence', that 'consciousness was nothing other than action' (Montag and Stolze 1997: 157). Philosophical knowledge, for Althusser, does not emanate from the subject, as it does for idealists, positivists and rationalists, but is rather 'stored' or 'transmitted' by texts. Accordingly, Althusser 'has not only separated mind and body, but has inserted between them the infinite space of the void through which they are destined to fall in parallel for all eternity' (Montag 2010: 157, 160). By rejecting humanist, rationalist and vulgar determinist accounts of history (or, in other words, a distinction between the subject or object of history in whatever configuration they may appear), 'Althusser endows the history of philosophy, with an object external to it: the nothingness that is the origin (or rather originary non-origin, a theoretical compromise which in no way escapes the implications of the concept of origins) and destiny of all things' (Montag 2010: 161).[14] In other words, because neither subject nor object can be taken as the starting point, analysis must begin with that which is not either of those: a new object which contains the conditions for both theoretical procedure and result, yet a position which is un-sayable in its *a priori* non-existence. This starting point is, for Althusser, what he would call 'aleatory' materialism following a series of interviews in 1984 with Spanish philosopher Fernanda Navarro, in which Althusser derives 'aleatory' 'from the Latin *alea*, for the dice or games of chance' (Montag 2003: 12). As Williams puts it, it is through the 'paradox of *incessant rupture* that philosophy is able to occupy a position, develop a strategy, a thought of practice, to 'think practice via that thought', and through this process to create political (that is, ideological and material) effects (2013: 154). Locating it as indeed the '"sole materialist tradition," a lineage that embraces Epicurus, Lucretius, Machiavelli, Spinoza, Hobbes, Rousseau, Marx and Heidegger' (Althusser 1997, Montag 2003: 12, Althusser 2006: 167), aleatory materialism was Althusser's answer to criticisms (and indeed his own self-criticism) that accused his earlier work of lacking a justification for his structuralist alternative to traditional Marxist dialectical frameworks.

A '[m]aterialism of the encounter, and therefore of the aleatory and of contingency' relies, for Althusser, on what he calls 'the rain of parallelism' (Althusser 2006: 167). The rain of which Althusser writes refers to Epicurus's philosophical atomism, which Althusser expands upon with the work of Spinoza. According to Epicurus, an infinite number of atoms exist in an infinite void of space around them within which they exist in constant motion, forming an infinite number of different bodies (Epicurus 1925: §40–1). For Althusser, '[t]hey still are', and this implies both that matter (in its undifferentiated form) constitutes being without any consistency (in the same sense of Badiou's undifferentiated multiplicity), and that before the formation of the world, 'there was no Meaning, neither Cause nor End, nor Reason nor Unreason' (2006: 168–9).[15] Interrupting the atoms' free-fall is the clinamen: an 'infinitesimal *swerve*' which, 'breaking the parallelism in an almost negligible way at one point, [induces] *an encounter* with the atom next to it, and, from encounter to encounter, a pile-up and the birth of a world' (Althusser 2006: 169, original italics). Epicurus's clinamen thus functions for Althusser as the structure that confers meaning upon matter. The clinamen does not contain bodies (or meaning, or reason) and is merely a structure of void; bodies are the resultant encounter between different atoms which takes place within the structure. The structure, as the possibility for an encounter to take place, facilitates encounters between atoms, encounters which confer '*their reality upon the atoms themselves*, which, without swerve and encounter, would be nothing but *abstract* elements, lacking all consistency and existence' (Althusser 2006: 169, original italics). Althusser's criticism of ideology is clear (and similar to Badiou's): any form of thought that bases itself upon one (or several) encounters, which function as the transcendental basis of analysis, do not take into account that '*the accomplishment of the fact* is just a pure effect of contingency, since it depends on the aleatory encounter of the atoms due to the swerve of the clinamen' (Althusser 2006: 169–70). Because ideas of what are created by encounters appear after the fact, any presupposition of encounters results in the dominance of the man who has the ability somehow to actively make history. It is worth here quoting Althusser at length from his 'Reply to John Lewis':

> Do you know of any being under the sun endowed with such a power? Yes – there does exist such a being in the tradition of human culture: *God*. Only *God* 'makes' the raw material with which he 'makes' the world. But there is a very important difference. John Lewis's God is not outside of the world: the man-god who creates history is not outside of history – he is *inside*. This is something infinitely more complicated! And it is just because John Lewis's little human god – man – is *inside* history ('*en situation*', as Jean-Paul Sartre used to say) that Lewis does not endow him with a power of absolute creation (when one creates everything, it is relatively easy: there are no limitations!) but with something even more stupefying – the power of 'transcendence', of being able to progress by indefinitely *negating-superseding* the constraints of the history *in which* he lives, the power to transcend history by *human liberty*. John Lewis's man is a little lay god. Like every living being he is 'up to his neck' in reality, but endowed with the prodigious power of being able at any moment to step outside of that reality, of being able to change its character. (Althusser 1976: 43–4)

The lay god is thus the man who, even having revoked the idea of a theological God, nevertheless presumes to be able to shape the form of the world by his or her own will, their action constituting the determining encounter in the course of history. Instead, Althusser's world is constituted by the contingent swerve of the atom which forms objects, the thought of objects (which are different in kind to the objects themselves), and man itself. It is from here, and through discussion of Althusser's conception of relative autonomy, that Montag's problem with the split between body and mind in Althusser can be understood, alongside Althusser's claim that everything starts with the void.

Relative autonomy within unity

The concepts of historical development and social determination are commonly thought to have been introduced by Hegel but were, according to Althusser, in fact introduced by Montesquieu. As a humanist, Montesquieu 'must also be credited with originating the materialist conception of history as "the concrete behaviour of men in their relations with nature and with their past"' (Resch 1992: 59). Montesquieu's thought was then developed by Hegel, who was to rediscover 'the Spinozist perspective of the absolute (God/nature) and [imbue] it with the social totality derived from Montesquieu' (Resch 1992: 59). Thus, for Hegel, every historical event or phenomenon is always in dialectic and contradictory relation to the Idea of it, which is the 'concrete historical process itself, in its totality' (Gordy 1983: 3). Change occurs as every 'historical entity demonstrates its finitude by passing away, by transcending itself into a new and higher phase of the Idea, its positive contribution to the historical process both preserved and transformed' (Gordy 1983: 3). This is, in Hegel, what Althusser terms an 'expressive totality' (Althusser and Balibar 1970: 94). Yet the Hegelian synthesis pushes the materialist tradition of both Spinoza and Montesquieu into the lofty clouds of idealism, an ideology *par excellence* for Althusser, and one which consists of a 'secret alliance between Subject and Goal which "mystifies" the Hegelian dialectic' (Althusser 1976: 137–8, Diefenbach *et al.* 2013: 172).[16] Althusser's problem with Hegel's synthesis is twofold: first it maintains a subject/object distinction (which, for Althusser can only be maintained whilst already in the realm of ideology (Williams 2001: 63)) and then, secondly, it confuses the distinction between the two, creating a denegated, empirical form of historical unfolding. As Chambers puts it, 'Hegel's philosophy cannot account for the socio formation as formed by contradictions that are not necessarily resolved in the march of history award its inevitable *telos*' (Chambers 2014: 67–8).

As Gordy puts it, unlike 'the simple unity of the Hegelian totality, the Marxist whole is essentially complex. Effectivity does not take place from the centre outward but displays a mutuality through which any structure might have a determining influence on any other' (1983: 9). What is particular about Althusser's philosophy is that, due to the aleatory nature of each encounter happening prior to any unity within a body, each of the traditional Marxist histories (economic, ideological, political), that together form an essential unity in Hegel, function in Althusser's work in 'relative autonomy' (Althusser and Balibar 1970: 100). Indeed, referring to the *a posteriori* nature of the knowledge of encounters, Althusser argued that each of these 'peculiar histories is punctuated with peculiar rhythms and can only be known on condition that we have defined the *concept* of the specificity of its historical temporality and its punctuations (continuous development, revolutions, breaks, etc.)' (1970: 100). The relative autonomy of each particular structure is to be known only through the creation of concepts, and the non-anteriority of meanings (a position derived from Epicurus) stands Althusser in opposition to Plato and Aristotle. For Althusser, the world happens and is only then established in the 'reign of Reason, Meaning, Necessity and End [*Fin*]' (Althusser 2006: 169).

It is with the concept of relative autonomy that Althusser can tie his ontology to his political claims. As Gordy points out, 'Marx had a holistic conception of society. Indeed, it is by emphasising that holism exclusively that many have concluded that the Marxist conception is simply the Hegelian one inverted, the rational kernel of Hegel's thought without its mystical shell' (1983: 9). However, Althusser is clear that the holism is only that which he calls the 'final analysis' of the relative autonomy of each particular history (economic, scientific, ideological, etc.). As he clarifies, the 'history of philosophy, for example, is not an independent history by divine right: the right of this history to exist as a specific history is determined by the articulating relations, i.e., relations of relative effectivity, which exist within the whole' (Althusser and Balibar 1970: 100).[17] So it is not, as with Heidegger, that each history opens up as a 'gift' from a given totality that already is (*Dasein*), but rather that the social totality is constructed after the 'accomplished fact' of various relatively autonomous histories unifying immanently in one identifiable event (Heidegger 1977: 235, Althusser 2006: 169–70). Althusser is thus at pains to point out that the emergence of history is still contingent and may never happen at all; the fact that things have happened is not guaranteed (because they have not been determined by an *a priori* given). With a line of reasoning that Meillassoux extends to its fullest in *After Finitude* (2008), Althusser argues that 'the encounter may not take place, just as it may take place. Nothing determines, no principle of decision determines this alternative in advance; it is of the order of a game of dice' (Althusser 2006: 174). Whereas, for Meillassoux, it is precisely this foundational lack of determination that questions the facticity of the world (the fact that what is given in the world is given at all), Althusser argues that the world is given by virtue of its existence in the final analysis.[18] Meillassoux's position will be examined more fully in the next chapter, but provides a useful contrast here. For Meillassoux, the conclusion that the encounter may not have happened (i.e. it is contingent) has to be enforced throughout all subsequent claims. What Meillassoux terms the 'necessity of contingency' (Meillassoux 2008: 67) means that even the claim about the necessity of contingency *is itself* contingent. Althusser does not go so far – he does not absolutise contingency – because, for him, the world *is* in the final analysis and this claim is not open to scepticism.

Philosophical dualisms

In 1991, Deleuze and Guattari stated in their last collaborative book that 'philosophy is the art of forming, inventing, and fabricating concepts' ([1991] 1994: 2). Furthermore, they agree that '[s]ubject and object give a poor approximation of thought. Thinking is neither a line drawn between subject and object nor a revolving of one around the other' ([1991] 1994: 85). In this regard, Althusser seems to anticipate Deleuze and Guattari in understanding philosophy as the creation of concepts. However, Althusser's use of philosophy is inconsistent in his work, at times emphasising the political nature of philosophy and at times reducing it to the level of the ideology he is tasked to criticise. For example, in a 1968 lecture to the Société Française de Philosophie entitled 'Lenin and Philosophy', Althusser maintained that '[p]hilosophy represents the people's class struggle in theory' (Althusser 1971b: 21), and yet he also quoted Lenin calling professors of philosophy 'graduated flunkeys' (Althusser 1971b: 30). What is to be made of this seeming irregularity? Following an outraged expression from the president of the society and facilitator of the event Jean Wahl, Althusser clarified that, by 'philosophy', he means 'the idealism of philosophies of history' that are to be replaced by a Marxist 'scientificity with respect to history' (1971b: 40). This new scientificity, Althusser declared, is to be the Marxist philosophy of science: 'dialectical materialism'. However, is Althusser entirely justified in conflating every mode of philosophy other than materialism under the banner of idealism, only in order to sweep them under the carpet?

In order to answer this, it is useful to see in more detail what Althusser suggested in the place of philosophy. Already, two definitions of Althusserian philosophy have been presented above: the first is 'theory of theoretical practice' and the second is 'representation of the class struggle with the sciences', both of which are confirmed by Badiou (Badiou 2005d: 61). These articulations are possible, for Badiou's Althusser, because the 'fundamental condition for philosophical activity is its dependence on politics, on political clarification' (Badiou 2005d: 61). Accordingly, the purpose of Althusserian philosophy, for Badiou, is to harness politics: a certain set of relations that make up the Marxist whole in relative autonomy to the other relations (of science and ideology). This allows philosophy to 'record, in the unfolding of previously unseen philosophical possibilities, the sign of a renewed "thinkability" [. . .] of politics *conceived on the basis of its own exercise*' (Badiou 2005d: 62, original italics). Bearing in mind the revelatory character of being through four truth procedures that Badiou develops within his own project, it is clear that Badiou's reading of Althusser here is glossed with his own terminology. Unlike Badiou, Althusser has no mathematical ontology conditioning the revelation of any (non) being in the particular configuration of politics, and so Badiou's characterisation of Althusser rarefying politics to a greater degree than any other set of relations is unwarranted. Badiou's mischaracterisation is found within his statement that, because 'Althusser posits that only the "militants of the revolutionary class struggle" really grasp the thought of the process in relations, [. . .] [t]herefore, genuine thought of process is possessed by those engaged in political practice' (2005d: 60). Badiou's strict delineation between politics and philosophy – and his prioritisation of the former – leads him to read into Althusser a concomitant distinction between those who both grasp the thought of a process of relations *and* act upon it (i.e. militants), and those who do not. Nevertheless, as the previous chapter concluded, there is no imperative for Badiou's militant to pay fidelity to the political outside of ideology (because fidelity to the event is constituted in the realm of ideology), and the same is true for Althusser – yet Althusser never makes claims to the contrary. Indeed, Althusser anticipates a reading of him in this manner and says, following a passage on Machiavelli's *Prince*, that:

> The reader may object that this is merely *political* philosophy, over-looking the fact that a philosophy is simultaneously at work here too. A curious *philosophy which is a 'materialism of the encounter' thought by way of politics*, and which, as such, does not take anything for granted. It is in the political *void* that the encounter must come about, and that [the] national unity [of Italy] must 'take hold'. But *this political void is first a philosophical void.* (Althusser 2006: 173, original italics)

Badiou's reading of Althusser is founded upon his own strong (axiomatic) distinction between the militants of the revolutionary class struggle and those who are not militants – a distinction that is based upon the primacy of the political event. As an ontological truth procedure, politics occurs prior to philosophy and axiomatically distinguishes between the militant and everything else. Politics, for Althusser, is a mode of thought that occurs after philosophy or, to rephrase in Badiouian terminology: politics constitutes a language with which philosophy (in its first configuration of a 'theory of theoretical practice') speaks. Politics is a second-order mode of thought that conditions the political activism of the revolutionary militant and is encapsulated by philosophy, which itself constitutes the terms and possibilities of politics. Unlike Badiou's strong, axiomatic distinction, there is thus a weak (empirical) distinction for Althusser between a militant and a non-militant which is defined by the extent to which an individual participates in the revolutionary class struggle or not. Rather than politics axiomatically determining the subject, for Althusser, theory is 'a weapon in the class struggle, and whether it serves progressive or conservative forces, whether it arms or disarms the exploited classes, is determined by the problematic that shapes its categories' (Gordy 1983: 19). So, Althusser's first definition of historical materialism is a philosophy that both avoids the 'dangers of *bourgeois* ideology' (i.e. idealism) and constitutes the ground for a political struggle against – or potentially in favour of – bourgeois politics (Althusser 1976: 105).

What of the second definition of philosophy, the "representation of the class struggle with the sciences"? As Althusser wrote in 'Elements of Self-Criticism', science is not, as he had defined it in his early work, the contrast between truth and error, or to be speculatively defined against ideology (1976: 106). His previous distinction between science and ideology, Althusser explained, was a *'rationalist'* explanation of the break that was necessary to '"prove" that there is an antagonism between Marxism and bourgeois ideology' (1976: 105–6). Yet this led to a 'theoreticist deviation' (1976: 105) which, as has already been argued, Althusser could not justify. Instead, Althusser defines science as a methodology whereby it is 'possible to produce (as Marx does in *Capital*) proven theoretical results, that is, results which can be verified by scientific *and* political practice, and are open to methodical rectification' (1976: 110, original italics). Conscious of being mistaken for an idealist himself, Althusser clarifies in an important footnote that '[w]hat follows should not be understood as a relapse into a theory of *science* (in the singular), which would be quite speculative, but as the *minimum of generality* necessary to be able to grasp a concrete object. *Science* (in the singular) does not exist. But nor does "production in general": and yet Marx talks about "production in general", and deliberately, consciously, *in order* to be able to analyse concrete modes of production' (1976: 112). Put simply, Althusser's conception of science is the set of minimum possible conditions for understanding an object (what is also referred to as a body), yet a set of conditions that are modified alongside change in the relatively autonomous totality to which it belongs. In line with Althusser's aleatory philosophy more generally – and in disagreement with rationalist conceptions of science such as Popper's – science does not come with any prerequisites for designating its practices *a priori* of its operation, aside from its immanent distinction from politics, ideology and other modes of thought.[19] Existing as it does within the umbrella of the first definition of philosophy, the terms of science are determined by theoretical practice – a practice with the world that is informed by the theory that it concomitantly generates. Williams puts this clearly: for Althusser, scientific knowledge (although this counts for all knowledge) is produced 'according to conditions internal to its own production' (Williams 2002: 34) and these conditions also include practical activity.[20] The second definition of philosophy is therefore the class struggle (or 'theoretical practice') represented as objective objects, whereby the conditions for the understanding of objectivity are determined by theoretical practice itself.[21] It is a result of this definition that Althusser could argue that 'philosophy, like theatre, cannot be suppressed; it is the perennial element in which scientific discoveries are attached and defended, exploited for apologetic purposes or protected from exploitation'

(Montag 2003: 35). Furthermore, Althusser can talk about a political void first of all being philosophical, as philosophy constitutes the first order method for constituting and understanding being, as presented by science which is political action described in objective terms.[22]

Can Althusser get away with distinguishing his materialist philosophy from all other forms of philosophy that are then placed under the banner of idealism? Althusser's philosophy can be distinguished from philosophies that either premise an explanation of the world purely based on epistemology (Kant), or an epistemology that is in some manner 'corrected' by ontology (Popper/Badiou) – both of which constitute, for Althusser, idealist positions. First, Althusser's concept of relative autonomy prevents an idealisation of philosophy through its constitution by theoretical practice – a practice which informs and, in turn, is delineated and differentiated by philosophy. The mutual co-constitution of the two attributes of theory (theoretical practice and the various modes of thought, such as ideology and science, etc.) means that Althusser's work avoids both understanding the form of being through pure epistemology and a scepticism that the real can only be understood in the form of a mind-independent world.[23] Secondly, the relative autonomy of science within the overall social structure, like that of ideology and economics, cements its materiality and further highlights its distance from idealist accounts of science; removed from rationalist/idealist/computationalist theories of analysis that foreground the subject as the active centre of epistemological explanation, modes of analysis are unhampered by the limitation of simply being able to work on the level of epistemology. As Williams puts it, ideology (and, by extension, science) 'is not to be associated solely with the realm of ideas; it is material and relational precisely because of its *structural existence*. Ideology is an element of the social totality and functions in a complex relation to the other elements or levels of the structure' (Williams 2002: 36). To this extent, therefore, Althusser's philosophy does avoid the trappings of idealising either thought or matter as lexically prior – and thus conditioning – of the other. However, there is a problem with Althusser's philosophy that must be addressed before he can truly be said to have avoided idealism: how can Althusser's relatively autonomous totality also be a void from which thought emerges? In order words, does Althusser not simply replace an idealisation of either thought or matter with an originary, inexplicable moment which itself constitutes both?

A very full void

To sum up Althusser's position so far: encounters between atoms occur due to shifts in their vectors within the clinamen, constituting an event. Knowledge of this event becomes intelligible through philosophy and then thinkable through politics, science, ideology, etc. All of these modes of thought are determined in relative autonomy to each other – and to objectivity itself – by atoms encountering each other. In Livingston's terms, philosophy is the language which provides the consistency of each mode of thought, yet it is non-totalising in its openness to the aleatory encounter. This means that, as Althusser puts it, Marxist philosophy is 'required to think the openness of the world towards the event, the as-yet-unimaginable, and also all living practice, politics included' (Althusser 2006: 264, Choat 2010: 28).[24] Whilst Althusser never discussed his philosophy in these formalist terms, Althusser's account of philosophy can never both totalise and fully consist in itself because aleatory materialism is prefaced upon an encounter that itself constitutes thought. As a result, his philosophy is consistent but non-totalising; knowledge is constantly reconfigured following the encounter or, as Althusser put it, history 'is the permanent revocation of the accomplished fact by another undecipherable fact to be accomplished, without our knowing in advance whether, or when, or how the event that revokes it will come about' (Althusser 2006: 174). However, this reliance on the encounter is where Althusser's later philosophy faces the problem of origins previously highlighted by Montag and finally falls to the charge of idealism.

Althusser's 'originary non-origin [and] theoretical compromise which in no way escapes the implications of the concept of origins' (drawn attention to above) is, for Montag, a problem to do with persistence, or 'a fear of that which, in Althusser's words, *dure longtemps*, lasts a long time, that which fails to end on time, as expected and predicted' (Montag 2010: 181). Montag highlights the unexplored possibility that, for Althusser, atoms might not just encounter one another, but become interlocked ('*accrocher*'), forming an order from whence there was originally none. A possible result of this order is the 'primacy of the structure over its elements' (Althusser in Montag 2010: 181), whereby future encounters are limited in their ability to create new knowledge by the dominance of their precursors, which extend further into the future than they should. In suggesting that Althusser introduces the concept of interlocking that incorporates objects in the structure and prevents radical change,

Montag nods towards Althusser's essay 'Ideology and Ideological State Apparatuses' (ISAs), where Althusser describes the interpellative effects of ideology that serve to reproduce the 'conditions of production' (Althusser 1971a: 127).

Indeed, the ISA essay provides a sobering read as Althusser sets out how 'children at school also learn the "rules" of good behaviour, i.e. the attitude that should be observed by every agent in the division of labour, according to the job he is "destined" for: rules of morality, civic and professional conscience, which actually means rules of respect for the socio-technical division of labour and ultimately the rules of the order established by class domination' (Althusser 1971a: 132). However, this description is sociological, not philosophical, and taking it for philosophy would be to mistake it for the materialist philosophy underpinning Althusser's social theory – the philosophical content of the essay comes later in describing ISAs. In his social commentary, Althusser does not, of course, advocate for the reproduction of the relations of capitalist production so much as highlight their existence and then set out in the essay their philosophical conditions. Therefore, placing the ISA essay into Althusser's (oftentimes contradictory) oeuvre as 'constitutive and necessary to its very unfolding' (Montag 2010: 173), ISAs – as interlocking encounters with individuals – do not necessarily extend further into the future than they should. Rather, any presupposition that social forms should die out earlier than they do must give an account of why this is so and, in doing so, will explain itself into a position of idealism with an anterior account of death. Montag misplaces the problem with Althusser's concept of origin as being with his account of persistence, when in fact it lies in his over-reliance on death; the problem with Althusser's concept of origin is precisely the lack of an account of persistence at all.[25]

Choat puts the problem clearly: Althusser succumbs 'to the seduction of a theory that prioritizes the aleatory but which thence can discern no patterns in the chaos and offer no explanations for what become apparently random events' (Choat 2010: 28). The void in Althusser, which as Montag has pointed out is an originary nothingness, is posited by Althusser in order to escape the transcendentalism implicated in idealism, and yet also necessitates a new transcendental plane at every moment of analysis. The difference between Althusser's transcendental plane and the idealists' that he criticises is that his plane is *in*consistent to the extent that nothing can be said of it (in the same manner as the void in Badiou's ontology). However, the very objectivity of the void – the fact that it is named at all by Althusser – is a conceptualisation that cannot exist lexically prior to philosophy because, for Althusser, all knowledge is always-already philosophical and ideological. The void is a concept that must be posited by philosophy in the very act of theoretical practice and, thus, if Althusser cannot account for its existence within knowledge (i.e. philosophy), it constitutes an idealism akin to the accounts of philosophy that Althusser takes aim at. In this sense, Althusser's void is as idealist as Badiou's void was shown to be in the previous chapter.

The challenge of idealism is not strange to either Althusser or Montag, who attempt to account for it by stating that 'philosophy must constantly pose to itself the question of its orientation, of the place it occupies and that which the conjuncture demands it accomplish; it must constantly ask: "what is to be done?"' (Montag 2010: 161). Philosophical practice, for Althusser, is an attempt to avoid idealism by constant engagement with matter. However, can Althusser really argue that philosophy '*begins by evacuating all philosophical problems*' whilst both keeping a coherency between philosophy, objects, social forms or modes of thought – whilst continuously instituting a transcendental empty void – and avoid the charge of idealism (Althusser 2006: 174)? To reformulate this question: if Althusser is to be taken at his word, that the void is indeed devoid of all content whatsoever, how are series to be understood? It seems that, rather than an *empty* void, Althusser's must in fact be a very *full* void. In fact, true to Althusser's own methodology of symptomatic reading, a different kind of void can be read into Althusser's philosophy that addresses its non-foundational transcendency. This void must contain the conditions for the constitution of knowledge, yet also avoid the unity that Althusser took Hegel to task over. Furthermore, it must also be able to account for the persistence of past objects, and the non-immediate effects of ideological, scientific and political practices into future encounters.[26]

Time and persistence

In order to understand series, i.e. to conceptualise the new within the context of what was (even on the condition that the new might have changed), a conceptualisation of persistence is necessary. As has been argued, positing a void in the assumption that this will then constitute knowledge equates to idealism. Positing an empty void at each moment of philosophy breaks thought's consistency: the explanation of events is prohibited because, following the void, knowledge could never be more than the result of raw sensory output – a series of impressions. It is necessary to *make sense* of this raw output. What is missing in Althusser's philosophy is a conceptualisation of persistence, or the state of objects' protraction into the new.

This is not to say that Althusser did not conceptualise time, for Althusser was careful to remove time from the reign of idealism to the same extent as philosophy and the modes of thought:

> The coexistence of the different structured levels, the economic, the political, the ideological, etc., and therefore of the economic infrastructure, of the legal and political superstructure, of ideologies and theoretical formations philosophy, sciences) can no longer be thought in the co-existence of the Hegelian *present*, of the ideological present in which temporal presence coincides with the presence of the essence with its phenomena. And in consequence, the model of a *continuous and homogeneous time* which takes the place of immediate existence, which is the place of the immediate existence of the continuing presence, can no longer be regarded as the time of history. (Althusser and Balibar 1970: 99)

Just as Althusser distinguished between ideology, science and politics, arguing that each mode exists in relative autonomy to the others, so does he argue the same with regard to time.[27] Althusser does not however posit a single, continuous time, essentialised in opposition to thought, which would unify Althusser's relatively autonomous totality and result in an empirical time against which philosophy and the modes of thought would be measured. Althusser shows that as each mode of thought 'does not have the same type of historical existence', i.e. they are in relative autonomy with each other, and rather 'we have to assign to each level a *peculiar time*, relatively autonomous and hence relatively independent, even in its dependence, of the "times" of the other levels' (1970: 99). Furthermore, in contradiction to what the 'best historians' are satisfied with (this being one of the criticisms that E. P. Thompson reacted so strongly to), 'we cannot be satisfied [. . .] by *observing* the existence of different times and rhythms, without relating them to the concept of their difference' (1970: 100). Time, for Althusser, is an attribute of being that exists in as many different modes of thought as it reciprocally constitutes. Differentially articulated as part of the relatively autonomous totality, time exists for Althusser in rhythms and punctuations which must be thought 'in the type of articulation, displacement and torsion which harmonises these different times with one another' (Althusser and Balibar 1970: 100, see also Chambers 2010: 207–8).

Importantly for Althusser's structural temporality was his insistence, first, that time is made up of both visible and invisible times and that, secondly, time is identified in the last instance in its concept, a concept which must be '*produced, constructed*' (Althusser and Balibar 1970: 101). Althusser was clear that time had 'nothing to do with the obviousness of everyday practice's ideological time' and that 'in no sense is it a time that can be *read immediately* in the flow of any given process' (1970: 101). Both of these accounts of time, for Althusser, are empirical and rely upon the Hegelian process of uncovering essence that, according to Althusser, Marx corrected in his latter work.[28] Empiricism, for Althusser, is the act of extracting the essential kernel of knowledge from its shell in a process which denegates its own methodology.[29] Althusser pointed out that the extraction of knowledge from a given object relies on it first being understood in enough detail to know the distinction between it and from what it is to be abstracted, as only from that point is an appropriate method of extraction able to be selected. By this point, however, the object has been abstracted from so much that the object of knowledge created by the process of empiricism has very little to do with the real object and more to do with the choice of the process of extraction. Empirical time, for Althusser, is thus a concession to time's subordination under ideology, for only within ideology can an object be framed in such detail as to constitute the basis for knowledge extraction. As per his criticism of idealist philosophy, the *a priori* specification of empirical time places it within the realm of ideology, that which must be put back within relative autonomy. Following its placement within the relative autonomy of the structure, time must therefore be constructed as a concept in accordance with the self-reciprocating construction of each mode of thought.

Althusser develops this much in *Reading Capital* but refuses to go further, despite his acceptance that the theory has 'hardly been elaborated at all' (1970: 107). What is left therefore is a conceptualisation of time that has been stripped of its object (time itself as a continuity), with the assumption remaining that time will re-constitute itself in the structure, as part of encounters and with the same objecticity as previous times. As a result, his aleatory conception of time thus falls at the same hurdle as his aleatory philosophical void, i.e. there is no guarantee that knowledge – in any of its forms – can cross over the eliminative anti-foundationalism that Althusser's aleatory moment institutes. Althusser's atomist ontology thereby removes the epistemic conditions for each individual time to be constructed in the void; why would there necessarily be time as a constitutive part of an event, given that every encounter instantiates a new void?[30] It is not as necessary as Althusser thought to throw the baby out with the bathwater, as what is needed in order to bring consistency to Althusser's conception of time is a foundation upon which to ground it. The conceptualisation of series as found within Hume, sutured to Althusser's temporality can account for the objecticity of time and the potential for duration within events in the form of duration developed by Bergson.

A turn to Hume might seem like one in the wrong direction, given Althusser's repudiation of empiricism in *Reading Capital*. As Reed puts it, Althusser 'urges us to work our way out of the ideological circle which encloses idealism and empiricism alike through a particular combination of theory and practice in which the truth of the theory precedes the reality it analyses, though the results of analysis are fed back into the theory itself ' (Reed 2005: 210). Explaining the problematic at stake, Reed argues that 'Hume's analysis of the origins of mental impressions is not fundamentally materialist, since he fails to prove that physical changes in the brain produce thoughts and perceptions, but he argues such a conclusion cannot be disproven, either, and that the reason for drawing a causal connection between physiological motion and mental effect is as sound as that for making any other causal link between action and reaction' (2005: 211). To put this in the terms used in the previous chapter: for Reed, Hume cannot demonstrate that thought is constituted by the empirical (or matter) whilst, at the same time, he uses negative argumentation to show that thought is as causally connected to matter as in any other explanation. Thus, Hume's thought lies half way between a failed materialist dogmatism and an assumed correlationism for lack of a better account of causality. Althusser's criticism (that empiricism lacks a sufficient authority to justify its own theoretical practices) would seem to strike Hume out of contention as an empiricist *par excellence*. Yet the fact that one question pervades Hume studies – was Hume a materialist or an idealist? – sheds light on a complexity in Hume's philosophy that nevertheless explains why he can provide a crucial addition to Althusser's philosophy (see Buckle 2007). Indeed, Althusser himself invited his readers to 'recover a "materialism of the encounter" from within a series of denegations, condemnations, and forgettings; from within philosophy this form of materialism rejects the presence that Reason, Origin, and End have maintained throughout philosophy, including, he suggests, throughout the history of materialism' (Reed 2005: 214).

In his essay on Hume, Deleuze undercuts the unresolved tension regarding Hume's materialism and idealism, declaring this to be precisely the strength found in Hume's work (Deleuze 2001: 35–52). For Deleuze's Hume, echoing Althusser's account of philosophy, theory is 'an enquiry, which is to say, a practice: a practice of the seemingly fictive world that empiricism describes; a study of the conditions of legitimacy of practices in this empirical world that is in fact our own' (2001: 36). Again, as with Althusser's own historical materialism, Deleuze argues that Hume's philosophy necessitates a constant practical engagement by the individual as part of the world, in what various commentators have termed naturalism (see, for example, Ansell-Pearson 2014a). Hume's 'theory of association finds its direction and its truth in a casuistry of relations, the practice of law, of politics, economics, that completely changes the law of philosophical reflection' (Deleuze 2001: 36). If this is the case, then the legitimation of theory in the work of Hume seems to anticipate the relative autonomy of Althusser's dialectical materialism – a theory of theoretical *practice*. However, the issue facing Althusser's materialism was that of an initiatory void which subordinated each mode of thought to it and thus eliminated the coherency of each passing moment in an (always-already impossible) series – how did Hume avoid this pitfall?

To help address this, Althusser's problem can be reframed as a 'problem of the origin of knowledge or of ideas, according to which everything finds its origin in the sensible and in the operations of the mind upon the sensible' (Deleuze 2001: 37). Althusserian philosophy, as Deleuze frames it, is a fight for the exteriority of relations (a fight which is also taken on in empiricism), by either 'finding a way of making relations internal to their own terms or by finding a deeper and more comprehensive term to which the relation would itself be internal' (2001: 37). In other words, the object of knowledge in Althusser's *Reading Capital* would either have to be idealised to the extent that it exists externally to the materialism of the world (i.e. "being" in Badiou), or subject to an infinitely repeating hermeneutic circle (and thus never actually arriving at a "true" object at all). Either way, Althusserian philosophy – through its insistence on both the aleatory void and the existence of the modes of thought – necessitates a constant search for the relations that determine its modes of thought *within* the *a priori* specification of the modes. The void requires questions such as "what is time and how is it generated with every new instance?", and yet even this question presupposes the existence of time which, according to the void, might not be. As Deleuze writes of Hume however, 'genesis is always understood in terms of principles, and itself as a principle' (Deleuze 1991: 66) and, furthermore, *'relations are external to their terms'* (Deleuze 2001: 37, original italics). Accordingly, genesis is misunderstood as a principle that determines a relation between knowledge and an object. For Deleuze's Hume, it is instead a term used to govern a relation that exists in excess of it; rather than terms (or objects of knowledge in Althusserian parlance) existing unto themselves, as kernels of essential knowledge that determine relations, terms are created as effects of relations themselves.[31]

What then is a relation, and how can it be used to conjoin philosophy with materiality without idealising the conjunction? For Deleuze's Hume, a 'relation is itself the fact of so-called principles of association, contiguity, resemblance, and causality, all of which constitute, precisely, a *human nature*' (Hume [1888] 1967: 368, Deleuze 1991: 39). A relation for Hume is that which conjoins ideas with other ideas in order to make up the mind, so the mind of the human, for Hume, is never one idea fixed as a term, but 'only the ways of passing from one particular idea to another' (Deleuze 1991: 39). As Bell puts it, it is a subjective synthesis which transcends itself in order to creatively engage with the world (Bell 2006: 412). Thus, contra Descartes's rationalism, whereby the subject is a principle by which to assert incontrovertible proofs (ideas of objects), Hume's subject 'breaks with the constraining form of predicative judgement' and is, instead, based upon 'an autonomous logic of relations' (Deleuze 1991: 38). Two sets of relations, the principles of association (the 'affective circumstances [which] guide the association of ideas' (Deleuze 2001: 45)) are combined with the principles of passion (those principles which 'have the effect of restricting the range of the mind, fixating it on privileged ideas and objects' (2001: 46)) to form human nature, or the characteristics of the mind (see Hume [1888] 1967: 234–9).

Why does Hume introduce this associationism in preference over the Cartesian rationalist unity? As Deleuze explains, there are two problems with Cartesian thought. First, Descartes advocates a *'spontaneity of relations'* (Deleuze 1991: 96) according to which, if ideas are to be found within the mind 'which are *tied* to the one that the mind wanted to see, it is, first, necessary that the ideas themselves be associated in the mind' (1991: 96). This originary 'apperception' however would necessarily resemble an impossibly all-knowing figure who could think all ideas (including all ideas of the relations of ideas) *a priori* of their manifestation in the world. The criticism of originary apperception is thus the same that Badiou leverages against Plato in order to justify his ontological reversal that prioritises the void over the One (Badiou 2011: 23–5). Secondly, Descartes argues in favour of the '*spontaneity of disposition* (1991: 97), according to which the distinction between two kinds of impressions (and thus the unity of the differentiated objects) must exist in the world *a priori* of the mind's ability to sense them. This is also found in Althusser's materialism, whereby the clinamen structures the world in a radically new manner with every passing present. The problem with this scenario is that there is no epistemic foundation upon which to comprehend difference; any change in the world would come as random to the mind, also randomly changing the constitution of the mind as the basis for thought. In answer to this problem with philosophies of spontaneity, Deleuze highlights Hume's argument that ideas are inferentially created from impressions, which are themselves the raw product of sense (Hume [1888] 1967: 92–3, Deleuze 1991: 96).

How does Hume then overcome the aleatory void between each passing present? Or, put differently, how are ideas created from impressions? Hume introduces the concepts of inference and habit to account for how the subject pushes beyond itself in the present and part-constitutes the present-to-come. Deleuze gives the following example: 'When I see the sun rise, I say that it will rise tomorrow; having seen water boil at 100 degrees, I say that it necessarily boils at 100 degrees. Yet expressions such as "tomorrow", "always", "necessarily", convey something that cannot be given in experience: tomorrow isn't given in experience without becoming today, without ceasing to be tomorrow, and all experience is experience of a contingent particular' (Deleuze 2001: 40). For both Hume and Deleuze, memory 'is the reappearance of an impression in the form of an idea that is still vivid' (Deleuze 1991: 94). This concept is similar to the object of knowledge in Althusser, yet with the process of 'extraction' which is denegated by Althusser and accounted for by Hume with his conception of human nature. However, the idea in the present (in the form of memory) cannot account for change because it does not contain within it that which it is not; the new situation in the next present will present a new set of impressions, upon which ideas are then to be formed by the mind. Thus, the subject in the immediate present is required to infer, or believe, that a situation will change in a particular way, according to the habit that they have previously developed. This inference is characterised by certain principles: '[w]hen the mind, therefore, passes from the idea of impression of one object to the idea or belief of another, it is not determin'd by reason, but by certain principles which associate together the ideas of these objects, and unite them in the imagination' (Hume [1888] 1967: 92).

The imagination is thus the faculty of the subject which extends past the present, allowing the ideas in memory to persist into the future and forming the basis for Hume's originary apperception. In the next present, the mind forms new ideas from new impressions in relation to the principles of association and passion. However, as Deleuze warns, 'memory alone does not bring about a synthesis of time; it does not transcend the structure, its essential role becomes the reproduction of the different structures of the given. It is rather habit which presents itself as a synthesis, and habit belongs to the subject' (Deleuze 1991: 94). Habit is the transcendental synthesis that 'gives the subject its real origin and source' (Deleuze 1991: 95), and it is upon this source that the subject pushes itself into the future in imagination and forms the conditions for future understanding.

The problem for Hume then is not to demonstrate that the past and present are synthesised because, in understanding the past and present, the subject has already shown itself as that which synthesises them; this is what Ansell-Pearson means when he argues that the repetition of a sequence produces an 'originary subjectivity' in the mind (Ansell-Pearson 1999: 100). Instead, the problem is how to demonstrate the persistence of the present into the future. For Deleuze's Hume, the past and present are 'constituted within time, under the influence of certain principles, and [. . .] the synthesis of time itself is nothing but this constitution, organisation, and double affection' (Deleuze 1991: 96).[32] In contrast to Althusser, for whom each individual time is constructed as part of the encounter, for Hume, the subject synthesises *within* time and, in doing so, provides the consistency of thought necessary to make inferential predictions about the future. Whilst Hume's scepticism – which denies the possibility of knowing the world in-itself and foregrounds only the belief and potential delirium of knowledge – might seem to leave him open to the same randomly changing world and, therefore, randomly changing modes of thought that are present in Althusser, this is not so. For Hume, 'affective circumstances' (i.e. the material conditions in the world) 'guide the association of ideas' (Deleuze 2001: 45) and thus, the subject's principles of association are developed on the back of the individual's embodiment within the world. Hume's scepticism – the argument that a static and unchanging world of either being or presentation (Plato or Badiou) is not the starting point for knowledge – conditioned his argument that the understanding of the world is based precisely on a synthesis of change and the struggle to understand and adapt to an essentially different world. When imagination is found wanting by the subject-synthesis of the future present, habit is modified to take account of the new situation and the subject's lack of ability to account for it in its projection of the future. Thus, Hume remained a materialist to the extent that there exists a realm of affective materiality separate to thought, but also an idealist to the extent that ideas are the subject's understanding of the world. Rather than idealising either of the two realms as existing separately to each other, however (this would itself fall foul of the Humean criticism of the spontaneity of relations, prefiguring the world in a manner which must then be understood), Hume's significant contribution to empiricism is, as was highlighted above, his emphasis on practice. An understanding of the world, for Hume, is an inquiry into 'this empirical world that is in fact our own' (Deleuze 2001: 36); not our own because our pre-constituted sovereign individuality claims property over parts of it (*qua* Locke), but because the subject, according to Hume, exhibits a constant fascination with – and a deep-seated need to make its way through – the world that constitutes its understanding.

The subject as practice

The suture of Hume's conception of human nature to Althusser's historical materialism furnishes the latter with a conceptualisation of persistence and overcomes the otherwise eliminative effect of a philosophical void. Without this addition, Althusser's void undermined the contiguity and consistency of series, breaking each idea with every passing present in instantiating itself as the *a priori* condition of historical materialism. Instead, and contra Althusser's theoretical anti-humanism insisting that the subject could only exist within the realm of ideology (Althusser 1984: 84, Williams 2013: 158–9), Deleuze shows that, for Hume, it is precisely human nature that is needed in order to synthesise ideas and impressions.

It is only the human mind that can synthesise ideas and impressions according to the two types of principles (association and passion), and these principles constitute the subject's habit. Whilst Althusser's anti-humanism avoids an idealism present in both rationalism (the reduction of being to either a thinking subject *qua* Descartes) and vulgar materialism (an empiricism *qua* Smith or Ricardo), it fails to account for the contiguity of series as it is incapable of thinking that which pushes itself beyond itself or, in other words, transcendentalism. For Deleuze's Hume, it is the relations of belief and invention which allow the subject to transcend itself, pushing itself into the future whilst conditioning series. Bell argues that this is the answer to Deleuze's problem of 'transforming a multiplicity into a system [that] is related to the problem of accounting for the constitution of a subject within the given that nonetheless transcends the given, or is irreducible to the given' (Bell 2006: 411) and, furthermore, highlighting the importance of practice, he says that 'it is precisely through the creativity of invention and belief that the multiplicity of ideas is transformed into a system' which is both part of, yet goes beyond, the given (2006: 412).

This practical creativity is important for both the social and political: as Deleuze puts it, the 'principles of association find their true sense in a casuistry of relations that works out the details of the worlds of culture and of law. And this is the true object of Hume's philosophy: relations as the means of an activity and a practice – juridical, economic and political' (Deleuze 2001: 51). Hume's philosophy can be characterised therefore as way of thinking the individuation of life by way of the individuated life, whereby Hume locates the grounds of subjectivity, not in either epistemology or ontology, but in practice. Avoiding an idealisation of either, subjectivity emerges as the practically creative locus of epistemology and ontology. In this way, does Hume not anticipate Althusser's relative autonomy, yet imbue it with a practical relationality that conditions the creation of the new?

Hume's emphasis on the practical can be favourably compared to both Badiou's and Althusser's. Unlike Badiou's and Althusser's goals of understanding the emergence of the new from aleatory events whereby, on the one hand, the ontologically prescribed militant grasps an event and actualises it within his immediate milieu or, on the other, one must understand the event as 'the principle in relation to which all things are resolved into the identity of pure nothingness, the origin and destiny of all things' (Montag 2010: 168), Hume offers a practical, affective philosophy. Deleuze goes further, suggesting that Hume offers a 'radical change in the practical way the problem of society is posed' (Deleuze 2001: 46). Rather than framing the social in the manner of the sovereign social contract theories of the seventeenth and eighteenth centuries, Hume's institutions are premised upon artifice and the question 'how can we create institutions that force passions to go beyond their partialities and form moral, judicial, political sentiments (for example, the feeling of justice)?' (Deleuze 2001: 47). For Hume, as developed in book II of the *Treatise* ([1888] 1967) and the essay *A Dissertation on the Passions* (Hume [1757] 1777), the passions – either indirect (pride, humility, love and hatred) or direct (joy, grief, fear and hope) – are psychological states that are created by the individual when they carry out either good or bad acts (Hume [1757] 1777: Bea 3, P 1.3).[33] Humean institutions then are social arrangements that structure passions through principles of association that themselves structure the institutions and, as such, these institutions are an extension of human artifice.[34] Bell describes two processes that transform the multiplicity of ideas in the Humean social. On the one hand, ideas are transformed within the mind 'into impressions of reflection that create beliefs, habits, and tendencies which constitutes within the given, that which transcends it' (Bell 2006: 413). On the other hand, this process happens within the social, 'though this time the multiplicity that comes to be transformed into a system or unity are partialities, passions, and interests of individuals' (2006: 413). Thus, argues Bell, for Deleuze, Hume understands society not as a necessary stage in human history that is predicated upon our *a priori* conception of human nature (i.e. for Hobbes), but rather 'as invented institutions, inventions that are themselves indistinguishable from human nature in that they follow from the principles of human nature' (2006: 413); Humean institutions are transcendent not from law, or a formal epistemology from which their moral norms can be discerned, but from practice itself.

It is here that comparisons can be made to Badiou's mathematico-ontological philosophy. To summarise Badiou's position: Being is obfuscated by the representation of itself in the world of appearance (*doxa*) and only a radical rupture in the state of nature will determine the emergence of the subject as the local phenomena of a truth procedure.[35] Put in the terms Deleuze uses to discuss Hume, Badiou's reliance on ontology to condition the thought of itself in the subject creates a dislocation between the relations that constitute ideas in the truthful subject and the animal human. Whereas, as was shown in the previous chapter, Badiou's militant is a suture to the animal human by the virtue of mathematics's scriptural productivity, the truth-event's negation of the presented world eliminates any relations of association or passion in the mind of the subject. So, given the radical break from the presented and the lack of a foundation for epistemology in ontology, where would the subject's ideas come from? Badiou denegates the importance of institutions (either ideational or socio-political) in the constitution of truthful thought and replaces them with the event. As Žižek has shown, however, the event is only knowable to those already interpellated within an ontological truth procedure and so, whilst denegating the thought of the animal human and its relation to institutions in favour of the ontological, Badiou's consistent individual (the animal human and its truthful supplement) represses its own schizophrenia. A consistent individual, on the one hand, continues to live its life in relation to its natural world yet, on the other hand, haemorrhages the emergence of Being.[36] Due both to the individual's inability to incorporate the event into its understanding (Badiou's ontological event actively rejects any incorporation of itself into knowledge (Badiou 2011: 189–90)) and the event's originary lack of relation to the individual's thought, the consistent individual can only but involuntarily be associated with the subject in its own lack of knowledge.

Thus, if Althusser idealises the aleatory event, Badiou idealises not the event, but the ont*ology* of mathematics and, particularly, the distinctions contained within mathematical logic that formalise the differentiation of the event from the representation of being.[37] Whilst Badiou's event distinctly apes Christian imagery in its revelatory nature (Badiou 1997, Žižek 2000: 137–8, Phelps 2013), the evental site (within which the event occurs) is in fact formulated by the scriptural materiality of mathematics. It is thus not that the event is idealised in Badiou's work, but mathematical ontology from which the event is made known. Indeed, as Badiou makes clear, the 'grand style' of mathematics is the only form of thought that thinks 'first principles' and 'has paradigmatic value because it *cannot* submit anything to the regime of opinion' (Badiou [1992] 2008: 93–105, original italics). It is clear that both Althusser and Badiou foreground their philosophies with a dogmatic use of an ideal form: the aleatory event itself on the one hand, mathematical ontology on the other, and that only after positing the existence of one of these forms can either philosophy set about understanding the creation of the new. Deleuze expresses his dissatisfaction with this way of thinking, stating that 'a literature is disappointing if it interprets signs by referring them to objects that can be designated (observation and description), if it surrounds itself with pseudo-objective guarantees of evidence and communication (*causerie*, investigation), and if it confuses meaning with intelligible, explicit, and formulated signification (major subjects)' (Deleuze [1964] 2008: 22).[38] In contrast, Hume does not idealise either ontology or epistemology, nor does he idealise an originary event that mystically produces consistent thought and being. Instead, Hume foregrounds the practical and affective engagement of the mind in the world that both individuates the subject *as part of the world* (contra Badiou), and as the naturalised locus of the world's consistency (contra Althusser). As Deleuze puts it, 'the natural constitution of the mind under the influence of the principles of the passions does not only involve the movement of an affection seeking out its object, it also involves the reaction of a mind responding to the supposedly known totality of circumstances and relations' (Deleuze 1991: 130). Of course, Deleuze is not arguing that Hume conceives of circumstances and relations as actually totalised. Rather, he is saying that the subject has ideas (or 'general views' (1991: 130)) that have been both engendered and constituted in part by circumstances and relations and, in part, by the passions. These passions, themselves also having been subject to the same constitution, are thus not a component of an essential subject (*qua* Descartes or Kant), but a localised and immanent production of it.[39] In other words, Hume does not rely dogmatically on essentialised forms to ground his philosophy and, instead, his is a non-dogmatic philosophy of humanity as practical invention.

Nevertheless, despite the criticism that Althusser's philosophy has received in this chapter so far, his philosophy's conceptualisation of the relationship between modes of thought in relation to matter is a significant departure from – and, more importantly, an attempt to explain – the idealism in philosophies of essence. For example, Althusser's method of symptomatic reading – illuminating the invisible presence of concepts in discourses as a result of their interaction with other discourses – is a method of reading which avoids transcendental claims of authority (such as the Kantian intellect), remaining – in this sense – critical and non-dogmatic. Whilst undermined by his reliance on the aleatory void in order to justify his anti-idealism, Althusser provides an important obstacle to structuralism, formalism, humanist and idealist Marxists (Lukács 1966, Sayers 2003), as well as idealism more generally, in his insistence that these accounts must answer for the constitution of their concepts. Furthermore, whilst Althusser does not rely on the concept of practice in the same way as Hume – in the sense that practice co-constitutes the subject and its world in differential relationship – two forms of practice do nevertheless feature in his work.

The first conceptualisation of practice in Althusser's work is the practice of 'philosophy which *creates the philosophical void* in order to endow itself with existence' (Althusser 2006: 174). Historical materialism requires an initial void that clears the way of *a priori* (essential) concepts in order to allow the encounter of two atoms; as Althusser puts it, philosophy 'begins by evacuating all philosophical problems' (2006: 174). As has been argued, however, wiping the philosophical slate clean in order to re-instantiate philosophy at every moment removes the objecticity of thought in itself, rupturing the coherence of ideas. Philosophical practice, in this configuration, has its legs pulled out from under it and, in the act of removing ideas from philosophy, Althusser prevents the very act of philosophy. Under Althusser, philosophy becomes arbitrary, as the meaning of ideas is evacuated from it by the very act of doing philosophy. As will be developed in the next chapter, the practice of philosophy needs ideas.

The second of Althusser's concepts of practice is that which occurs within the unconscious and, here, Althusser's work takes aim at both the Lacanian school of psychoanalysis and the ethnographical work of Lévi-Strauss. On 28 October 1966, four years after publishing his first major work of philosophy *For Marx*, yet two years before its development into a manual for philosophical practice in *Reading Capital*, Althusser sent the first of three Notes to his colleagues (Alain Badiou, Étienne Balibar, Yves Duroux and Pierre Macherey) in the Theoretical Working Group on Spinoza he convened, outlining his idea of the work to be carried out by the group (Althusser and Matheron 2003: 34–5). Although this collective project never fully came to fruition, the Notes are an almost entirely understudied aspect of Althusser's work that shed light on the role of practice in constituting an otherwise federated, and therefore non-totalising philosophy ('historical materialism'). As Corpet and Matheron put it in their introduction to *The Humanist Controversy*, rather than the often presumed Althusserian hegemonic system, 'what we find in these texts is quite the opposite: a mode of thought that attends to the singularity of the sciences and carefully eschews, at a time when "structuralism" was at its apogee, any unification of the "human sciences" under the hegemony of one of them, "historical materialism" and "dialectical materialism" not excepted – even while attempting a differential definition of the states of each one of them (in the present instance, psychoanalysis)' (2003: 36–7).

In the first Note, Althusser's criticism of Lacan and Lévi-Strauss centres on the statement that psychoanalytic theory 'takes the form, in the best of cases, of a *regional theory* which lacks a *general theory*, although it is, *in principle*, the realisation of this general theory' (2003: 38, original italics). Psychoanalytic theory is, for Althusser, a regional theory of the unconscious that accounts for its structure and function within the terms that are generated within a therapeutic practice upon the unconscious itself. An empirical theory, psychoanalytic theory 'goes beyond' its 'point of departure' to produce its own theoretical object (i.e. it conceptualises a phenomena), but the theory of conceptual production is denegated to the extent that psychoanalytic theory assumes that it speaks directly to the empirical object (2003: 39). Anticipating Livingston's description of thought as either consistent or totalising, Althusser claims that,

> we can observe, within the regional theory itself, the absence of the general theory (the effects of this absence) at the theoretical level: for as long as the general theory is lacking, the regional theory strives to 'achieve closure', but fails to; or, to put it in other terms, it tries to define its own object *differentially* (in contradistinction to other theoretical objects: in the present case, the of biology, psychology, sociology, etc.), but *fails to*. This attempt and failure are the presence of this *de facto absence* of a general theory, the existence of which is nevertheless called for, *de jure*, in order to found these attempts. (2003: 40)

Accordingly, psychoanalytic theory, in presuming that its general theory is in fact a regional theory, cannot account for the conceptualisation of its terms outside of its own discourse and therefore falls to the criticism of idealism. There are three possible upshots of a lack of a general theory to inform psychoanalytic thought's regional theory for Althusser: practitioners practise regional theory and, by chance, practise it correctly; practitioners practise false theory; or psychoanalysts master the regional theory in terms of a general theory, yet practise it badly. Althusser does not elaborate on how he understands either 'correct' or 'bad' practice, inferring instead that practice would be correct if it were corroborated by the support of the general theory, yet Althusser does however claim provisionally that support of regional theory by a general theory would have two benefits for practitioners. The first would be to prevent the conflation of psychoanalytic theory with other regional theories, such as biology and psychology, the second being the removal of conservative and limiting hesitation that often prevents the change of terms that are created internally to a theory.

What then is a general theory, and how does it effect a regional theory? A general theory is both the foundation and product of all the differential regional theories, or that which provides and forms the differentiating reference points, which are deployed and modified by regional theories.[40] For Althusser, and in accordance with Spinoza's claim that substance is not a unity to be explained by its effects but rather 'exists in its effects', a general theory can only be explained in terms of regional theories (Althusser and Matheron 2003: 47, original italics). Using the example of the psychoanalytic regional theory of the unconscious, in the first Note, Althusser argues that 'the unconscious is a structure whose elements are signifiers' (of the unconscious and not those of other systems such as 'ideology, art, science, etc.') and that the general theory 'allows us to think [the] specific difference' between the structures (2003: 48).

Cautious of the trappings of formalist structuralism, Althusser warns that 'it does not seem as if a general theory of the signifier can by itself produce (by deduction) the specific difference that distinguishes the discourse of science from the discourses of ideology, art, and the unconscious', and instead goes on to argue that the general theory 'should make this difference possible through the play of the possible variations inscribed in the theory of discourse' (2003: 48). To the extent that a discourse is a structure of epistemological indicators that, in expressing an object of knowledge, signify a material object, a general theory therefore constitutes the discourse of discourse.[41] And yet it is not turtles all the way down, for the general structure is comprised (in a clear tautology), for Althusser, only of regional theories and the differential relations that define the regional theories against themselves (2003: 49). The relative autonomy of each regional theory constitutes the consistency of the general theory, a position from which the further development of regional discourses is able to take place. For Althusser, a general theory cannot be reduced to an empirical operation on one or two regional theories (such as the regional theory of linguistics and the regional theory of psychoanalysis) but instead, 'it must be developed in a very different perspective, by means of very different confrontations, through the intervention of very different regional theories and their differential relations' (Althusser and Matheron 2003: 46). Indeed, Althusser clarifies the relationship between general and regional theories, describing the effect of general theory: 'whenever it clarifies a given regional theory about itself, helping it to formulate and rectify its concepts, it necessarily has the same effect of *rectification-reclassification* on the concepts of the other regional theory brought into play in this operation of differential definition' (2003: 44). In Livingston's terms, the reformulation of terms in one regional theory alters the consistency of the general theory which, in turn, has a determinate effect on the totalising potential of each of the other regional theories.

It is clear that, in the Notes, Althusser is, unintentionally or otherwise, laying the groundwork for the different modes of thought that are set out in *Essays in Self-Criticism*. Here, he explains that a science of history (i.e. dialectical materialism) 'is born out of the unpredictable, incredibly complex and paradoxical – but, in its contingency, necessary – *conjunction* of ideological, political, scientific (related to other sciences), philosophical and other "*elements*", which at some moment "*discover*", *but after the event, that they needed each other*' (Althusser 1976: 112, original italics).[42] Despite Althusser's admission to a 'theoreticist deviation' in his early work which rationalised the epistemological break between the early and late work of Marx (Althusser 1976: 105), there is an important continuity running through Althusser's work that involves understanding the performative effectivity of discourses and practices in accordance with their differential relationships.[43] A general theory, then, is a realm of expressive difference, totalised by regional theories, that constitutes the foundation for regional theories to define themselves and, in doing so, specify their relation to other regional theories. In other words, a general theory provides the non-totalised consistency that is totalised by regional theories, which themselves are inconsistent without their transcendental basis in the general theory.[44]

How then does practice relate to the two levels of theory for Althusser? For Althusser, practice does not relate to theory, but in fact practice relates theories; it is the passage from one local theory to another, using the signification of one discourse as a transcendental basis for another.[45] Deleuze refers to Althusser's 'structural causality in order to account for the very particular presence of a structure in its effects, and for the way in which it differentiates these effects, at the same time as these latter assimilate and integrate it' (Deleuze 2004a: 181); it is from the immanent, affective differentiation of the different theories that practice moves one theory to the other as a singular point of conjuncture. Whereas

Deleuze refers to *Reading Capital* and how 'Althusser can present the economic structure of a society as the field of problems that the society poses for itself [. . .] and that it resolves according to its own means', Althusser himself explains his position most clearly within the first Note with regard to psychoanalytic theory:[46] again within the context of a discourse of the unconscious, Althusser describes the effect common to all the discourses (unconscious, scientific, ideological and aesthetic) of the subject. According to Althusser, every discourse has a 'lieu-tenant', a 'necessary correlate, a subject, which is one of the effects, if not the major effect, of its functioning' (Althusser and Matheron 2003: 48). The subject *itself* remains a formation and function only of the ideological discourse which then '"produces" or "induces" a subject-effect' (2003: 48) within the other discourses and this subject-effect is a composition which presents the ideological subject in terms local to each of the other discourses. Given that the relatively autonomous relationship between the regional theories implies differences in kind between their discourses, Althusser argues that '[if] we compare the various subject-effects produced by the different forms of discourse, we observe that (i) the relationship these subjects bear to the discourses in question is not the same; (ii) in other words, the subject position "produced" or induced by the discourse vis-à-vis that discourse varies' (2003: 48–9).[47]

The consequence of induced subject effects in each of the relatively autonomous discourses is that, as a result of subjective interpellation in the ideological discourse, each of the other discourses constitute a knowledge object in the unconscious (in this case the subject effect) that is both specific to, and constructed within, the specific terms of each discourse. Thus, when Althusser speculates that the function of the four different discourses might be knowledge (science), recognition-misrecognition (ideology), recognition-perception (art) and the circulation of signifiers (language), and that the subject effect in each discourse acts as a particular object of knowledge to be worked on, he paves the way for an inquiry (that he never fully completed) into how practice within each discourse might create new objects of knowledge in other discourses. These new objects of knowledge are important for Althusser's theory of structural causality insofar as the 'structural unconscious is at once differential, problematising and questioning', enabling Althusser to 'show how contradictions are thus born in the structure' (Deleuze 2004a: 183, 191). Unlike a Hegelian conception of contradiction, whereby each phenomena has as its essential correlate both a place and an antithesis, Althusserian structural causality determines contradiction of the knowledge object as a necessary, productive feature of relative autonomy. This necessity is not a strong, metaphysical necessity, bounded as it is within the terms of the structural determination of Althusser's philosophy (and its reliance upon the void); rather, an object of knowledge, by creating an effect in the other discourses that acts as the object's 'lieu-tenant (sic)' (Althusser and Matheron 2003: 49), thus creates a new foundation – immanent with the structure of which it is part of – that acts as the imperative for theoretical practice.[48]

The differential relations that determine the place of each regional theory (existing externally to the terms of each discourse in the Humean sense) concomitantly determine the Althusserian unconscious as the foundation for practice itself. However Althusser's ambition for a theory of structural causality and an associated anti-humanist conception of practice is undermined by the reliance on the aleatory void. As has been argued, each passing present in Althusser's historical materialism implies the instantiation of the philosophical void and, therefore, the clearing of the objecticity of thought. In the terms of the first Note, therefore, although a subject effect might create a new object of knowledge within the relatively autonomous regional theories that neighbour ideology, this object is eradicated as soon as it is constituted, and it is impossible for series to be formed. As Deleuze puts it, a 'structure only starts to move, and become animated, if we restore its other half', and this other half is the relation to another series that 'derives from the terms and relations of the first, but are not limited simply to reproducing or reflecting them' (Deleuze 2004a: 182). The construction of the terms and relations of a second series, used as the imperative for movement in a structure, is impossible if, at every new present, philosophy necessitates the superimposition of the void in order to render neutral any previous thought. Thus, without the suture of Hume's conceptualisation of persistence, Althusser's philosophy of general and regional theories remains an inconsistent and non-foundational collection of structures. Without a foundation for persistence and thus noetic coherency, Althusser's philosophy has no basis to establish the objecticity of any of the discourses. It is only when Hume's human nature is sutured onto Althusser's structural determination, adding the possibility for the persistency of both the objecticity and consistency of ideas, that the ground is paved for a practical philosophy that avoids entrapment within either epistemology or ontology. In other words, when the persistence of ideas through time is accounted for within a differential structure of relatively autonomous discourse, philosophy can be defined as the singular practice of constituting epistemology and ontology as it itself is constituted.

Non-dogmatic philosophy?

If Chapter 1 was an effort to identify the idealist principles that underpin Badiou's philosophy, whilst attempting to hold onto two important facets of his work (the concept of truth and a way to think ethics), then the path this chapter has taken may seem divergent. So far, little has been mentioned of Althusser's politics, his conception of ethics, or truth. Indeed, this chapter will not discuss these concepts, as what is at stake here is the contribution Althusser's thought makes to a non-dogmatic philosophy as an alternative to Badiou and a contribution to the work of Deleuze. As discussed, the task Althusser set himself (becoming explicit in 'The Only Materialist Tradition' and 'Lenin and Philosophy') was similar to that undertaken hitherto in this project, i.e. to develop an account of philosophy that does not premise itself upon idealism and, as such, Althusser's historical materialism is important (but not sufficient) for the development of a non-dogmatic ethics in the final chapter. Yet, whilst exposition of Althusser's work centred in this chapter predominantly on his appropriation of Epicurean atomism, the conjuncture within the clinamen and the associated problem of the evental rupture, this was necessary in order to examine the status of idealism within his own thought.

It was concluded that Althusser did indeed manage to avoid the various trappings of idealism (such as those of subject, object, epistemology and practice) in his later work only by idealising an initiatory void from which thought's consistency emerged. It is strange then that, whilst the coherence of Althusser's oeuvre lies in the attempt to subtract idealism from philosophy, he nevertheless injects it back in with his concept of the event which, like Badiou's, remains obstinately aleatory. Both Badiou's and Althusser's event present a rupture within being that, by design, cannot be explained and therefore remains an idealism *par excellence*. This is particularly strange, given the first Note's insistence that an object of knowledge (in this case the concept of an event itself) cannot be explained by the axiomatic postulates of a regional theory and must be placed within the differential context of the general theory. In this respect, and not forgetting the important correction of his 'theoreticism' within the book, Althusser's progression in *Essays in Self-Criticism* is a retrograde movement in his philosophy. The reasons for this (which may be more personal and sociological than philosophical) would make important contributions to both the study of Althusser and of continental philosophy more generally.

To reiterate the argument so far: the conjunction of Hume (or, more precisely, Deleuze's reading of Hume) to Althusser is an attempt to supplement this retrogression with an account of persistence in order to overcome, or subvert, a charge of idealism. The persistence of Althusser's event as an idea, constituted by relations that exist externally to the terms of the idea (and which are, in turn, artefactual in the Humean sense), immunises the event against charges of idealism. This immunisation is achieved by accounting for Althusser's concept of structural causality; the structure is causal because of the (dialectical) differential relationships between the relatively autonomous modes of thought (or regional theories) producing a new object of thought and concomitant knowledge effects.[49] Hume's encounter, forcing thought into action and the creation of ideas from relations external to their terms, thus impels the persistence of past thought into each passing present, within the structure of the subconscious.[50] The persistence of thought into the intellect, whilst avoiding the charge of idealism present in Althusser's aleatory materialism, puts thought into practical relationship with itself. In other words, politics can be thought in practical relationship with other modes of thought, paving the way to the think politics of art and science, or the aesthetics of politics, etc.

In contrast to Badiou's position, for whom politics was a prescription that could only be deployed by the militant *a posteriori* of the aleatory event (Hallward 2005: 772), Hume's and Althusser's relocation of politics from the start to a part of the differential structure has the effect of turning politics from a prescription into a practical interrogation. Without ontologising thought to either the prescription of a Badiouian event, or to the *telos* of a *polis* (*qua*, for example, Aristotle) – both operations hypostasise a particular form of thought which remains transcendent to the form of the *polis* – Althusser and Hume suggest that politics is essential within epistemology itself. Thus, removing the formal distinction that Badiou instantiates between (ontological) truth and *doxa,* practice alternates epistemology and the ontology of the encounter in a practical relay, located within the human (Hume) and the unconscious (Althusser).[51] It is in the foregrounding of practice that philosophy can undo the first Platonic dyad of truth/ *doxa*. Furthermore, in addition to avoiding the charge of idealising either ontology or epistemology, the conjunction of Hume's idea of human nature to Althusser's structuralism supplements the latter with a conception of time that circumvents the breaks in temporal continuity that are necessitated by the aleatory event.

For Althusser, each mode of thought has an inherent temporality, with both visible and invisible times that could be brought into visibility by the practice of philosophy. For Hume, time is not local to the modes of thought, but to the event, and time is constituted by the relations that make up human nature. For both thinkers, there is no single, linear time along which human nature or the unconscious travels, however, only Hume's idea of the subject accounts for duration. As Boundas explains in his introduction to *Empiricism and Subjectivity*, Hume's 'anticipating and inventing subject constitutes the past which weighs on the present, making it pass, while positing the past as the rule for the future. Time as the constitutive force of subjectivity, responsible for the bending and folding of the given and the formation of interiority, is indeed intensive' (Boundas in Deleuze 1991: 16). Hume's account of time, as opposed to Althusser's, exists separately to the ideas that form the intellect and condition the intellect's formation, although the synthesis of the subjective intellect understands time only as it shapes time, as time shapes it. In this sense, the conjunction of Hume to Althusser's aleatory materialism, suturing the aleatory event with the persistence of the past, allows for the continuity of the objects of knowledge and their relative effects within the series of practical philosophy. In the creation of the new, the past is preserved within time, but the object of knowledge is created anew with each passing present. Contra Badiou, for whom the new could only be thought on the impossible condition that some-one had already been interpellated as a subject of the ontological event, a relational Althusserianism allows for the thinking of the new *as part of* the event, without any formal delineation between the event and its subject. As has been argued, Althusser is not entirely successful in ridding philosophy of idealism and, in addition to a reliance on the event, Althusser's focus upon the unconscious remains a dogmatic concept in his work that is never fully accounted for. Althusser was well aware that the concept of the unconscious has latent Freudian connotations that would eventually necessitate its replacement (Althusser and Matheron 2003: 53). However, after observing in the Notes that, even within Freud's work, the unconscious had acquired enough considerable negative connotations to suggest a surrogate, Althusser does not offer a suggestion as to what concept should take its place. Whilst, in his later work, Althusser does move away from problematic and explicitly psychoanalytic terminology, a certain synthesis of thought nevertheless pervades throughout his oeuvre. For example, in *Essays in Self-Criticism*, Althusser develops Marx's comment in the *Eighteenth Brumaire* that 'Men make their own history' to argue that 'the constitution of individuals as historical *subjects*, active *in* history, has nothing in principle to do with the question of the "*Subject* of history", or even with that of the "*subjects* of history"' (Althusser 1976: 95; original emphasis). For Althusser, associating men as the agent that constructs history is an example of the classical humanism of the Enlightenment, an ideological distortion that constructs an abstract understanding of history (1976: 97). Rather, history must be understood through the Marxist concept of dialectical materialism, which explains the constitution of the subject as an ideological object which has scientific, artistic and philosophical effects. Here, it is worth quoting Althusser at length from his 'Reply to John Lewis':

> It is precisely the Thesis of the *Communist Manifesto* – 'the class struggle is the motor of history' – that *displaces the question*, that brings the problem into the open, that shows us how to pose it properly and therefore how to solve it. It is the masses which 'make' history, but 'it is the class struggle which is the motor of history'. To John Lewis' question: 'how does man make history?', Marxism-Leninism replies by replacing his idealist philosophical categories with categories of a quite different kind. (Althusser 1976: 48)

The philosophical categories that Althusser highlights are the relatively autonomous modes of thought which, in the above passage, form the Marxist-Leninist understanding of history. Later in the 'Reply', Althusser argues that even the concept of 'making' must be done away with as it connotes too much importance to a centralised artifice. And yet, Althusser never addresses the relationship of the unconscious (the singular, practical locus of the four forms of thought) that is set out programmatically in the Note and dialectical materialism more generally. Is dialectical materialism to be understood as "populated" by unconsciousnesses, and how would this new objecticity (the being-in-the-world of unconsciousness) be explained? In identifying a unifying locus within which the four forms of thought locate themselves in synthesis, does Althusser not institute a Kantian/Badiouian subject: a transcendental unity that provides the minimum criteria for further epistemological practice? As well as the hypostatisation of an aleatory event, Althusser specifies a subconscious that understands the world in four – and only four – modes of thought (or regional practices). Again then, the problem of origins that Montag highlights raises its head: a synthesis of the modes of thought is necessary in Althusser's later work in order to account for the new, however Althusser does not develop this in any more detail within his later work to draw a connection between his initial psychoanalytic influence and his later materialism. Furthermore, in the first Note, although Althusser tentatively suggests the four functions of the regional theories that make up the unconscious, there is no given reason as to why these are to be the particular theories that make up Althusser's epistemology and, concomitantly, the minimum criteria of the subconscious. Whilst he acknowledges the danger of relying on definitions based upon their function, the fact that he does not proffer any further explanation for differentiation within the rest of his work leaves him open to the charge of defining the modes of thought upon the phenomenology of established discourse – precisely what his conception of relative autonomy was established to undermine. Whilst the distinctions employed are of use to Marxist sociology and activism, in philosophy, the concept of the unconscious, as the pre-defined locus of epistemological practice, falls to the criticism of idealist dogmatism to the same extent as Althusser's aleatory void.

Similarly, does Hume not also commit a similar act when he posits a *particular* unity, with *particular* relations (i.e. association, contiguity, resemblance and causality) that happen to constitute ideas? Boundas puts it clearly when he differentiates the subject as 'the product of the principles of human nature; but then the mind, or the given, is the product of the powers of nature' (Boundas in Deleuze 1991: 17). Here, Boundas highlights the lack of explanation for why some particular relations condition the mind, as opposed to others. Indeed Kant also recognised in Hume a metaphysical dogmatism on which, he claims, all indifferentists (philosophers who rely on common sense to ground a metaphysics of scepticism) 'inevitably fall back, in so far as they think at all, into those very metaphysical assertions which they profess so greatly to despise' (Kuehn 1983: 182, Kant [1787] 1996: Ax). For Kant, causality is an *a priori* concept that, as a concept, exists prior to the constitution of the subject which only then attributes it to certain phenomena. The realisation of this in Hume's work began a process of realisation in Kant who found 'that the concept of causality was only one among many *a priori* concepts of the understanding and that all of metaphysics consisted of them' (Kuehn 1983: 182). So whilst, as has been shown, Kant's project does not successfully avoid the criticism of dogmatism itself, both Boundas and Kant nevertheless highlight the *a priori* condition whereby certain relations constitute the mind which themselves require explanation. Not everyone has the same cognitive apparatus because of the differential relations, superior to the subject, that nonetheless constitute it. Although, for Hume, the subject is indeed only a product of relations which are superior to it, nevertheless the specification of certain relations idealises them to a transcendental position above the subject. Hume and Althusser then rely upon certain dogmatic claims, constituted by ideal terms that, despite their foregrounding practice, nevertheless undermine their positions as non-dogmatic.

It is the pragmatist John Dewey who characterises best the underlying condition of Badiou, Althusser and Hume as prescribing 'modes of thought [that assume and foreground] the intelligibility of the world, assuming that this is the only way in which the world can be "managed"' (Dewey 1958: 128). Tracing this lineage back to its Platonic inspiration and an appropriation of artisanship by ancient philosophy, Dewey argues that the 'very conception of cognitive meaning, intellectual significance, is that things in their immediacy are subordinated to what they portend and give evidence of. An intellectual sign denotes that a thing is not taken immediately but is referred to something that may come in consequence of it' (1958: 128). Dewey argues that, in both the Platonic ideal form and Aristotle's efficient and final causes, things are appropriated by philosophy in a problematic and unjustified attempt to instrumentalise the world in a process that rids the thing of its other intrinsic qualities, whatever they may be. The intellectual instrumentalisation of things serves management, for Dewey, because the mode of management conspires with the mode of instrumentalisation of the world itself.[52] In service of this appropriation, '[s]elf-evidence ceases to be a characteristic trait of the fundamental objects of either sensory or noetic objects. Primary propositions are statements of objects in terms which procure the simplest and completest forming and checking of other propositions', meaning that '[m]any systems of axioms and postulates are possible, the more the merrier, since new propositions as consequences are brought to light' (1958: 130). Dewey's description rings true of Badiou's explicitly axiomatic philosophy in terms of the latter's ontological axiomatic structure and its claims to "understand" the new according to the category theory developed in *Logics of Worlds* (Badiou 2009). His description also applies to Hume's and Althusser's philosophies, which both seek to theorise an understanding of the world by a propositional intellect. Yet, as Dewey argues, according to this understanding, '[o]bjects are possessed and appreciated, but they are not *known*' (1958: 131).

For Dewey, to know 'means that men have become willing to turn away from precious possessions; willing to let drop what they own, however precious, in behalf of a grasp of objects which they do not as yet own' (1958: 131). But what does this mean? In *Proust and Signs*, Deleuze develops the concepts of series and groups with regard to love in an account that sheds light on what it means for both to know. It is helpful to quote him at length in order to understand his account of the progression from one object to the other:

> The image or the theme [of love] contains the particular character of our loves. But we repeat this image only all the more, and all the better, in that it escapes us in fact and remains unconscious. Far from expressing the idea's immediate power, repetition testifies to a discrepancy here, an inadequation of consciousness and idea. Experience is no help to us because we deny that we repeat and still believe in something new, but also because we are unaware of the difference that makes our loves intelligible and refers them to a law that is in a sense their living source. The unconscious, in love, is the separation of the two aspects of essence: difference and repetition. (Deleuze [1964] 2008: 44)

According to Deleuze then, love exists as an idea, but this idea is not 'placed' upon a particular experience in an act that attributes sense to the idea but, rather, it is an idea that unites different experiences in what then becomes a repeating series. In other words, a series of relationships only becomes a series in retrospect, once each relationship has begun and reached the stage which can then be called love. Yet the love of one individual at one moment will not be identical to its antecedent love, for everything involved is different – even if the partners are the same – and it is in this sense that love repeats differently with every experience.[53] As Deleuze reveals, 'the beloved belongs initially to a group, in which she is not yet individualised'. 'Who will be the girl', he asks, 'the hero loves in the homogeneous group?' ([1964] 2008: 49). Thus, people must be willing to let things drop in order to place them into the condition where they may form series with that which is yet to come; one enjoys a thing in itself whilst being open to its placement within a series. In this sense, the experience is a sign of enjoyment for Deleuze, but it is only fully enjoyed when it is part of a series which only occurs in retrospect of its becoming ([1964] 2008: 47). It is not sufficient to allow things to remain appropriated within an intellectual system of management, or an 'abstract truth that a thinker might discover by the effort of a method or of a free reflection' ([1964] 2008: 47) because this would limit the potential to understand the thing as part of a series that is itself constituted with the thing.[54] Accordingly, for both Dewey and Deleuze, it is important to let things drop – or die – which is not itself an enjoyable experience, but is the only possibility for joy; whilst 'the phenomena are always unhappy and particular' in their fleeting singularity, 'the idea extracted from them is general and joyous' ([1964] 2008: 47). Indeed, Deleuze argues that we 'extract from our particular despairs a general Idea; this is because the Idea was primary, was already there' as part of the things, and joy is the unification of a series under the remit of the Idea ([1964] 2008: 47). If Badiou, Hume and Althusser all instantiate an idealism in their philosophies, it is because they all attempt to make intelligible a world which they, in turn, idealise as intelligible. For Deleuze, all three are sad thinkers as they deny the creative potential of life in their attempts to subordinate it under the thinkable (Deleuze 2001: 68–74). In order to bring joy to philosophy – i.e. to affirm it and the novelty it creates – and to construct an ethics of this joyful philosophy, it is necessary to understand the thing as a singularity, within its place in a series considered only retrospectively.

Notes

1. In the previous chapter, this 'purely formal logic' was shown in Badiou to be the matheme, or the scriptural materiality of Badiou's mathematical, subtractive ontology.
2. In 1978, Althusser published an essay entitled 'What Must Change in the Party' (1978), which 'denounced the weakness of democracy and the entrenched bureaucracy within the party' (Hewlett 2010: 22). Althusser's wife, Hélène, had been a Marxist activist for most of her life and had encouraged Althusser to remain within the PCF, leading Althusser to avoid the sort of strong criticism afforded the party by Badiou (Althusser *et al.* 1993).
3. Badiou is correct in his assertion that Althusser's aleatory materialism is without an active subject, but underplays the importance of Althusser's formulation of the unconscious which provides the synthesis of thought and matter.
4. I have often been accused in presentations of trying to argue that Deleuze was a Marxist (as if that would be such a terrible thing). Indeed, inserting the work of Deleuze into a discussion with that of Althusser and Badiou might seem as if I was attempting to place Deleuze within the Marxist cannon. I am not interested, however, in what Chambers calls 'petty intellectual squabbles' with regard to Althusser (Chambers 2014: 93), and I am not trying to place Deleuze anywhere. This is not because Deleuze was not a Marxist, but because it doesn't matter if he was or not (here I disagree with Resch's argument that it does matter and, furthermore, that Deleuze had a 'hostility to Marxism' (Resch 1992: 2–10). The coherence of any canon – Marxist or otherwise – is maintained either out of reductive simplicity (i.e. a pragmatic necessity to stick to certain terms and assumptions in order to carry out productive research) or the defence of key territories, figures or both. Whereas E. P. Thompson's critique of Althusser in *The Poverty of Theory* is a defence of both the territory of Marxism and the figure of Marx, arguing that 'Althusser and his acolytes challenge, centrally, historical materialism itself ' and that 'Althusser's structuralism is a structuralism of *status*, departing from Marx's own historical method' (Thompson 1978: 196–7, original italics), Badiou goes so far as to argue that, following a radical rupture between Marx and Lenin as identified by Lazarus, '*Marxism doesn't exist*' (2005c: 58). A portrayal of the 'conjunctures in the international Communist movement' and the competing claims to an authoritative Marxism can be found in Elliot's *Althusser: The Detour of Theory* (2006: 1–54) and a discussion of his status as a Marxist in a conference paper presented by Elliot, *Althusser's Solitude* (1993). I argue that, whilst a certain practical focus on central concepts is a central part of academic research,

the paternalist defence of canon belies either an unwillingness or inability to do the intellectual labour of philosophy, relying on the authority of names to do the work instead. As such, and whilst a discussion of their relations can be found in Garo (2011), no claims are made by this chapter regarding whether or not either Althusser or Deleuze were Marxists (or even Spinozists), aside from the authors' own claims to their intellectual inheritance.

5. Deleuze's two main works on Spinoza are *Expressionism and Philosophy: Spinoza* (1992) and *Spinoza: Practical Philosophy* (1988) with a chapter entitled "Spinoza and the Three 'Ethics'" in Montag and Stolze (1997: 21–32). However, Spinoza is also to be found mentioned in every book he authored since *Difference and Repetition* (2004). Badiou's work also regularly features references to Spinoza and discusses his use by Deleuze in *The Clamour of Being* (2000).

6. There are a small number of works on Badiou and Hume which include Johnston (2011) and Bell (2006). Those on Althusser and Hume include (Peden 2008) and (Reed 2005). The literature on Deleuze and Hume is more substantive, although Jeffery Bell provides the most comprehensive study of Deleuze's reading of Hume. See Bell (2006, 2008, 2009).

7. Montag's discussion of Althusser's autobiography is indeed excellent in highlighting its rupture with the latter's oeuvre. See Montag (2003: 117–31).

8. In personal communication, Richard Sakwa went so far as to say that everyone has, at one time or another, been an Althusserian – if only to repent later. Williams echoes this comment, writing that '[e]very theory of ideology which takes its genealogy through Marx has also to pass by way of Althusser' (Williams 2002: 29).

9. In a particularly vitriolic polemic, directed as much against Althusser's persona as against his philosophy, E. P. Thompson labeled Althusser 'a freak of intellectual fashion, which, if [historical materialists] close their eyes, will in time go away' (1978: 195). Freaks, according to Thompson, 'if tolerated – and even flattered and fed – can show astonishing influence and longevity' (1978: 195). This longevity, demonstrated by the continued interest in Althusser, evidenced by the repudiation of his biographical history and internal to the work of Althusser itself, says perhaps as much about Althusser's anti-humanism as his theory.

10. In *Negotiations*, Deleuze addresses his distaste for the prominence of the history of philosophy, stating that 'the main way I coped with it at the time was to see the history of philosophy as a sort of buggery or (it comes to the same thing) immaculate conception. I saw myself as taking an author *from behind* and giving him a child that would be his own off-spring, yet monstrous' (1995: 6).

11. According to Williams, Althusser's conception of ideology was one of 'an imaginary, albeit wholly necessary, relation to reality' (2002: 30). Williams lists various incarnations of ideology that Althusser took aim at as 'all forms of Hegelian Marxism, notably that of Lukács with its attendant historicism and humanism as well as its residual idealism' and 'other forms of humanism, particularly the existential variety that remains tied to a conception of the subject as cogito' (2002: 31). The task of replacing ideology with a science was one that Althusser saw begun by Marx: 'He replaced postulates (empiricism/idealism of the subject, empiricism/idealism of the essence) which were the basis not only for idealism but also for pre-Marxist materialism, by a historic-dialectical materialism of *praxis*: that is, by a theory of the different specific *levels* of *human practice* (economic practice, political practice, ideological practice, scientific practice) in their characteristic articulations, based upon the specific articulations of the unity of human society' (Althusser [1965] 2005: 229, original italics).
12. As Bryant puts it, Deleuze would later make a similar criticism of this form of knowledge, calling it one of the forms of the 'dogmatic of thought' (Bryant 2008: 80–1, Deleuze [1994] 2011: 164–214).
13. Although Deleuze revised his definition of philosophy, alongside Guattari in *What is Philosophy?*, as the 'discipline that involves the creation of concepts' – and thus as a practice itself – his prior definition was more akin to Althusser's definition of philosophy as the theory of theoretical practice (Deleuze and Guattari [1991] 1994: 5). Roffe outlines how Deleuze's work on Hume in *Empiricism and Subjectivity* (1991) led him to argue that subjectivity must be perpetually reconstituted in the light of encounters and, as such, philosophy was the account of how this occurs (Roffe 2017: 184). Whilst Deleuze and Guattari's latter definition is perhaps richer, adding a productive and affective component to the otherwise descriptive role of the former definition, it is clear that both Althusser and Deleuze were at one point united by their pursuit of a structuralist account of the individual's relation to the social formation.
14. This criticism of Althusser is very similar to that made of Badiou, i.e. that he is unable to account for the split between the rational and empirical in his ontology.
15. Badiou also incorporates a latent atomism in his ontology and explains that 'if a property is attested for at least one natural multiple, then there will always exist an *ultimate* natural element with this property' (Badiou 2011: 135). This natural element, for Badiou, is the minimal property of belonging $\in$, or the '"smallest" element for which the [natural] property is appropriate' (Badiou 2011: 139). However, because, for Badiou, a totalised nature does not exist, it is not the case that everything belongs to nature. Instead, as he argues,

'everything (which is natural) is (belongs) in everything, save that there is no everything', thus confirming the undifferentiated and unnameable status of the void.

16. In *Logic of Sense*, Deleuze argues that the importance of structuralism in philosophy was to displace frontiers that had traditionally been set up, on the one hand by humanists and rationalists, and on the other by idealists who, primarily referring to Heidegger, he describes as the '[n]ew theologians of a misty sky (the sky of Koenigsberg) [...] who sprang upon the stage in the name of the God-man or the Man-god as the secret of sense' (Deleuze [1969] 2004: 83). Deleuze's frustration with both is evident as he wonders 'whether it is the ass which loads man or man who loads the ass and himself' ([1969] 2004: 83). Deleuze argues that the sense of whether one loads the other or not is an argument to create, rather than to discover, predating by seven years the argument made by Althusser in 'Reply to John Lewis'. Other than Stolze's article specifically connecting Deleuze and Althusser, there is no literature to show whether Deleuze also influenced Althusser in this regard, yet the similarity of the argumentation used is certainly uncanny.

17. Diefenbach *et al.* put this clearly when they state that by 'assuming that the social instances mutually condition one another in their existence, Althusser infers that they internalise the position that they occupy in the structure'. Relations are 'not thought', they argue, 'as in Spinoza, through the intervals that they articulate, but through their [own] terms' (Diefenbach *et al.* 2013: 174).

18. The importance of unveiling new words – or theoretical concepts – has large implications for Althusser's 'symptomatic' reading of texts, as developed in *Reading Capital*. Althusser reveals that, 'Marx criticised Smith and Ricardo for constantly *confusing* surplus-value with its forms of existence: profit, rent and interest. The great Economists' analyses are therefore lacking a word' (Althusser and Balibar 1970: 146). It is by introducing a new term into analysis ('surplus-value') that, for Althusser, Marx allows for the correct theoretical analysis of capitalism, corrected against the myopia suffered by both Smith and Ricardo (1970: 19). Althusser is clear that not every word can function as a theoretical concept but, rather, if 'the word surplus-value has such importance it is because it directly affects the structure of the object whose future is at stake in the simple act of naming' (1970: 146). Thus, new terminology both unveils and stipulates the affective extents of encounters that have been arrogated under previously myopic classifications. Whilst this could, at first, appear as if Althusser is setting up a simple positivism – whereby matter takes the form of the concept that is applied to it – to claim that this were so would be to ignore the *a posteriori* nature of concepts with respect to the encounter. As in the work of Hume, for

Althusser, relations are external to (and in excess of) their terms. The encounter forms the basis upon which concepts can be constructed, not the other way around, and there is not necessarily any assumption that the new concept, once constructed, is entirely adequate to the task of capturing the affective capability of the encounter.

19. Although more commonly known as an empiricist, and following the distinction between the work of Hume and Popper developed within Meillassoux's *Science Fiction and Extro-Science Fiction* (2013), Popper's account of scientific methodology places him better within the rationalist camp. As Meillassoux convincingly argues, Popper's description of verification as the criteria that judges the truthfulness of scientific claims is an epistemological claim regarding the ability of science to prove its own results and says nothing of the ontological (Meillassoux 2013: 14). The upshot of Popperian methodology is that science is unable to guarantee whether or not previously unforeseen material behaviours or scientific laws might emerge or indeed, paradoxically, *have* emerged. According to Meillassoux, however, empiricism itself is not necessarily guilty of this inability (indeed Hume examined precisely this problem in his work), thus the distinction between rationalism and empiricism here is useful.

20. That knowledge is produced according to conditions of its own production was important for Althusser. He wrote frequently of analysis 'in the last instance' and this last instance is the point at which all relatively autonomous forms of analysis (scientific/ideological/economic) have concentrated into one moment that can be articulated (Althusser 1976: 50–1). As Gordy puts it, the 'concept of class struggle thus emerges as the fundamental category of historical materialism, for to say that the economy is determinant in the last instance is precisely to say that class struggle is the motor of history (Gordy 1983: 11). The mode of production is a significant evaluative concept for Marx and Althusser, and determines the nature of class struggle in the form of its social hierarchies and different property claims. Yet it should not be assumed that Althusser ignores ideology when he discusses economics, as all knowledge in Althusser's work is in fact interpellated by ideology. Instead, analysis in the last instance should be taken to mean 'analysis taking into account all modes of analysis, but from the perspective of (the most significant) one'.

21. Objecticity is used here in the Deleuzian sense to denote the understanding of what an object is, as opposed to objectivity, which would be the study of these objects once defined. See Deleuze (2004b: 164).

22. Althusser clarifies that '[p]hilosophy is not Absolute Knowledge; it is neither the Science of Sciences, nor the Science of Practices. Which means: it does not possess the Absolute Truth, either about any science or about any practice' (Althusser 1976: 58). Although philosophy does take lexical priority over science, philosophy has no claim

to objecticity or, concomitantly, objectivity; this remains within the realm of science. Philosophy, existing as it does in the void and remaining devoid of transcendental truth conditions, is the space within which the terms of science (and its outcomes) are hashed out by the relatively autonomous collection of other theoretical modes. As Matheron and Post put it, philosophy is 'the full field in which nothing occurs but the repetition of a void' – this void being the aleatory and inconsistent foundation of all thought (Matheron and Post 1998: 28–9).

23. Markus Gabriel provides an argument as to why such worlds (mind-independent or not) do not exist in his books *Fields of Sense* (2015), *Why the World Does Not Exist* (2015) and his TED talk of the same name (2013).

24. Althusser conceptualises history in two types. The first is that of historical laws, which are developed by 'vulgar historians and sociologists' who 'consider only the accomplished fact of past history' (Althusser 2006: 263–4). The second type is what Althusser calls history '*in the present*', the study of tendential laws whose future paths cannot be seen because they are aleatory (2006: 264). The latter history is the aleatory materialism, open to the event, that Althusser attributes to Marx.

25. For Lampert, the problem of origins in Althusser's concept of interpellation appears in Butler's appropriation of it for her own work. According to Lampert, Butler's commits Althusser to a theological understanding of ideology, whereby the act of 'hailing' an individual interpellates an individual by virtue of the hail's assumed authority. This reading of Althusser, however, forgets that the task of the ISA essay is 'to undo the idealist schema of ideology-as-belief and words-as-actions' (2015: 129). Instead, 'it is not' as Lampert puts it, 'that the words spoken in a [. . .] ritual compel belief; rather, it is that a ritual is followed *as if* those words were true, whether we believe them or not. The words themselves – "I now pronounce you man and wife," etc. – may in fact be a necessary part of the ritual (utterances can in this way be one "modality" of material practice, as Althusser puts it). But the utterances themselves are not interpellations in some performative sense' (2015: 129). As such, whilst Lampert is wrong to claim that the words are true by necessity, he is correct to emphasise the importance of the event within which the always-already there field of ideology relates to the individual. This event, which encompasses ideology and the individual, also accounts for the reproduction of ideology following the act of the individual's interpellation.

26. Deleuze and Guattari conceptualise philosophy in a manner which accounts for these factors in *What is Philosophy?* ([1991] 1994). According to the authors, concepts are created by a conceptual persona from an immanent pre-conceptual plane of immanence, which

synthesises a concept's conditions. This text is not drawn from in this chapter, however, as it says little of either time or persistence, two ideas which are necessary for the discussion of ethics to come.

27. As such, Chambers calls Althusser the 'untimely discoverer of the untimely' (Chambers 2014: 143).
28. Althusser explained that any attempt to account for obvious chronological passages constitutes an '"empirical history" [that] is merely the bare face of the empiricist ideology of history' (Althusser and Balibar 1970: 105, Chambers 2010: 208–9).
29. Althusser develops this criticism, directed predominantly against Hegel, in the introduction to *Reading Capital* (Althusser and Balibar 1970: 1–78). The criticism will not be fully expanded here, only to note that it is similar to the critique of ideology found in his later work.
30. In *After Finitude* (2008), Meillassoux argues precisely that there is no necessity for this at all as, indeed, there is no necessity for the coming into existence (or 'facticity') of anything at all. A more substantive engagement with Meillassoux is reserved for Chapter 3, yet, leaving to one side the probability or contingency of an object existing, the issue at stake for Althusser and Deleuze is not whether or not an object exists but, to the extent that it does, what its affective characteristics are and what the object does. To this extent, this chapter concentrates on the construction of series before their facticity.
31. In *Reading Capital*, Althusser criticises empiricism with the Hegelian imagery of a nut waiting to be cracked. The kernel of the nut is analogous to the idea which must be attained by an empirical process of extraction, the use of which is then denied. Althusser describes this denial as 'denegation' or 'an unconscious denial masked by a conscious acceptance' (Althusser and Balibar 1970: 312). In other words, denegation occurs when a process is used to understand an object, the knowledge of which is thus an *addition* to the object, but the specificities of the process are ignored in the assumption that the process used is the same as all other empirical processes.
32. Deleuze discusses this only briefly with regard to Hume, instead developing his theory of time more fully in *Bergsonism* ([1988] 1991), *Cinema 1 & 2* (2005) and *Difference and Repetition* (2004). His development of Hume is expanded on here due to its importance in Deleuze's conceptualisation of series and the individual.
33. A discussion of Hume's passions that does them justice is too much for this book. Put simply, they are Hume's account of the motivations according to which individuals act in relation to others, and the second book of the *Treatise* (Hume [1888] 1967), in which they are discussed in their fullest, gives an account of the underlying cause of the different passions (McIntyre 2000: 78). For a full discussion, see Ardal's *Passion and Value in Hume's Treatise* (1966),

which Immerwahr references as the most important book-length discussion of Hume's idea of passions (Immerwahr 1994: 225, ff. 222). With regard to Deleuze's relation to the passions, see the edited book, *Deleuze and the Passions* (Meiborg and Tuinen 2016).

34. When sutured to Althusser's aleatory philosophy and as part of the Althusserian encounter, Hume's institutions are examples of persistence. Like Hume's concept of habit (the transcendental source of the subject for Deleuze's Hume), institutions affect the constitution of ideas in the mind in accordance with their temporal specificity and contingency. As Deleuze says of the mind, although it applies to both the mind and institutions, it '"*advises* certain ideas rather than others." "To transcend" means exactly this' (Deleuze 1991: 127). In this sense, both institutions and habit can be viewed as what Stiegler terms 'technical objects'. Stiegler argues that the history of western philosophy has systematically underplayed the role of technics as the organisation of inorganic matter. In *Technics and Time 1* (1998) and *For a New Critique of Political Economy* (2010), Stiegler argues that technical objects are constituted by primary retention (the act of remembering in itself) and secondary retention (memories), and are known as tertiary retention (memories that are extended into technical objects external to the subject) (Stiegler 1998, Roberts 2016: 93). Whilst it is is not within the scope of the current book to develop it, research into the relationship between Stiegler's and Hume's conceptions of artifice could produce important conclusions regarding the temporal, pharmacological and ethical natures of social institutions.

35. Badiou aligns himself more to Rousseau than any other social contract theorist and draws from him this concept of political subjectivity (Power 2006: 318). Indeed, Badiou goes so far as to argue that if 'Rousseau forever establishes the modern concept of politics, it is because he posits, in the most radical fashion, that politics is a procedure which originates in an event, and not in a structure supported within being' (Badiou 2011: 345). Badiou cannot name the event in Rousseau (as the event, according to Badiou, is unnameable in itself), but where the "evental form" is the social pact, what Badiou terms '*eventness*' (where in the event 'any political procedure finds its truth' is in the form of the pact (2011: 345). It is in this sense that both Badiou and Badiou's Rousseau can claim to break from the state of nature, as each citizen within the general will claims a pure form of fidelity. Badiou cannot completely support Rousseau's position, however, because, as Power explains, when Rousseau considers the practicality of the general will in singular situations, he 'submits the general will to the "law of number" and thus turns a generic, egalitarian political programme into a majoritarian one' (Power 2006: 319). The turn to numbers – counting each individual within the general will – is simply, for Badiou, a case of torsion (see Chapter 1 above)

or the 'fetishism of universal suffrage' (Badiou 2011: 350). Instead of relying on Rousseau's return to a theory of individual subjects within the general will, Badiou relies on axiomatic subjectification and forcing to account for the subject's actions within singular situations. For an illuminating discussion of Badiou's relationship to Rousseau, and a criticism of the generic approach to singular situations, see Critchley (2012).

36. As Badiou argues, '[n]ature has no sayable being. There are only *some* natural beings' (Badiou 2011: 140). This declaration, a result of the illegitimacy of the count-as-one operation, allows Badiou to then describe the 'unlimited opening of a chain of name-numbers, such that each is composed of all those which precede it' (2011: 141). In other words, there are natural multiples that structure the world in which the individual perseveres, yet these multiples are not totalising and condition the possibility of the truth-event.
37. See the previous chapter's discussion of the two Platonic and the one Parmenidean axioms.
38. Although Deleuze does not expand on his distaste for major subjects after this passage, his preference for minoritarian practices run throughout his works, including those with Guattari. For a discussion of his appropriation of minor mathematics, see Evans (2006) and Chapter 5 of *Difference and Repetition* (Deleuze [1994] 2011). For Deleuze and Guattari's conceptualisation of a 'minor literature', see *Kafka: Toward a Minor Literature* (Deleuze and Guattari 1986) and for their idea of 'becoming minoritarian' see the fourth plateau, 'November 20, 1923: Postulates of Linguistics' in *A Thousand Plateaus* (Deleuze and Guattari 2004b).
39. Deleuze insists that principles of both association and passion are 'not entities; they are functions' and 'are defined by their effects' (Deleuze 1991). To present a definition of the principles by defining their effects, i.e. to ask 'what they are', would be to foreclose the possibility of the passions becoming other than what is specified by the *a priori* description. In other words, this would be to instantiate a dogmatism into Hume's conception of the subject. The virtue of transcendental empiricism for Deleuze is precisely the understanding that what is given as real can transcend *itself* to become radically new, regardless of the predictable possibilities contained within the given. For this reason, the principles in Hume are to be understood as pure production and defined *a posteriori* in their effects, only in the understanding that they may still become other.
40. Althusser is unclear as to whether there are one or a plurality of general theories. In the first Note, he criticises Lacan for confusing the regional theory of psychoanalysis as the general theory of linguistics and vice versa. This leads, according to Althusser, to a conceptualisation of discourses as 'confrontation' (or, in other words, dialectics)

and the various ideological problems associated with such idealism (Althusser and Matheron 2003: 45). What is needed instead, for Althusser, is a third element – the general theory – which forms the transcendental synthesis for the two regional theories of psychoanalysis and linguistics.

41. In his 1971 debate with Chomsky, Foucault coins the term 'epistemological indicator' to mean a concept that has a 'classifying, delimiting and other [function]' to define one discourse against another (Chomsky and Foucault 1971: 2). Foucault says of the concept 'human nature' that it 'played the role of an epistemological indicator to designate certain types of discourse in relation to or in opposition to theology or biology or history' and was not, as Chomsky would have it, a scientific concept (1971: 2). Epistemological indicators are thus used here as contingent reference points to certain discourses that have a problematic relationship to their designation with other, relatively autonomous, discourses.

42. The differential relationship between modes of thought that unify within a non-totalising whole is reminiscent of Spinoza's concept of substance and its expression in attributes and modes. Much of the recent secondary literature on Spinoza concentrates on Althusser's relationship with Spinoza (see Kaplan and Sprinker 1993, Montag and Stolze 1997, Fourtounis 2005, Diefenbach et al. 2013, Williams 2013) and this chapter defers discussion of this relationship to these studies.

43. Chambers makes a similar argument, pointing out that it is not necessary to highlight Althusser's 'so-called aleatory materialism' in the 'later Althusser', particularly given that Althusser himself 'took drafts of *early manuscripts* and went through in later years crossing out "historical" in the phrase "historical materialism" and writing in "aleatory"' (Chambers 2014: 148). For Chambers, Althusser's conceptualisation of social formations always was aleatory to the extent that he recognised that *'temporality is not a variable distinct or separate from the social order; any (theory of the) social formation contains its own temporality'* (2014: 149).

44. Deleuze credits Althusser by saying that no one has better thought the status of the structure in terms of Theory, confirming that the object of knowledge is the production of a regional theory by stating that 'the symbolic must be understood as the production of the original and specific theoretical object' (Deleuze 2004a: 173).

45. As previously noted, Althusser himself recognises his early works' 'theoreticist deviation' in *Essays in Self-Criticism* (Althusser 1976: 105–6). He clarifies his position to remove its rationalist foundations and counter-actualise it as a historical (and therefore practical) argument. Whilst, as has been argued, this counter-actualisation may serve to immunise Althusser against claims to rationalism (and therefore

idealism) with regard to *a priori* claims in this regard, his argument is ultimately founded upon the aleatory event which opens him up once more to criticism.

46. For Deleuze, a society resolves problems according to its own means because the society itself has formulated the problems in its own terms, these being terms that society is able to understand and work with. Anticipating work on Bergson that he would publish sixteen years later – itself a development of an argument in Marx's work (Deleuze [1988] 1991: 16) – Deleuze argues that 'a problem always gains the solution that it deserves based on the manner in which it is posed, and on the symbolic field used to pose it' (Deleuze 2004a: 181). The economic structure of society is, for Althusser and Deleuze, not pre-given as an object that empirical problems can 'find out' about but, rather, it is only what is expressed *as expression*. In other words, solutions are veridical to their problems only on the terms of the latter and, as such, the whole of society is constituted by either well-formed, non-existent, or badly-formed problems (where non-existent problems contain a 'confusion of the "more" and the "less"'; and '"badly stated" questions [are] so defined because their terms represent badly analysed composites' ([1988] 1991: 16–17)). Importantly for politics – and echoing Hume's conceptualisation of social institutions – Althusser and Deleuze highlight that the freedom, as well as 'the history of man, from the theoretical as much as from the practical point of view is that of the construction of problems' (Deleuze [1988] 1991: 16).

47. Caroline Williams objects to Althusser's account of subjectification, arguing that 'Althusser offered no account of the link between the materiality of ideological state apparatuses and the constitution of the subject, that is, how ideology is internalised and how it produces the effects of subjectification' (Williams 2001: 106). This objection, however, misses the emphasis that Althusser places on regional theories or, in other words, the socio-historically specific nature of the subjectifying events. Althusser could not have given specific accounts of subjectification because each process of subjectification is singularly unique to the individual. Furthermore, the effects of subjectification are, for Althusser, not articulable by ideology and must be expressed by one of the other discourses.

48. The foundational status of necessity within practice will be discussed more fully in the next chapter. Within Althusser's work, the concept of necessity is subordinated to the contingency of the originary void, this being the basis for the prior criticism of his evacuation of ideas from philosophy (Morfino 2005: §37). As Morfino highlights, 'Althusser uses the notion of the "fact" in an anti-metaphysical sense' in the sense that he must submit 'the fact to the most radical contingency', i.e. the void (2005: §43). The construction of the subject effect is an example of what Deleuze calls a 'sign'. See Deleuze ([1964] 2008: 3–17).

49. The use of the term "causal" here is not to be read in the strict Hegelian sense by which a dialectic relationship is synthesised by way of logical progression which formally determines its outcome. Instead, it is used here to designate the functional relationship of relatively autonomous modes of thought, whereby the causal outcome of the dialectic is determined by the differential relationship itself.
50. With regard to the relations conjoining the encounter, Reed demonstrates that this 'notion of a spontaneous disposition is paradoxical, or even oxymoronic: it might be termed an "unconstrained constraint." Yet, with this oxymoron Hume is pointing to the ways a particular association erupts from the field of the possible' (Reed 2005: 218). It is not purely the passive objectivity of an association which impels the intellect, but rather that there are *different* 'ways' to associate which both call on and motivate the intellect to form new ideas. Reed goes on to argue that the 'quality of one thing to cause another is a power, as Hume points out, but by his system of analysis, that power exists only in associations we draw between the two things, not as an inherent quality of the thing' (Reed 2005: 219). Things therefore condition associations between themselves (through what Deleuze elsewhere calls the 'sign' (see Deleuze [1964] 2008)) which nevertheless then need associating. It is this practice of association which Hume calls human nature, and Althusser calls practice in its second form.
51. This does not necessarily mean that rejecting the distinction between truth and *doxa* also necessitates giving up on the concept of truth. Instead, Deleuze argues that truth is a 'matter of production, not of adequation' or, in other words, truth is produced internally as an answer to a well formed question, one that does not pre-suppose its answers in the question itself (Deleuze [1994] 2011: 192, 197).
52. Dewey argues that '[i]ntellectual meanings may themselves be appropriated, enjoyed and appreciated; but the character of intellectual meaning is instrumental', sardonically adding that '[f]ortunate for us is it that tools and their using can be directly enjoyed; otherwise all work would be drudgery' (Dewey 1958: 128). Dewey here points out the complicity between the intellectual appropriation of the world and the forms of work that found themselves upon, and reinforce, this appropriation, forms of work which also interpellate the individual into enjoying them for lack of a fuller knowledge of the world. This argument is expanded on by, amongst others, the situationists (for example, see Debord 2002 and Bernard Stiegler, especially Stiegler 2010).
53. Contra Deleuze, for whom singular difference must be conceptualised in and for itself, Badiou argues that one is able to say 'this is the same thing as that' because this 'only differs from that by the statement of the difference, by the literal placement' (Badiou [1982] 2013: 12). Borrowing from Hegelian dialectics, for Badiou, the difference between the thing (A) and the thing placed (Ap) is

the difference between what Heidegger calls the ontological and the ontic being. This means that the thing never exists in itself and relies upon a placing operation which results from the operation of theory ([1982] 2013: 12). Badiou's reliance on theory in order to place the object, however, is another example of the management strategy that Dewey locates as reverberating throughout western philosophy from Plato. How fortunate it is for Badiou that the theory he advocates happens to result in the proto-Maoist political prescription that he holds dear.

54. It is here that the foundations for an ethics of the new can be seen to emerge in Deleuze, and this will be further developed in Chapter 4.

Chapter 3

A Time for Practice

Speculative or problematic?

Chapter 1 demonstrated the inheritance of Platonic and Parmenidean dogmatism in Badiou's philosophy and Chapter 2 showed Althusser's efforts to overcome such dogmas and develop a non-idealist philosophy. It concluded that Althusser did indeed avoid the idealist position of either epistemology or ontology grounding the other, though he accomplished this with his concept of an aleatory void to dispel any latent dogmas that might pre-condition thought. This, it was argued, constituted a new dogmatic idealism as a replacement for the transcendent idealism that determined thought at each moment in the practice of philosophy. Simply put, Althusser replaces idealism in philosophical practice with the idea of a philosophical void which is, of course, another idealism. In order to overcome the reliance upon chance that Althusser's void forces upon thought, Hume's concept of the subject was sutured to the latter's thought in order to account for the persistence of ideas through the aleatory void. It is because, for Hume, the subject invents and anticipates – indeed *practises* – thought that ideas persist through time. Hume's concept of human nature is that of a synthetic product of relations which, it was argued, can connect each otherwise-aleatory moment as the result of (in Althusser's terms) its theoretical practice. Nevertheless, the suture of Hume's work to Althusser's leaves some scar tissue: whereas Hume's relational subject was shown to provide persistence and coherence in thought, it is not clear why it is the subject *per se* that accomplishes this.[1] The lack of an account of what constitutes the subject as such leads to two immediate questions. Firstly, what is it that specifies the particular relations (as opposed to others) that constitute human nature for Hume? Secondly, why are there three principles of association (resemblance, contiguity in time and place, and causation) rather than more or less? Having previously identified the problem of idealism in Badiou's thought and having attempted to address it with Althusser and Hume, only then to find the problem once more in Hume's account of human nature, this chapter will show that it is Deleuze's three syntheses of time that are needed to overcome idealism (or what Deleuze refers to as postulates of the dogmatic 'image of thought' (Deleuze [1994] 2011: 167)).

Before turning to Deleuze, however, Meillassoux's account of the relation between ideas and matter in *After Finitude* (2008) will be examined as an important, contemporary rendition of materialism. In this, his first monograph, Meillassoux's ambitious task is to rid contemporary philosophy of what he calls 'correlationism'. Defining correlationism as the position whereby 'we only ever have access to the correlation between thinking and being, and never to either term considered apart from the other' (2008: 5), Meillassoux takes aim not only at all philosophical positions that fall within Kant's distinctions of '"dogmatism", "scepticism", and "critique"' (Badiou in Meillassoux 2008: vii), but also at metaphysics and many post-metaphysical positions (2008: 33–42). In trying to account for how we can make 'ancestral' statements about 'any reality anterior to the emergence of the human species' (2008: 10), Meillassoux argues that a world of absolute contingency can still be thought by 'grafting the Humean thesis onto that of Cantorian intotality' (Meillassoux 2007a: 232). By this, Meillassoux refers to a world comprised of an infinite number of laws (which are held as regular only by the denegated belief that they are so) that can be indexed by mathematics. In showing how this might be so, he can be aligned with authors such as Ray Brassier, Ian Hamilton Grant and Graham Harman, who argue in favour of varieties of 'non-metaphysical speculation' (Meillassoux 2008: 111).

Meillassoux has been particularly influential in recent debates on ontology (particularly with regard to speculative realism) and presents a novel articulation of set theory in contrast to its appropriation by Meillassoux's one-time mentor Badiou.[2] The pertinent difference between Badiou and Meillassoux, in terms of their studies of ontology, is that whereas the former argues that politics, science, art and love are the four categories in which ontology presents itself, Meillassoux makes no such foundational claim. Whilst Meillassoux couches both *After Finitude* and *Science Fiction and*

Extro-Science Fiction in terms of the factual claims about natural laws, and therefore seems to gesture in the direction of Badiou's category of science, there is nothing in his work that indicates a strong differentiation between different discourses. Therefore, it is the speculative nature of Meillassoux's ancestral question which makes him of interest here, rather than the fact that he (again, speculatively) posits a mathematical answer to it.

Meillassoux's argument will be rejected, not because his criticism of a large set of correlationist philosophers is necessarily wrong, but because his solution, in avoiding the correlationist position, currently relies (as Badiou does) on the 'ontological pertinence of Cantor's theorem' (Meillassoux 2008: 103). Despite Meillassoux's convincing argument that post-Kantian correlationism cannot account for claims about the in-itself, his solution falls to the same criticism that Chapter 1 brought against Badiou's reliance on the matheme. However, Meillassoux's reliance upon mathematics is a symptom of a different issue in his work from that of Badiou and, so, although they share the same criticism (that they rely upon an 'Emperor's new clothes' rationalism), this criticism takes different forms. Meillassoux's efforts to address what he calls 'Hume's Problem' demonstrate the emphasis that Meillassoux places on constancy (in his case, the constancy of natural laws). By maintaining the Parmenidean hypothesis that 'being and thinking are the same' (Meillassoux 2008: 44), reductively thinking ontology as mathematics and maintaining the importance of the sensible as the verification of mathematics' veracity with the world, Meillassoux argues that, as far as we can currently think, only mathematics can move from the question of 'What can I know?' towards two other problems: 'What must I do?' and 'What can I hope?' (Badiou in Meillassoux 2008: vii). However, as will be argued, Meillassoux nevertheless relies upon both the sensible and nonmathematic thought in order to measure and verify the claims of mathematics. As such, in contrast to Deleuze's appropriation of Hume, Meillassoux's speculative realism highlights the problem of denigrating the sensible in favour of mathematics. A turn (back) towards Marx will then show that it is necessary to account for the constitution of knowledge as a process of social production that takes into account the affectivity of matter. Furthermore, it is important to go not from the concrete (Meillassoux's idea of mathematics) to the abstract as Meillassoux advocates, but from the abstract to the concrete.[3]

This turn will be carried out with Chambers's (2014) work on Marx and Althusser and a return to the three Notes of the previous chapter. Chambers argues that when, in the Introduction to the *Contribution to the Critique of Political Economy* (henceforth the '1857 Introduction'), Marx collapses epistemology into ontology, he places thought back into a social mode of production (Chambers 2014: 106). There are several important ramifications of knowledge being part of social production, but this chapter will emphasise the political and ethical territories which knowledge must traverse as it is being socially produced. To be precise – and counter to the claims of Badiou and Meillassoux (as well as Object Oriented Ontologists more generally) – this chapter makes the argument that there is no such thing as neutral, universal or truthful knowledge; all knowledge is subject to political and ethical constraints that condition its constitution. Concomitantly, as part of its social construction, knowledge is politically and ethically problematic. The openness of knowledge to its problematisation as a condition of its production forms part of the conditions for further learning and ethical action, conditions which Deleuze terms the 'encounter' (Deleuze [1964] 2008: 12). In particular, then, this chapter will demonstrate that Althusser's anti-humanist philosophy was not, as has been accused, anti-subjective and this is because the concept of the subject is a productive component of one of Althusser's four modes of thought (the ideological).

By showing that knowledge develops as part of social production, this chapter will therefore serve as the foundation for Chapter 4, which will develop a latent, yet hitherto undefined ethical component to Deleuze's metaphysics. In contradistinction to Meillassoux's speculative replacement for correlationism's supposed inability to make metaphysical statements, this chapter will argue for the necessity of metaphysics in the first place. However, this will not be a metaphysics of the form Meillassoux describes as 'demonstrating the existence of a supreme principle governing our world', such as God (Meillassoux 2008: 87). Rather, Deleuze's temporal metaphysics shall be read, not as a foundational principle which *governs* the world, but as a constitutive part of it, itself constituted by its practical, synthetic function. Taking heed of Livingston's warning that a philosophy can be coherent, totalising or paradoxical, this chapter shall conclude in favour of the former. Indeed it is this non-totalised coherence – distinct from Meillassoux's mathematically founded speculative position in its lack of any foundation whatsoever – that constitutes the grounds for future ethical decisions, the topic to be developed in the next chapter. Ultimately then, this chapter will demonstrate how Deleuze's synthetic metaphysics of time can inform Althusser's conclusion that thought does not occur without an individual that thinks, and lay the foundations of a socially embodied theory of individuation.

Meillassoux's problem with Hume

Ancestral statements – statements about the world anterior to the emergence of human life – constitute the problem that Meillassoux addresses in *After Finitude*. How, he asks, is 'science able to think such statements, and in what sense can we eventually ascribe truth to them' (Meillassoux 2008: 10)? In posing such a problem, Meillassoux follows in the footsteps of Badiou, for whom it is necessary to tell the truth of a situation before any philosophy is possible, to the extent that there is no explicit normative philosophy in Meillassoux's text at all (Johnston 2011: 103). Instead, the political implications of Meillassoux's project are made clear in his criticism of the ramifications of correlationism: the absolutisation of fideism, which Meillassoux claims was announced by Montaigne, the 'founding father' of the Counter-Reformation. As Zalloua puts it in his essay 'Of Cripples', 'Montaigne ridiculed philosophers who incessantly discourse about causes (he called them "plaisants causeurs," punning on the double meaning of "causer" – "to talk about something/to someone" and "to cause something")' (Zalloua 2015: 397). Meillassoux is correct to argue that the renunciation of causal thinking in contemporary philosophy has, through a generalised scepticism and the 'destruction of the metaphysical absolute [. . .] resulted in a generalised becoming-religious of thought, viz., in *a fideism of any belief whatsoever*' (Meillassoux 2008: 46). His political argument, then – and it is an argument that this book is very much aligned to – is summed up by his claim that, because contemporary philosophy has capitulated to faith, 'there is no reason why the worst forms of violence could not claim to have been sanctioned by a transcendence that is only accessible to the elect few' (Meillassoux 2008: 47).

Instead of offering up a competing set of normative statements, Meillassoux demonstrates the grounds upon which it is possible to make statements about the world, given that any absolutist statement made about it is usually couched in terms of its truth, as Hegel put it, 'for us' (2008: 4, 13). For Brassier, Meillassoux's portrayal of 'correlationist' thought 'affirms the indissoluble primacy of the relation between thought and its correlate over the metaphysical hypostatisation or representationalist reification of either term of the relation' (Brassier 2007: 51). In other words, Meillassoux successfully demonstrates that there is a relation between thought and being, but also that contemporary philosophy jumps straight to *re*presenting this relationship instead of simply stating it. Brassier insists that correlationism 'never denies that our thoughts or utterances *aim at* or *intend* mind-independent or language-independent realities; it merely stipulates that this apparently independent dimension remains internally related to thought and language' (2007: 51).[4] To make his way out of this 'correlationist two-step', Meillassoux thus needs a way to make non-metaphysical, absolutist claims about the in-itself. These claims must not be grounded upon, on the one hand, the presumption of a past transcendental event that theorises an in-itself of which we can only know its appearance (this would be 'weak' correlationism; see Kant [1787] 1996: A 495, B 523, Brassier 2007: 52), or, on the other hand, the assumption that the in-itself is *entirely* unthinkable, except for the fact that we can think *about* it ('strong' correlationism) (Meillassoux 2008: 39). Indeed, for Meillassoux, the only absolutist claim that can be made about the world is that it is absolutely contingent, and that this contingency is itself absolutely necessary, i.e. *not contingent* (Zalloua 2015: 396).

It is upon this understanding that Meillassoux takes up what he describes as 'Hume's Problem'. Is it possible, he asks, 'to demonstrate that the same effects will always follow from the same causes *ceteris paribus*, i.e. all other things being equal?' (Meillassoux 2008: 85).[5] In asking this, Meillassoux attempts to account for the stability of what is, for him, an absolutely contingent world, despite its manifestly stable appearance, given his thesis that correlationism is unable to think the in-itself.[6] Only by accounting for this stability, Meillassoux argues, can one say anything determinate about ancestral objects. Putting his argument terms already familiar to this discussion, Meillassoux distrusts the *doxa* of empirical discussion in the same manner as Badiou, but nevertheless wants to gain knowledge of what, borrowing from Descartes and Locke, he calls the 'primary' qualities of things.[7] This involves addressing what Johnston, following David Chalmers, calls the 'hard problem' of philosophy: 'an account of the relationship between mind and matter not just in terms of the former's epistemological access to the absolute being of the latter in itself, but in terms of whether or not mind can be explained as emergent from and/or immanent to matter (and, if so, what such an explanation requires epistemologically, ontologically, and scientifically)' (Johnston 2011: 96). In avoiding the standard gesture of correlationism which, according to Meillassoux, would simply posit a relationship between mind and matter in order to then denegate it in favour of an explanation of how the world appears to the mind, it is necessary for him to come up with an ontological answer to the hard problem, albeit a speculative one that avoids any absolute other than that of contingency.[8] To do this, Meillassoux ontologises Hume's epistemological theory of induction (Johnston 2011: 95).

Johnston summarises Hume's position well and it is worth quoting him at length:

> as Hume insists, the mind is (naturally and instinctively) attuned to the world – albeit attuned in modes such that an attenuated skepticism equivalent to a non-dogmatic openness to the perpetual possibility of needing to revise one's ideationally mediated knowledge of extra-ideational reality (in the form of conceptual structures of cause-and-effect patterns) ought to be embraced as eminently reasonable and realistic. (Johnston 2011: 99)[9]

In Meillassoux's terms, Hume is not satisfied with statements about universalist laws and simply claims that 'it would be perfectly compatible with the requirements of logic and experience for everything to become other than it is' (Meillassoux 2008: 88). The only reason that it does not do so randomly is because individuals' habit has been constructed in attunement to the (now only *potentially*) random nature of existence. Indeed, because causality lies within habit and not within the 'extra-ideational relation', for Hume, the individual's notion of causality will come to expect causality in whatever form it has learned. Hume nevertheless remains a correlationist for Meillassoux precisely because his 'causal necessity is a necessary condition for the existence of consciousness and the world it experiences' (2008: 89), despite the fact that, by Hume's own admission, causality is not necessary, but contingent. Thus, in line with Badiou's criticism of Kant, namely that the latter posits an originary subject in order to guarantee the synthesis of percepts and concepts, Meillassoux criticises Hume for positing *a priori* '*the truth of the causal necessity*' (2008: 90, original emphasis). Despite Meillassoux's admission that our senses say that the world is not entirely random (2008: 91), he problematises (what he sees as) Hume's dogmatic use of causal necessity precisely because of its reduction to an epistemological property of the subject. It is *because* Hume's is not an ontological argument that Meillassoux takes issue with him in the first place. Meillassoux thus lays out his speculative argument: 'instead of asking how we might demonstrate the supposedly genuine necessity of physical laws, *we must ask how we are to explain the manifest stability of physical laws given that we take these to be contingent*' (2008: 91–2).

The way the world really works

For individuals who wish to grapple with 'the way things are', Meillassoux's speculative approach is a seductive path towards political action, even if he does not expand his approach beyond its theoretical components (Hallward 2011: 131). The speculative approach will be developed more below, but here it suffices to say that, in offering a non-correlationist explanation for the stability of natural laws, Meillassoux offers the individual what seems to be a solid ground upon which to make convincing political claims. By developing plans founded upon Meillassoux's speculative ontology, the activist can boast of talking directly about the world, without any representative distortion. Nevertheless, this chapter will demonstrate how Meillassoux's insistence that natural laws do remain constant, *despite* his acknowledgement that they are fundamentally contingent, illuminates the idealism in how he measures this constancy. In other words, Meillassoux assumes the stability of the world through the sensible and fits his ontology to match it; is it a surprise then that there is compatibility between the sensible and the ontological? Ultimately, this chapter will argue that grounding the knowledge of a situation in one particular structure is not a problem – indeed, the next chapter will show that it is a significant part of thinking ethically. The problem with the speculative account, however, is the assumption that mathematics is – and should be – the *only* structure to use.

In order to show this, it is necessary to develop Chambers's work on Marx and Althusser. Chambers shows, in *Bearing Society in Mind* (2014), that the epistemology/ontology distinction that underpins much of the problematic motivating the work of both

Meillassoux and Badiou is misconceived. In fact, Chambers circumvents the debate over whether ontology or epistemology can ever ground each other by maintaining the position that thought is itself ontological: 'thinking always remains in a relation to the real because the thinker is always rooted in a social formation' (2014: 119).[10] Put negatively, thought can only be in relation to the real lest either thought or the real assume a foundation for the other. This foundation would then be subject to the same conditions that were highlighted by Livingston earlier in Chapter 1, namely that a philosophy can either be totalising or coherent, but not both. However, by making the connection between thought and the real relational – rather than foundational – Chambers attempts to avoid this problem. Whilst Chambers is not saying that there is no such thing as epistemology *per se*, he collapses the distinction between thought of the real and formal epistemology, where signification is reserved solely for either linguistic acts or properties. In terms of Badiou's distinction between politics and philosophy, for Chambers, philosophy would not be the discourse that actualises a (political) truth procedure, but rather a discourse in differential relation with politics.

Chambers identifies a problem within the works of Hegel, Butler and Hall that he draws on to unfold his relational ontology. Ultimately, for Chambers, the three authors are related by the assumption that one cannot think the way the world really works without *at the same time* also thinking the social constitution of knowledge. Taking his criticism of Butler as an example, Chambers argues that she 'approaches Althusser as if he, like Hegel, were describing relations among abstract philosophical subjects' (2014: 60). For Chambers, Butler reads Althusser through her own distinction between abstract subjects and the language through which they come into being as a consequence (Butler 1997: 107, Chambers 2014: 61). A theory whereby language 'populates' an otherwise empty subject has the advantage for Butler of being able to create, as the subtitle of her book *The Psychic Life of Power: Theories in Subjection* demonstrates, a number of different theories of subjection and moral distinctions between them. In this book, Butler outlines Althusser's famous example of 'ideological interpellation' in the ISA essay, which features an individual walking down the road, a policeman hailing them and the individual turning around, suspecting or knowing the hail is for them. Butler's criticism of Althusser is then based upon his statement that 'these things happen without any succession', thus vacating the account of any temporal or causal process (Althusser 1971a: 174). Butler's distinction allows her to criticise Althusser by pointing out that 'Althusser does not offer a clue as to why the individual turns around' (Butler 1997: 5). Butler then offers her own explanation: the subject turns because they already know that they are guilty, they self-attribute their own guilt and then turn to the policeman knowing that he must be hailing them. As Chambers highlights, Butler reads Althusser's scene of interpellation in order to show her ontology of the subject as 'an openness or vulnerability before the law' (Butler 1997: 108, Chambers 2014: 62). This openness is the guilt that, for Butler, leads to individuals desiring the law and explains our willingness to be subjectified under it. It is difficult to see however how this claim is given philosophically, because as Chambers points out, 'guilt has a very particular, and specifically Judaeo-Christian, history' and Butler 'implicitly conceptualises guilt as lying outside history' (2014: 62). Presumably, societies built on non-Judaeo-Christian thought might not feature guilt as a foundational aspect of the subject, and so Butler's account of interpellation is historically and socially inconsistent. More importantly, Butler misses the point of the ISA essay, which is to establish 'how the material conditions of production are themselves *reproduced*' (Chambers 2014: 63, original emphasis). Indeed, as Chambers clarifies, 'Althusser seeks to show that we cannot understand any concept of "ideology" without first grasping it as fully material, as embedded within practices *that are themselves embedded within the material structures of a social formation*' (2014: 63, original italics).[11]

Before showing how Althusser illuminates the material conditions of reproduction in Marx, it is worthwhile elaborating on Chambers's criticism of Butler's work in order to show what is at stake. This is because Chambers uses his criticism of Butler to make a claim about both empiricism and idealism which is central to the argument within this book. Specifically, Chambers shows that Butler starts her social analysis with an essentialised psychic subject, drawn heavily from the work of Freud (Chambers 2014: 59). With this pre-given, empty subject, Chambers claims, Butler develops a theory of the social using a Hegelian theory of 'dyadic recognition'. As he puts it, Butler 'evacuates the social-historical context [of her social theory] so that she may construct a philosophical account of recognition, and then she turns recognition itself into the context for the emergence of her new, thin, account of the social' (2014: 76–7). In other words, the liberal individualistic ontology that underpins her social thought is shrouded with a philosophical gloss that is her criticism of Althusser. However, Butler's concept of the subject is not at the same level of Althusser's: whereas she relies on an idealised (thus empirical) ontology which is then populated with meaning through discourses (used problematically as a synonym for the social (2014: 77)), Althusser's subject is conceived as part of the social structure itself. Butler's fault lies in her formal separation between the ontic and epistemic characteristics of the subject, pre-supposing the former whilst offering only the latter up to critical thought. Chambers summarises that 'for Hegel, *thought is the Real*; for empiricism, the real is given and thought must find a way to correspond to it, to map it, perhaps even to grasp it, but certainly not approach it' (2014: 105–6). Put more generally, both empiricism and idealism posit a radical differentiation between thought and matter, and occupy the same position that Badiou was in at the end of Chapter 1: an inability to account for the veracity of the translation between the ontological and epistemological. There is no way to account for the relation between ontology and epistemology if one is grounded by the other, as this split would necessarily have to be defined within the terms of one or the other, and self-reflexive explanation is tautological.

Lampert characterises the political issue at stake clearly. Demonstrating in the same vein as Chambers that Butler's ethics of resistance is based upon the subject's internal reflections, he goes on to state that 'such an ethics seems ineffectual, and even nihilistic' (Lampert 2015: 137). By focusing on how a pre-given subject is only influenced by social structures, Butler cannot conceive of subjectification other than as a process of subordination, or as all ideology in terms of a dominant ideology. Yet, again, this places her in the same position as Badiou, for whom the militant could never escape the State's authoritative counting against which the truth procedure was measured. For Butler, as Lampert argues, the subject would forever be entrapped by the dominant ideology, without which they would cease to be a subject. In comparison, Althusser's ISA essay focuses on the reproduction of the relations of production, which treats ideological interpellation as a contingent process. Lambert suggests that this allows him to advance a 'politics of resistance', and one might ask of individuals: 'what behaviour does a particular individual engage in, in order to be recognised as such-and-such kind of subject' (2015: 137). While it is not clear why the individual could not ask themselves this same question, thus turning Althusser's politics of resistance into an ethics of a different form than Butler's, two points can be taken from Lampert's comparison. First, subjectification must not be conceptualised as synonymous with subordination, and secondly, in order not to do this, the individual and subjectification must be conceptualised immanently within the mode of production.

The hope of speculative resistance

Chambers's criticism of both idealism and empiricism provides the means to show how Meillassoux's speculative approach is beguiling in its promises, but that it hides a misconceived relationship between the formal and the sensible. This will be highlighted below but, first, having identified the problem which Meillassoux addresses, it is worthwhile looking at what his approach entails. Meillassoux's first move is to establish what he calls an 'anhypothetical' principle which, 'by working through the intra-systemic consequences of his opponents' logic and the relations between their positions, marks an acknowledgement that any and all philosophical hypothesis are already immersed in the conjunctural field within which one establishes a position' (Brown 2009: 11). This method is the same as Althusser's 'symptomatic reading', and the purpose of both is to identify denegated foundational claims in arguments which are then shown to be illegitimate. Using this principle, Meillassoux makes the obvious claim that knowledge is historically and socially conditioned, but makes the more subtle claim that the weakness shared by all the positions he criticises is that they all unwittingly subscribe to the 'principle of facticity'. According to Meillassoux, the principle of facticity demonstrates that 'we can only describe the logical principles inherent in every thinkable proposition, but we cannot deduce their truth'. 'Consequently', he continues, 'there is no sense in claiming to know that contradiction is absolutely impossible' (Meillassoux 2008: 39). The principle of facticity clearly has significant implications for any attempts to understand the arché-fossil as, prior to human experience, there is nothing to say that the world was not entirely other than what it is now (i.e. contradictory). Secondly, it is a problem for the activist because they cannot guarantee that the world tomorrow will accord to the same rules that they have deduced for the world today. Why should anyone else – or activists themselves for that matter – commit to action in the knowledge that tomorrow everything could change for no reason whatsoever?[12] However, identifying the principle of facticity simply shows that the logical propositions we use to describe the world's stability cannot account for why it is necessarily so; Meillassoux still has to give an explanation for what might provide such an account.

The second move of the speculative gesture therefore involves taking the principle of facticity at face value, i.e. accepting that factual claims about the world are necessarily contingent, and then inducing from this position a (non-sufficient) reason for why the world is nevertheless manifestly stable. Meillassoux rejects any claim that the constancy of phenomena guarantees the stability of an ultimately contingent world because both constancy and chance (i.e that which accounts for the fact that some things appear unconfined by a scientific understanding of the world) form two sides of the same coin that is Epicurean aleatory reasoning. Chance presupposes the existence of other natural laws and, as such, is subject to the principle of facticity to the same extent. However, Meillassoux is keen to maintain the difference between chance and contingency, making it clear that the latter is capable of 'affecting the very conditions that allow chance events to occur and exist' (Meillassoux 2008: 101). Thus, in order to account for the radically non-totalising condition of contingency, whilst acknowledging the inadequacy of sufficient reason to account for its own veridicality (i.e. the principle of facticity), Meillassoux turns to (and references) the same ZFC set theory that Badiou calls the language of being *qua* being. The specific claim that Meillassoux makes is that 'there is a mathematical way of rigorously distinguishing contingency from chance, and it is provided by the transfinite' (2008: 104).

For Meillassoux, Cantor's work in showing that quantities are unable to be indexed by any finite number can be taken to make a further ontological claim. Because a set of infinite numbers cannot contain the quantity of the parts of the set, it is demonstrably impossible to totalise any given set of laws – including, for Meillassoux, natural laws.[13] Thus, mathematics (at least in its specific variant of ZFC set theory read through Badiou's *Being and Event*), provides Meillassoux with an ontological answer to Hume's epistemic problem: 'in what sense of truth can we think and talk of ancestral statements?'. By positing that mathematical axiomatisation provides a way to think the untotalisable *without totalising it*, Meillassoux is comfortable concluding that one can 'think the stability of laws without having to redouble them with an enigmatic physical necessity' (Meillassoux 2008: 107). In other words, the stability of laws becomes indexed by the application of an absolutised mathematics, where what is mathematically conceivable is absolutely possible, even if it is not necessarily true or actual. Whilst Meillassoux accepts that he does not show how this conclusion demonstrates itself how to answer ancestral questions, he is content to claim it shows that the in-itself can be thought absolutely, through axiomatised mathematics.

Yet, is Meillassoux's ontological gesture being grounded on the problem of ancestral questions precisely the reason why it cannot answer them? For Hallward, no stranger to Badiou's mathematic ontology, this is just the case. He describes Meillassoux's project as 'seductive', but concludes his criticism of it by stating that the 'critique of metaphysical necessity and an appeal to transfinite mathematics will not provide, on their own, the basis upon which we might renew a transformative materialism' (Hallward 2011: 140–1). Hallward doubts that, if the point of philosophy is to conceptualise how one can change the way things are, the pure mathematics of transfinite set theory can function as an applied mathematics able to think both secondary qualities (such as colour and texture), but most primary qualities as well (length, mass and date) (2011: 140). How would one construct a concrete process of social and political change, without being able to think the most basic qualities of objects? It is precisely the fact that mathematics indexes the stability of laws *and does nothing else* that leaves it mute to thinking either primary or secondary relations, let alone social relations. Thus, Hallward is right to firmly insist that 'Meillassoux's acausal ontology [. . .] includes no account of an actual process of transformation or development', and that his 'insistence that anything might happen can only amount to an insistence on the bare possibility of radical change' (Hallward 2011: 139).

However, taking Hallward to task for extending Meillassoux's arguments past their original intent, Nathan Brown argues that the former misses the point in the speculative account of qualities. For Brown, Meillassoux does not argue that 'units of measurement or mathematical descriptions of objects "might be independent of the mind"', but that Meillassoux follows Descartes in arguing that 'mathematical descriptions of physics or cosmology *index* primary qualities' (Brown 2011: 145, emphasis added). Relations of measurement (i.e. length, mass and date), according to Brown, are therefore *relative* to primary qualities which are properties of the in-itself. Thus, science can talk of the way things really are, even if talk of this is subject-specific, because it builds on the formal prescriptions of mathematics. Hallward's attempt to dismiss Meillassoux's thought as a result of its inability to think specific historical events is thus, for Brown, to criticise him for not thinking something that Meillassoux never says he will think in the first place. That is to say: speculative materialism cannot account for, or explain, historical events, but Meillassoux never pretends to the contrary. Rather, Brown argues that Meillassoux simply shows that any account of 'those structural invariants which govern our world' are necessarily open to contingent change, built as they are upon mathematical grounds (Meillassoux 2008: 38). As he summarises, 'the principle of factiality requires that we think relation as a fact, rather than an absolute' (Brown 2011: 149). For Brown then, no: the reason why Meillassoux accepts that he cannot answer ancestral questions is not because he cannot do so, but because he cannot do so *and* was never trying to do so in the first place. Indeed, Meillassoux might argue that speculative materialism shines a light in front of the activist by showing the possibility that dominant and seemingly-determining social structures are in fact, necessarily, open to being radically other. The political argument, which Meillassoux has so far not made in his published works, might be that the activist must work to transform social structures to their liking given the rallying call that they are contingent after all.[14]

Nevertheless, Hallward is right to insist that Meillassoux's promise is beguiling. Despite Brown's caution against reading too much into Meillassoux's philosophy, there is a sense in which the activist must demand more than speculative materialism can offer. For, when Meillassoux concludes that all relations are necessarily contingent (rather than necessary in themselves) he gives the activist hope that s/he can change them. In other words, there is a formal prescription that results from his ontology that declares resistance to the given possible. And yet, this formal prescription says nothing of the activist's ability to produce any significant change whatsoever. Hallward puts it well, reasoning that the 'abstract logical possibility of change (given the absence of any ultimately sufficient reason) has little to do with any concrete process of actual change' (Hallward 2011: 139). Meillassoux tells the activist that resistance is necessarily possible, but not necessarily probable.[15] In doing so, he demonstrates a radical disconnection between the formal and empirical, and there are two upshots of this.

First, any hope derived from speculative materialism may well be only false hope. Meillassoux's philosophy (in its current form) can say nothing about the potentially insurmountable difficulty which faces the activist. For, although his future work may bridge the gap between the formal and the empirical, like Badiou, Meillassoux's current insistence in subtracting the empirical from his ontology ensures that he can say nothing about the actual nature of social relations. It is all well and good pointing out to the slave, the *sans-papier* or the subaltern that their condition is necessarily changeable but, unless this helps them conceptualise how to escape their condition, it will be of little use to them. This is not to say that the activist should necessarily demand a normative philosophy or political formulae from Meillassoux, but that speculative materialism is unable (and indeed unwilling) to provide any positive commentary on the empirical whatsoever (Hallward 2011: 139). Furthermore, it is hard to see that Meillassoux's conclusion (i.e. that factual relations are actually contingent) is any significant development upon what correlationist philosophy already concludes. The idea of contingency is not new to post-Kantian philosophy and, whilst this criticism does not reduce the academic importance of Meillassoux's work, it will be of no surprise to the individual (activist or otherwise) that historical conditions change, or that they have little say in both why and how they do so. It seems rather that Meillassoux's argument provides little in the way of conclusions that empirical investigation hasn't already demonstrated, i.e. that the world might change at any moment, for no reason, but that it hasn't. Meillassoux's rejoinder, that speculative materialism demonstrates how chance has nothing to do with *why* the world doesn't change, seems like an unsatisfactory trump card.

The second upshot of speculative materialism's absolutisation of contingency is that, according to its conclusions, activists have no reason to suppose that their efforts won't be in vain, regardless of the difficulty they find themselves facing. Brown's defence of Meillassoux must accept that, if Meillassoux shows that the structural invariants that govern our world are contingent and open to change, he also shows the same for those of the activist. Despite Meillassoux's argument that chance is as much at the mercy of his critique of sufficient reason as all other relational claims, it is precisely Meillassoux's insistence that anything at all might happen for no reason (although there is no reason that it would) that undermines the efforts of the activist. Of course, the activist will accept, even without Meillassoux, that politics is precarious and that political resistance is fraught with unforeseen challenges to be overcome. But Meillassoux's argument is more radical, pointing out that the laws governing the results of their efforts might instantly change for no predictable reason. The fact that, for Meillassoux, chance is necessarily contingent does not necessarily mean that chance won't occur. Furthermore, the reduction of all other laws to the same status of absolutely contingent does not immunise them from chance either. Resistance, according to speculative materialism, would therefore be practised in the constant fear that, on the one hand, the hope of change to come is not after all a false hope and, on the other, that it is not all for nothing, because the world has simply become other for no particular reason. Meillassoux has invented the Infinite Improbability Drive, and how frustrating it must have been for the sperm whale, which was previously a nuclear missile, to fall headlong from the sky for the second time (Adams 1979: 117).

Thus, the disconnection between the formal and the empirical in speculative realism results in Meillassoux's ability to show how thought may formally think its own index of primary qualities, yet remain unable to think the empirical. Indeed Meillassoux understands this perfectly well when he states that '[p]hilosophy's task consists in re-absolutising the scope of mathematics' and, further, that 'the task of the principle of factiality' is to derive 'the capacity, proper to every mathematical statement, through which the latter is capable of formulating a possibility that can be absolutised, even if only hypothetically' (2008: 126). Again, this is a reiteration of his position that what is mathematically conceivable is absolutely possible, but only hypothetically so. In separating the formal from the empirical, Meillassoux thereby shows the same rationalist assertions that both underpinned and undermined Badiou's ontology. Meillassoux seems surprised that this would be an issue, stating that 'it is astonishing to note how [. . .] philosophers, who are generally the partisans of thought rather than of the senses, have opted overwhelmingly to trust their habitual perceptions rather than the luminous clarity of intellection' (Meillassoux 2008: 91). And yet Meillassoux seems to have forgotten, and therefore not accounted for, the fact that he also trusts his habitual perceptions as well as his intellect, and subordinates the former to the latter. Meillassoux's subordination of perceptions to the intellect, and concomitant inability to think new perceptions, will be shown in order to contrast Althusser's account of the formation of knowledge, which does take into account the conceptualisation of new perceptions.

Meillassoux claims that the 'condition of possibility for physics is the repeatability of experiments, which is the fundamental guarantor of the validity of a theory' (Meillassoux 2008: 86). However, he then goes on to pose the situation that leads to Hume's problem in terms of the ability of experiments to achieve the same results after repetition. So, for Meillassoux, it is not just the ability for experiments to be reproduced which is necessary for science, but for them to come out with the same results when they are. The former criterion – the possibility of reproduction – is a formal criterion which has to do only with the hypothetical possibility of the experiment being undertaken. It is only the latter criterion – the veracity of the experiments' results to each other – which actually constitutes the validity of science, according to Meillassoux. This distinction is important, not least because it describes the working differentiation between theoretical physics on the one hand (which has no need of empirical validity) and applied physics on the other (which does). The fact that Meillassoux does not account for the difference between the two sub-disciplines brings into question exactly what idea of science he has in mind. Yet his unwillingness to take into account the formation of the description of scientific results – or, specifically, the description of the *phenomena* that result from scientific experimentation – means that Meillassoux cannot account for the veracity of scientific results from the perspective of the phenomena. Scientific practice, according to speculative materialism, can only go by a formal description of what science looks for and must necessarily ignore new phenomena that it has not developed (necessarily contingent) laws to explain. In other words, Meillassoux assumes the stability of the world because he has no way of conceptualising new sensible criteria by which to establish its instability.[16]

Meillassoux thereby falls to the same criticism at the hands of Osborne as Badiou did in Chapter 1: he advocates 'a full-blown idealism struggling with the limitations of its grasp on actuality, which *redefines reality* in terms of the gap that structures the limitation (Osborne 2013: 22, original emphasis). To be precise, when Meillassoux argues that 'the refutation of the frequential implication cannot consist in demonstrating that the stability of the world conforms to the laws of chance – rather, it should demonstrate that the contingency of natural laws remains *inaccessible to* aleatory reasoning' (Meillassoux 2008: 100, original emphasis), he misses the point that the categories (such as aleatory reasoning) are *part* of what he calls the stability of the world. In other words, Meillassoux's subtraction of everything except for the mathematical transfinite from what he intends to explain allows him only then to index explanations against the mathematical. Yet it is not clear what benefits this might bring and, instead, it seems that a suitable investigation into the world must account for the constitution of the terms it uses as part of this investigation, as well as their stability.

Ideas and the social formation

In contrast to Meillassoux's account of speculative materialism, and the previous discussions of idealism, the rest of this chapter will demonstrate how Althusser and Marx conceptualise thought as an immanent part of what Chambers calls the 'social formation'. Secondly, it will show that Deleuze's philosophy of time can suture the aleatory void that renders Althusser's philosophy idealist. Once sutured with Deleuze's philosophy of time, Althusser's dialectical materialism avoids the charge of idealism by accounting for the constitution of the terms it uses in its analysis (unlike Meillassoux's speculative theory with regard to contingent laws). The key to this avoidance is that Deleuze's syntheses account for the constitution of the individual in time, as the individual synthesises these very conditions.[17] For Althusser, then, the individual is populated (but not constituted) by its relationship with the social formation, and does not exist outside of those relations.[18] The term population, rather than constitution, is used with regard to Althusser because of the originary philosophical decision that his philosophy necessitates. For the same reason that Badiou criticises Kant, i.e. that there is an assumed originary unity that makes synthetic judgements possible, Althusser also assumes an originary void within philosophical practice. This void is posited as necessarily inconsistent and therefore requires population. When sutured to Deleuze's concept of individuation, however, and by taking into account Deleuze's three syntheses of time, which overcome the idealism in Althusser's work, a synthetic conception of the individual can be thought as part of the latter's social theory. Thus, the path will be paved to develop an ontological theory of ethics that is latent in Deleuze's work and is furnished by Althusser's social theory. Lest it be thought that Althusser's work was an attempt to de-politicise Marxism, as indeed it was by a number of his political opponents in the PCF, it is important to remember at this stage that, by destabilising the ontologically primary subject (such as that found in Butler), to quote Lampert, 'Althusser is advancing a politics of resistance' (Lampert 2015: 137). This is not a resistance against the subject *per se*, and Williams is wrong to claim that it was 'precisely the phantasm of the subject which Althusser strove to eliminate in Reading Capital' (Williams 2001: 58). Rather, as Althusser develops in his essay on ISAs, the subject is the object of ideology, which is the theory of social relations (Althusser 1971a: 170). Thus, Althusser cannot eliminate the subject, because it is a constituent function of ideology: how else would the individual (for better or worse) think their place in the world, or their relationship to other individuals, movements and institutions? Through his idea of the subject interpellated by ideology, Althusser destabilises dogmatic conceptions of the subject (such as that found in Badiou) and subverts conservative social relations that are grounded upon concepts such as tradition or nature. Such a destabilisation impels the individual to take an active interest in their political and social situation, and it is this interest which constitutes the ethics to be developed in the next chapter.[19]

To reiterate Chambers's argument as developed so far: philosophy that posits a radical differentiation between the ontological and epistemological, and the grounding of one upon the other, cannot account for this grounding in the terms of either. As Deleuze asserted in his 1956–7 seminar series *What is Grounding?*, demonstrating further similarity with Althusser's project, in order to make a claim, one needs to assert one's right (or authority) to do so and this involves positing a ground (Deleuze [1956–7] 2015: 22). As the authority by which a claim makes sense is not to be found within the claim itself, nor is it inherent within the subject that makes the claim, Deleuze argues that it must be grounded in a 'third'. This third cannot simply be either ontological *or* epistemological, empirical *or* formal, as this would make an empirical claim about the nature of the ground and, thus, open the ground up to the problem of circular justification. Therefore, for Deleuze, 'ground is the instance invoked by and in the demand of the claim' ([1956–7] 2015: 24). The ground assumes no formal difference between ontology or epistemology in service of the claim, but uses what it needs in the practice of claiming. It is in this way that, for Deleuze, claims *make sense* and constitute, through the use of the third, their own coherence.[20] Whilst the invocation of the third may account for how sense is made by a claim, it does not explain the relationship between thought and matter. For Chambers, this relationship is constituted by the practices that make up the social formation.

Drawing on Marx's *The German Ideology*, Chambers argues that it is not thought that thinks, but human beings. Chambers does not however posit a crude rationalism himself, as 'human beings can only think from within the context of the social formation in which they find themselves' (Chambers 2014: 106). To this end, the material activities and structures in which individuals live condition them to think about these conditions or, put in the terms above, human beings are situated in material conditions that overdetermine their claims about the world.[21] Thus, as Chambers puts it, there is '*no such thing as epistemology, a theory of knowledge, that is not also and at the same time a theory of the social formation*' (2014: 106, original emphasis).[22]

Unlike Meillassoux, who does not think it necessary to account for the constitution of concepts by which the empirical is thought, Chambers emphasises the production of thought as part of the process of historical development. In doing so, Chambers complicates the assumption that Meillassoux uses throughout *After Finitude*, i.e. that we are able to think the in-itself because, for Chambers, to assume this would be to miss the point that the in-itself is *itself* a conceptual product of social formation.[23] In other words, what Meillassoux calls the in-itself does not exist outside the practices and structures that constitute both the real present *and* the thought of the present. It is this distinction between what Marx, Althusser and Chambers call the 'real' and the 'thought of the real' that solves the problem of grounding found in both Badiou's and Meillassoux's work; neither the real, nor the thought of the real, grounds the other, because they are both reciprocally produced and presupposed by the other. As such, Chambers does not have to undertake the circular task of accounting for grounds.

Marx's distinction between the real and thought follows Spinoza's distinction between the attributes of thought and extension. This is not the same as Badiou's distinction between ontology and epistemology, because it does not make sense to think of the real coherently expressing itself without thought. For Badiou, mathematics is ontology, i.e. the language of the ontic, irrespective of the relationship between the ontic and the individual, and irrespective of the latter thinking, writing or actualising mathematics. Indeed, this explains the title of Chapter 3 in Hallward's *Badiou: A Subject to Truth*, 'Infinite by Prescription' (2003: 49–78); the subject, for Badiou, is because it *must be* (on the condition of mathematics which, for Badiou, takes ontological priority over philosophy). Only on condition of the formalist subject can philosophy actualise mathematical prescriptions, and this priority leads to the problems regarding the conceptualisation of phenomena (more explicitly) shown in Meillassoux's work above. Instead, for Marx and Althusser, as Chambers puts it, there is an 'interweaving' of epistemology with the real, so that practices are always a major 'constituent part of any social formation' (Chambers 2014: 108). In this configuration, epistemology and the real are both concrete: they both reciprocally determine one another through theoretical and material practices, and are conditioned by their differential relation with each other. Thus, as Chambers puts it succinctly, '[t]he social formation is made up of practices, and it is made up of thoughts of practices. Above all, the conceptualisation of practices itself organises, structures, and potentially directs those practices' (Chambers 2014: 108). Whereas Badiou claims that ontology can express the ontic (or, the 'real') in spite of matter, Chambers shows that matter is a prerequisite for the expression of the real. Without material relations, there would be no way to organise, construct, direct or, ultimately, *think* the real.

What is the precise nature of the relation between theoretical practice and material practice? Chambers is keen to point out both that, for Marx, thought is not the thought '*of*' the real, and that 'thought does not grasp the real directly' (2014: 106). For both Chambers and Althusser, humans think objects, not as real objects, but as theoretical objects. Were the real object to be thought, then the real would always be reduced to the given, rather than also what is possible. Instead, Chambers and Althusser are in line with Hume, Kant, Hegel and Deleuze in arguing that we must study a theoretical object in order to theorise what may happen to the real object, because to 'know is to go beyond'; [. . .] 'it is to say more than what is given' (Deleuze [1956–7] 2015: 25). Althusser and Chambers thus show how the social formation conditions thought to go beyond what is given – the real – as thought thinks both itself (i.e. thought) *and* the 'relationship between the real and thought' (Chambers 2014: 107). In opposing a strict determinism, both authors escape the determinism of Hegelian Marxism (where being determines thought) and Badiou's and Meillassoux's rationalism (where thought presupposes what being then reciprocally determines). Rather, Althusser's emphasis on practice neither acts as nor constitutes a transcendental ground, but rather accounts for how thought, thought of the real and the real interact.[24] Similarly, Althusser's conception of philosophy, both as an example of and in relation to other, real, material practices, allows Althusser to theorise the practices and technologies that populate the social formation.[25] Furthermore, it is the practice of philosophy that accounts for the constitution of the third in Althusser's philosophy: it is the positing of the aleatory void at the 'front' of philosophy in order to clear the way for further thought. Chambers has therefore demonstrated how Althusser overcomes the problematic disjunction between thought and matter, as evinced in Badiou's onto-mathematics and Meillassoux's speculative materialism, and one important upshot of this disjunction that can now be seen is that Meillassoux is mistaken in his assumption that there is, in fact, an in-itself to think. Because the in-itself only exists to the extent that it is produced by the differential, productive relation of the real and thought of the real, any concept of the in-itself as such is a presentation of this relation. Were the language of the in-itself still necessary – and it is no longer clear that it is – the question to be asked would therefore be: what is the function of the in-itself (understood as a particular configuration of social practices) within the situation that requires thinking it?

However, the concept of the void in Althusser's philosophy must nevertheless be remembered because, as the previous chapter showed, the concept of the void prohibits an account of the persistence of thought within the event. Although Althusser accounts for differential times that are entirely separate from the standard understanding of linear time, he nevertheless can only account for the population of a pre-given event, and cannot account for the constitution of the event itself. Therefore, in order to fully remove all traces of idealism from his thought, this aleatory void must be constituted with an account of persistence, i.e. that which was in the past also being in the present. To bring Althusser's account of ontology and socially productive epistemology into accord with both his anti-humanist philosophy and Hume's concept of the relational individual, it is thus necessary to make a second suture. This suture is the addition of Deleuze's three syntheses of time which, although playing several functions within Deleuze's philosophy, together account for the passage from the virtual to the actual, and the persistence of the past into (and through) the present (Williams 2011: 15). Suturing Deleuze's three syntheses of time to Althusser's social theory will allow for the persistence of time in Althusser's philosophy and, together, provide the context for an ethics of resistance to be developed in the next chapter.

Time and the syntheses of Ideas

Deleuze conceptualises time, not in the sense of a homogeneous field of intuition as Kant argues, nor in the sense of Badiou's contradictory timelines that emerge from the event, but rather 'a series of heterogeneous syntheses, some passive and some active' (Williams 2013: 98).[26] Although the active syntheses (representation, contiguity, causality, resemblance and opposition) are important for the individual in order to 'live empirically', these are a second level of temporality for Deleuze ([1994] 2011: 92, 105). The 'empirical' syntheses are reminiscent of the relations that constitute human nature for Hume, and are a reminder for the reader of Deleuze who might wish to downplay the importance that Deleuze places on the 'reality' of events.[27] The passive syntheses are important for Deleuze because they are the metaphysical conditions of the individual or, in Deleuze's terms, a 'pre-reflexive impersonal' consciousness without the self-reflexive self (Deleuze 2001: 25).[28] There are three passive syntheses outlined in *Difference and Repetition* that constitute, first, memory (that of the 'passing present'); habit (that of the past); and thirdly, the fractured self (that of the future).[29] None of the syntheses are predominant in the sense that they ground the others; for example, were the first synthesis primary, then the present would become a 'dimension of the past' (Williams 2011: 5). Rather, each synthesis is differentially related and necessarily presupposes the others. This differential relation forms what Williams terms the 'ideal synthesis of difference', where pure difference is Deleuze's (non-)foundational ontological condition (Williams 2013: 30, 98, 151).[30] A detour via Deleuze's development of differential calculus is required in order to account for the determining potential of the second synthesis, which will therefore also be shown.

Following the work of Duns Scotus, and drawing upon Bergson's *Matter and* Memory ([1908] 1991), Deleuze's philosophy of time is an attempt to 'explain the relation of instants in time, without having to rest on an answer claiming that instants either somehow imply one another or are somehow contained in a larger entity that they are a subset of' (Williams 2011: 24).[31] There is no reason, for Deleuze, *a priori* of the individual's sense of the world, why two moments should be related to each other, and yet he acknowledges that individuals need to connect moments into series in order to live in a spatio-temporal world. As Bergson puts it in terms of an individual drumbeat in series, it is the 'best illuminated point of a moving zone which comprises all that we feel or think or will' (Bergson 1911: 3).

It is clear then that Deleuze is, however unwittingly, taking up the problem of time that Althusser falls foul of when he posits the aleatory void. In doing so, Althusser's approach clears the decks of any erstwhile philosophical idealism but, on the one hand, idealises the event in its place and, on the other, actively prohibits individuals from connecting series. By contrast, the position of Deleuze's syntheses with regard to aleatory theories is made clear when he claims that 'perceptual syntheses refer back to organic syntheses which are like the sensibility of the sense; they refer back to a primary sensibility that we *are*' (Deleuze [1994] 2011: 93). Here, and contra the purely disjunctive void, Deleuze argues that sensibility both conditions both the individual as such (in answer to this question being left open by Hume), and as the sense by which the individual goes about their life in the world. It is not enough for Deleuze, as it is for Kant, Badiou and Meillassoux, to presume the 'harmonious exercise of the faculties' (Bryant 2008: 92). Whereas these latter three authors develop the idea of a self-reflexive individual which recognises itself in its thought of the world (even if this individual is purely formal, as is the case with Badiou's idea of the subject), the individual, for Deleuze, is only an empirical subject and cannot properly be said to be a *life*, for it lacks the 'singularities and the events that constitute' it (Deleuze 2001: 29).[32] The task Deleuze sets himself is therefore to account for the conditions and delimitations of the individual, showing how the *non*-harmonious faculties construct the sense of the world *as it itself is made up of the world* (2001: 29, 31).

The individual's sense of the world, or 'habit' is produced in the first synthesis of time, that of '*habitus*' (Bryant 2008: 93, Deleuze [1994] 2011: 99). The importance of the first synthesis is to produce the ideas by which individuals might go about acting because, in Deleuze's terms, '[a]ction is constituted, in the order of generality and in the field of variables which correspond to it, only by the contraction of elements of repetition' ([1994] 2011: 96). As Deleuze points out in what follows, however, the contraction that constitutes the grounds for action cannot be constructed by action as its own presupposition. Rather, the contraction occurs in what Deleuze calls variously the 'contemplative self', a life, or the individual of the passive and active syntheses ([1994] 2011: 96). The *habitus* fulfils the goal of synthesising the sense of the past that forms the conditions for further synthesis (Williams 2011: 26). Importantly, then, there is nothing yet in the first synthesis that could be called Being. Rather, as Deleuze puts it in *Bergsonism*, 'the present *is not*; rather, it is pure becoming' (Deleuze [1988] 1991: 55) and later in *Difference and Repetition*, describing the first synthesis as the 'living present' (Deleuze [1994] 2011: 97). It is not that the present is simply one *instant* in a series of instances that form a continuous series, for this would both fall foul of the criticism of empirical time as outlined in the last chapter's discussion of Althusser, and would pre-suppose differences *between* instances that are, in fact, the product of reason. The first synthesis is responsible for contracting the past that is presented to the present: '[the first] synthesis constitutes time as a living present, and the past and the future as dimensions of this present' ([1994] 2011: 97). But what does the first synthesis contract?

This is the task of the second synthesis and is best explained through Deleuze's appropriation, and difference from, Bergson's theory of time. As Crocker puts it, memory is often thought to be the recollection of events which are no longer present. This might be a series of instances as measured against a clock, or in the sense of Althusser's plurality of different temporalities, each specific and in differential relation to the others. All recollections have in common a past that once was, but is ultimately no longer present. Crocker explains that this 'recollection' of the past 'involves only differences of degree between presents', and that 'the moment of association is derived from what is associated' (Crocker 2001: 54–5). Recollection, in other words, involves a judgement, rooted in the subject, of what happened in the past. This judgement compares and contrasts past presents, but cannot account for how the past constituted the present or the individual's ability to recollect certain instances and not others. For Bergson on the other hand, memory is itself creative; it does not contemplate past presents in the sense that these exist separately from each other, but instead 'past events participate in relations of association and resemblance with a new, present perception' (Deleuze [1988] 1991: 51, 54, Crocker 2001: 55). Memory is not a faculty for storing and it does not work only intermittently. The past is contracted by the mind as what Bergson calls the 'Past in General', or 'pure memory' (Crocker 2001: 55, Mullarkey 2004: 473), and the cerebral mechanism drives back into the subconscious what is not useful (or what it cannot immediately 'cast into light') (Bergson 1911: 5). Using the example of a musical tune, Bergson highlights how each note seems to meld into one another. '[M]ight it not be said', he questions, that 'even if these notes succeed one another, yet we perceive them in one another, and that their totality may be compared to a living being whose parts, although distinct, permeate one another just because they are so closely connected[?]' (Bergson [1960] 1989: 100).

As developed later by Deleuze, this is the 'virtual' structure of the tune which becomes 'actualised' when played, for example, on a piano by a student. The student, whose memory has contracted the notes into a tune so far (and also the information necessary to finish off the tune) has, as a result of this synthesis, a certain bed of knowledge from which to carry on playing. Of course, the student may not wish to carry on playing, or even carry on with the tune that they know how to play – they may improvise. This is to say that there is nothing strictly determinate in Bergson's theory of time, nor in Deleuze's appropriation of it. For the virtual structure to be determinate, there would have to be a fixed relationship between its elements and their relations, and this relationship would have to be defined by a conditioning principle that exists outside of the terms of the relationship itself. Instead, for Bergson, both elements and relations are in a state of mutual transformation and unable to achieve identity, for the repetition of an element is defined only by its difference to the previous elements in a series (Crocker 2001: 53, Mullarkey 2004: 473).[33] This is not to say that there aren't elements and relations in the virtual structure, but that they only become sensible after they have become actual.[34] The constitution of the virtual structure is the substantial issue over which Deleuze parts from Bergson, and a difference by which Deleuze's second synthesis can be understood.

Ansell-Pearson is clear about Deleuze's break from Bergson: it is 'over the question of the nature of intensity' (Ansell-Pearson 1999: 74). According to Bergson's *Time and Free Will*, psychic states (i.e. the virtual structure of an individual's mind) 'are seen to be more or less *intense*' (Bergson [1960] 1989: 222). Intensity, for Bergson, is the measure of qualitative states (such as 'redness'), insisting that '[i]ntensity is quality and not quantity or magnitude' ([1960] 1989: 224). Because, for Bergson, space is a homogeneous medium that life resists as it rises up through it, it makes no sense for there to be qualitative distinctions outside of the mind (Bergson 1911: 10–17); how would matter determine its own quality and, even if it could, wouldn't this also necessitate a subjective, qualitative judgement of matter's judgement in order to accept it? In dyadic opposition to matter, the differentiation of differences in kind is, for Bergson, a principle solely pertaining to life, and his idea of duration is the method that the mind uses to think the contraction and relaxation of qualitative states in relation to external matter. As Bergson puts it, only 'in consciousness we find states which succeed, without being distinguished from one another; and in space simultaneities which, without succeeding, are distinguished from one another, in the sense that one has ceased to exist when the other appears' (Bergson [1960] 1989: 226).[35]

Deleuze's criticism of Bergson's concept of intensity, as it appears in his 1956 essay 'Bergson's Conception of Difference' (1956), *Bergsonism* ([1988] 1991) and *Difference and Repetition* (Deleuze [1994] 2011: 299–301), concerns the fact that Bergson pre-supposes 'ready-made qualities and reconstituted extensities' (Ansell-Pearson 1999: 74). For Deleuze, everything 'Bergson has to say about [duration] comes down to this: duration is *what differs from itself*. Matter, on the other hand, is what does not differ from itself; it is what repeats itself ' (Deleuze 2004b: 37). However, because, as shown by his example of lightning, difference carries its difference 'within itself ' for Deleuze (1999: 74), he is thereby concerned with the order of difference that constitutes and informs *both* quality and quantity. In other words, Deleuze affords primacy, not to either quantity or quality (even at the risk of having to go to radical lengths to explain the constitution of the individual having given up internal qualitative distinctions), but to the principle of a difference of intensity. As Ansell-Pearson puts it, for Deleuze quite simply, 'difference *is* intensity' (Ansell-Pearson 1999: 74, original emphasis).

The question of what the second synthesis contracts then is complicated significantly by Deleuze's insistence that it is not populated, as Bergson argues, by qualities. Were this the case then he would have to explain, as Bergson does, how the process by which life, already imbued with the capability to discern qualities, makes its way through matter. In one way then, Deleuze is saved from the need to explain the existence of non-conditioned qualitative distinctions in the mind, but, of course, this means he must explain how both quantitative and qualitative distinctions are constituted according to the principle of difference. As difference is, for Deleuze, a metaphysical principle (Ansell-Pearson 1999: 65), Deleuze's criticism of Bergson's biological explanation, and his own account of time, must be developed on metaphysical grounds (Mullarkey 2004: 475). Deleuze has to account not just for the constitution (and, as will be shown, determination) of qualitative and quantitative distinctions, but also for the differentiation between the noetic and the ontic. His account is sourced from the work of Bergson – despite the latent duality – specifically in Bergson's criticism of Kant, and is developed predominantly in Chapter 4 of *Difference and Repetition* (Ansell-Pearson 1999: 33).

In *Matter and Memory*, Bergson explains that, when Kant argues that the mind can 'have no contact with matter', he does so by claiming that there can be no 'conceivable relation, no common measure' between the thing in-itself and the sensuous manifold from which knowledge is constructed (Bergson [1908] 1991: 230–1). Instead, Kant presupposes homogeneous space as the barrier interrupting and obfuscating the intellect from things, thus making both matter and spirit unknowable, and orientating conscious perception to pure knowledge (Bergson [1908] 1991: 231, Ansell-Pearson 1999: 33, Badiou 2004: 135). Bergson, however, insists that the idealisation of this barrier amounts to a 'true hallucination', whereby Kant would have to accept that either 'our conception of matter is false, or memory is radically distinct from perception' (Bergson [1908] 1991: 239). In other words, by formally separating knowledge of the thing from the thing in-itself (the noetic from the ontic), Kant cannot account for the relationship between the two, except as one of extensive differentiation. He is thereby obliged to develop his categorical theory of the faculty of understanding to account for how the subject might think synthetic concepts as the understanding of the noetic and the sensible. This problem is of course familiar, and is a variant of the same issue both Badiou and Meillassoux run into: formally separating thought and matter into two separate realms prohibits an account of how formal ideas think phenomena. So how does Deleuze negotiate the necessity to account for the difference between thought and matter, whilst accounting for their relation?

The key to Deleuze's reversal of Kant is found in his characterisation of differential calculus, itself an expression of his principle of difference: 'just as difference immediately reunites and articulates that which it distinguishes, and the fracture retains what it fractures, so Ideas contain their dismembered moments' (Deleuze [1994] 2011: 216). Here, Deleuze argues that difference has the dual function of both distinguishing and uniting things, and that things are not differentiated by any principle prior to this distinction. Ideas then are a problematic unity of difference, where a problem is defined as 'the constitution of a unitary and systematic field which orientates and subsumes the researches or investigation in such a manner that the answers, in turn, form precisely cases of solution' (Deleuze [1994] 2011: 215). In arguing this, Deleuze is not suggesting a vulgar rationalism, and indeed criticises Kant for maintaining that ideas (and thus problems as well) are only identifiable by their extensive characteristics in determinate relation to the *a priori* fields of experience and understanding (Bowden 2011: 103). Extensive characteristics would imply that Ideas are actual, i.e. are the product of a process of individuation. Rather, Deleuze clarifies that 'Ideas [. . .] possess no actuality. They are pure virtuality' (Deleuze [1994] 2011: 349). They are the open expression of the difference that distinguishes and articulates elements which 'play' in differential relations ([1994] 2011: 349). The differential relation provokes the question 'what else can be related, and what would this relation be?' (Deleuze [1994] 2011: 216–17). Williams summarises the openness of ideas well when he writes that 'Ideas must give determinacy to the chaos of pure differences but without rendering it finally determined in any way' (Williams 2013: 150).[36]

Deleuze's prioritisation of intensive difference reverses his priority of determination contra Kant. For Kant, the faculty of understanding is obligated the task of judgment, i.e. of establishing which categories were universal and, thus, properties of human intellect. The categories of the intellect are, for Kant, transcendental because, as he puts it in the first *Critique*, having removed intuition as a way of cognising, all that are left are concepts (Kant [1787] 1996: 121–2, A168, B193). Kant continues by distinguishing concepts and intuitions further: 'concepts are based on the spontaneity of thought, whereas sensible intuitions are based on the receptivity for impressions. Now the only use that the understanding can make of these concepts is to judge by means of them' ([1787] 1996: 121–2, A168, B193). Nevertheless, as Bergson shows, this amounts to admitting that intellect is simply a hallucination conditioned by homogeneous space, playing on the fact that Kant only *assumes* that appearances 'relate' to objects ([1787] 1996: 121–2, A168, B193). Drawing on Bergson's argument, Deleuze explains that, for Kant, 'problematic Ideas are both objective and undetermined' in the sense that Ideas are a necessary part of intellect, determinable by intuition, but ultimately not determined by any form of ontological ground (Deleuze [1994] 2011: 215, 220).[37] Deleuze's transcendental problem asks, however: how can we account for the rules and conditions of a transcendental philosophy, given that these conditions seem based upon an empiricism in the first place (Bryant 2008: 34)? For Deleuze, developing the contribution to calculus made by Salomon Maimon, both the terms of difference – i.e. 'the determinable intuition and the determinant concept' must 'equally be thought' (Deleuze [1994] 2011: 220). It is not enough to simply suppose the distinction between intuition (i.e. the sensible) and the concept as belonging to either different faculties of the subject (Kant), or a mind/world dyad (Bergson), but rather both distinctions must be explained according to an account of what Deleuze calls a 'principle of reciprocal determination' ([1994] 2011: 220). Reciprocal determination for Deleuze is when 'Ideas appear in the form of a system of ideal connections – in other words, a system of differential relations between reciprocally determined genetic elements' ([1994] 2011: 220). It is thus the differential relation that determines both quantity and quality, rather than the latter determining the former. The relation itself is, for Deleuze, the Idea which, according to Williams, is a determinable problem (to the extent that the Idea is not a totalised unity, but open to further relations) (Williams 2013: 152). In reversing the Kantian prioritisation of difference, then, 'Deleuze develops his concept of the problem in such a way that it accounts for the internal genesis of both the sense and the truth of propositions, along with the object which realises this truth, and without reference to anything transcending the problem and determining it from the outside' (Bowden 2011: 97). Furthermore, the radical differentiations between thought and matter, as present in Kant, Badiou and Meillassoux, are shown to be conditioned by an originary relation. This originary relation undermines the idea of dyads as completely determinate, as they must always be related to other differential relations and, thus, problems.[38]

In order to show how Deleuze conceptualises the necessity of both the passive and active syntheses of time, and thus the constitution of the individual in its social production, it is necessary to develop briefly his use of differential calculus. It is important to note, before embarking on an exposition of Deleuze's use of mathematics that might give the impression that he commits himself to the grand style of mathematics alongside Badiou, that Deleuze subscribes in fact to the minor style (Evans 2006). Daniel Smith distinguishes between the grand and the minor style of mathematics (which he calls the studies of theorematics and problematics respectively) as such:

> if in theorematics a deduction moves from axioms to theorems, in problematics a deduction moves from the problem to the ideal *events* that condition it and form the *cases* of solution that resolve it. (Smith 2006: 148, original emphasis)

In other words, rather than assuming that mathematical figures exist as ideas in the Platonic sense (in terms of essence and derived properties), mathematicians of the minor style define figures dynamically by their '*capacity to be affected*' (2006: 149, original emphasis). In particular, for Deleuze, differential calculus is only an *expression of the function* of differentiation, and cannot be called scriptural materiality in the same way that Brassier describes Badiou's use of mathematics.[39] Both group and set theory, for Deleuze, hide within them a teleology that combines both the necessity for the mathematical expression of problems with the manner by which problems are solved (Deleuze [1994] 2011: 228). It should therefore not be a surprise, as Deleuze explains, that some problems cannot be solved algebraically, as calculus is 'only a mathematical instrument which, even in its own domain, does not necessarily represent the most complete form of the expression of problems and the constitution of their solutions in relation to the order of dialectical Ideas which it incarnates' (Deleuze [1994] 2011: 228). The use of calculus in solving problems amounts to a 'counter-actualisation' for Deleuze, or the identification of the 'transcendental – yet immanent – conditions of the actual' (in this case mathematical) in order to 'then proceed to a different way of actualising them' (Egyed 2006: 82). In other words, mathematics is not an analytical framework *qua* Kant or

Badiou, but the productive synthesis of a particular multiple of different relations, some of which relate mathematical functions with the non-mathematical (i.e. empirical). Differential calculus identifies and expresses one manner in which problems, ideas, solutions and fields of solution are composed but, when it comes to actually solving problems, there are, for Deleuze, many ways to skin a cat. Deleuze begins his explanation of the differential relations of ideas by stating that, the 'symbol dx appears as simultaneously undetermined, determinable and determination' (Deleuze [1994] 2011: 217).[40] This is to say that the symbol presents the difference that determines both d and x as distinct from each other. Without relation to anything however, x is simply an axis (the abscissa) populated by singularities. Singularities, also described by Deleuze as 'vanishing quantities', are points on the abscissa where dx (the change in x) is zero (Deleuze 1981, Duffy 2006: 119).[41] Because the axis x is not yet in relation to anything else, this means that there are an infinite number of singular points along it. Yet, the relation dx is determinable in the sense that there *are* singularities along the line x with which another variable can be related.[42] A differential relation with another variable y (i.e. dx/dy) constitutes the reciprocal determination that allows Deleuze to account for the material production of the quality and quantity of Ideas. According to this relation, y changes in relation to x when subject to a function f, thus $y = f(x)$, and the Idea denotes this variation. As Deleuze puts it, 'the Idea has the differential relation as its object: it then integrates variation, not as a variable determination of a supposedly constant relation ("variability") but, on the contrary, as a degree of variation of the relation itself ("variety")' (Deleuze [1994] 2011: 219–20).[43] For example, it would make no sense to speak of a variable Idea of a painting (dx), because y, having been reciprocally determined by the relation df, would intersect x at separate points along the line and thus determine a series of different and distinct paintings. Deleuze's use of calculus thereby accounts for qualitative difference along the y axis and quantitative difference along the x axis and, following an exchange of letters with Althusser, who suggests the two terms, uses 'differen*t*iation' and 'differen*c*iation' respectively to distinguish between the two types of difference (Stolze 1998, Bryant 2008: 75, Deleuze [1994] 2011: 312–13).

This brief overview having introduced the ideas and relations of the second passive synthesis, it is important to note that, for Deleuze, variety necessitates the use of the active syntheses (representation, contiguity, causality, resemblance and opposition). For example, having determined a series of paintings according to one differential dx/dy, the comparison between different paintings constitutes what Deleuze calls a 'linear' relation dz. This new relation is populated by the paintings identified by what Deleuze refers to as their extensive coordinates, as opposed to the original relation dx ([1994] 2011: 223). Not a differential relation, Deleuze explains that this linear relation necessitates the use of a sum – an empirical counting of these pre-determined singularities – which themselves determine a second series that is 'completely determined' ([1994] 2011: 223). The complete determination of the second series renders its Ideas 'distinct', removed from the pure difference that constitutes differential relations. It is therefore clear why Deleuze argues that active syntheses are needed in order to think completely determined series (such as a collection of similar paintings): the first passive syntheses of the passing present is immanent with the creation of the paintings and is different at all times. Only in retrospect, after the initial series of painting, does an active series use and reproduce the image of the pure past, as presented by the past in the second passive synthesis.

This explains why, despite passages both in Deleuze's work with Guattari and the secondary literature which appear to the contrary, nowhere does Deleuze argue that the active syntheses are necessarily to be avoided, *per se*, and nor is there necessarily a priority of the second synthesis as directly determining the first.[44] The introduction of Deleuze and Guattari's *A Thousand Plateaus* is one such example where the reader might get such an impression, given the authors' instruction to 'make a map, not a tracing' (Deleuze and Guattari 2004b: 13). The authors place emphasis on the experimental method of drafting, rather than the reproductive method of tracing, because of the possibility that the former is open; 'it is detachable, reversible, susceptible to constant modification' (2004b: 13). In fact, however, whilst the active syntheses presuppose the passive syntheses (i.e the differential relations conditioned by the principle of difference), they are a crucial part of Deleuze's modification of Kant's principle of sufficient reason. As shown above, Deleuze recognises that individuals need a '*distinctness* of Ideas' in order to live life ([1994] 2011: 223, original emphasis). However, there is no point, for Deleuze, in trying to explain away the existence of objects, practices or ideas; rather, one must ask what is their function, and what purpose do they serve when placed in a certain structure or regime, such as the individual's life. The active syntheses are essential, therefore, in the determination and actualisation of singular practices – on the understanding that these practices are both metaphysically experimental, and also 'directed towards a clinical and critical affirmation of our actual lives' (Williams 2008: 99). Put in terms of Deleuze's example, the individual drafting the map needs the active syntheses in order to differentiate towns from roads, trees from elevation, yet the drawing of a map is a creative articulation of this differentiation – a counter-actualisation. Put technically, the determination of orders of distinction (which constitute the active syntheses) alongside the order of becoming (that is contracted by the passive syntheses) means that propositions express the sense of a situation, whilst concomitantly being determined by an *a priori* problem (Bowden 2011: 97–8).

Having taken a slight detour through Deleuze's use of differential calculus, it is now possible to show how, for Deleuze, the second synthesis of the pure past, which is referred to under different conditions as the virtual, is the structure of singularities and relations that form the potential conditions for the first synthesis. For Bergson, difference is the difference of duration (the internal tendency for the contraction of qualitative states) which, as Ansell-Pearson characterises, 'appears to be an indivisible global power' (Ansell-Pearson 1999: 66). Deleuze, however, insists on the necessity of differentiating both qualitative and quantitative relations, and the second synthesis provides the grounds upon which to differentiate such relations in the present. For this reason, whereas Deleuze calls the first synthesis that of 'Habit', the second is that of 'Memory'. Memory (the virtual structure of singularities and relations) is presented as a synthesis to Habit as its condition in the form of what Deleuze calls variously surface effects, ideal events or signs (Deleuze [1964] 2008). The first synthesis is thus of the differential relations themselves, whereby every relation constructs a new structure, constructing the second synthesis, via the principle of reciprocal determination. Active syntheses play upon the relations in the second syntheses, selecting elements of the virtual structure for processes of individuation alongside the first passive synthesis. Williams puts this concisely when he states that 'the past for passing presents is general and not particular, because it is a condition for any passing present which can then be aimed at and represented in active memory' (Williams 2011: 59).

An ontology proper to structuralism

In contrast to Althusser's aleatory void, it can now be seen how Deleuze accounts for the constitution of the present. Althusser argues that the void must be instituted in order to avoid idealism, because only in doing so could one remove the possibility of previous atomic collisions determining future ideas. Deleuze addresses this conceptualisation directly, where he corrects the denigration of the atomist *clinamen*: 'the *clinamen* is by no means a change of direction in the movement of an atom, much less an indetermination testifying to the existence of a physical freedom. It is the original determination of the directions of movement, the synthesis of movement and its direction which relates one atom to another' (Deleuze [1994] 2011: 232). For Deleuze, then, there is no need to take drastic measures to reconfigure the clinamen because it is simply the virtual plane of relations that affirm the place of singularities. Indeed, the *clinamen* is, for Deleuze, reciprocal determination itself, the removal of which (according to Deleuze's philosophy) would require the exercise of the active synthesis for its selection and counter-actualisation. Although Deleuze argues that the Epicurean atom 'still retains too much independence, a shape and an actuality' ([1994] 2011: 232), when conceptualised as a singularity that presents one relation to another, Althusser's atomism looks much more like that which differentiates the four regional theories in Althusser's first Note.

In accounting for the *clinamen* as the structure of atoms' falling, and bearing in mind that *Reading Capital* is grounded in atomist philosophy (even if this is not made specific), it is clear to see how Deleuze can state that 'Althusser and his collaborators are, therefore, profoundly correct in showing the presence of a genuine structure in *Capital*' ([1994] 2011: 234). He goes so far as to argue that, for a society, 'there are only economic social problems, even though the solutions may be juridical, political or ideological, and the problems may be expressed in these fields of resolvability' ([1994] 2011: 235). Notwithstanding Deleuze's criticism of structuralism (i.e. that there is too much emphasis placed on the actuality of the atom), there is a clear commensurability between the philosophies of Althusser and Deleuze.[45]

In a 2007 blog article, Bryant claims that '*Difference and Repetition* and *The Logic of Sense* [were], in part, an attempt to develop *the ontology proper to structuralism*' (Bryant 2007) and Deleuze's correction of Althusser's atomism should be seen as a contribution to his theory, not a repudiation.[46] In other words, the social theory of the latter can be supported by the philosophy of the former; Althusser's theory of social formation, as characterised by Chambers, thus acquires an ontological foundation.[47] For example, using Deleuze's work as ontological support for Althusser's concept of ideology, and contra to Butler's account, ideology does not need a psychic account of recognition in order to function. This is so because, according to Deleuze, concepts are not epistemological but ontological (Bryant 2008: 68). Ideology functions as part of the virtual, pre-personal field as the discourse of social relations; although these relations are of course open to change, this change would nevertheless remain part of the discourse of ideology and does not require any cognitive or psychic processes of a totalising subject. Buchanan reinforces this point, arguing that 'Deleuze and Guattari insist that there is no such thing as "psychic" reality, which would somehow be different from other kinds of reality' (Deleuze and Guattari 2004a: 27, Buchanan 2015: 386). For Deleuze and Guattari, there is only one 'reality' which is constructed by the reciprocal determination of the three passive syntheses of time. As per economics in *Capital*, ideology might be the discourse of study in a particular text (such as Althusser's ISAs essay), but this is on the understanding that it is only one field in which questions about social problems can be posed and solved, and one discourse does not articulate reality any more than any other.

Most important then is the question of the extent to which Deleuze's philosophy of time itself remains idealist. Badiou's, Meillassoux's and Althusser's philosophies have all been criticised so far for their idealism, to the extent that they all subordinate one aspect of being to the thought of another, from which being in its entirety can be known. Deleuze's position, then, is different, for Deleuze does not argue that philosophy is subtractive, but constructive (Deleuze and Guattari [1991] 1994: 2–3). Although he does not discuss the importance of time in Deleuze's escape from idealism, MacKenzie argues that Deleuze (and Guattari's) constructivism is the key to the cell door (MacKenzie 1997). In particular, MacKenzie emphasises the separation of the concept from what Deleuze and Guattari refer to as the 'plane of immanence' (Deleuze and Guattari [1991] 1994: 35, MacKenzie 1997: 8). The plane of immanence is a 'preconceptual field presupposed within the concept' that gives authority to the concept as its third (MacKenzie 1997: 8, Deleuze [1956–7] 2015: 43).

Recalling then the problems of idealism for Badiou, Meillassoux and Althusser, it was clear that they confused planes and concepts, thus making their theories transcendent to one or more concepts (mathematics, transfinite logic or the void). In MacKenzie's terms, within idealism, 'the privileged concept is considered coextensive with the plane of immanence, rendering both the concept and the plane transcendental' (1997: 9). Yet, for Deleuze, concepts construct their sense from a selection of their virtual structure by the active syntheses. These concepts, now actualised, nevertheless constitute the new virtual conditions for counter-actualisation. Deleuze therefore does not conflate the concept and its transcendental conditions by way of emphasising the passage from the virtual to the actual and then back to the virtual. In MacKenzie's terms, Deleuze does not succumb to the 'charge of attributing immanence "to" something' (1997: 9), because the concept reciprocally determines its plane of immanence and is immanent *with* it (1997: 10). The same is true for the first and second syntheses of time: whilst the active syntheses select the specific singularities from within the pure past, the past is itself only determined as such by the passing present. Likewise, the past only contracts what has passed on the condition that it is not present, yet forms the present's immanent grounds. The reciprocal determination of the passive syntheses thus ensures that neither formally grounds the other, leaving both open to change via the active syntheses.

Philosophy and idealism

It has been argued that Deleuze's ontology can form the structure for a non-idealist conceptualisation of resistance. First, by accounting for the constitution of novelty via the differential relation of ideas, Deleuze ensures that no Idea or concept is rarefied above another, and therefore avoids the trappings of idealism. Whereby Kant's transcendental idealism subordinates knowledge of the world to the knowledge that we can't know the thing in-itself in the first place, and the dogmatic use of logically deduced categories, Deleuze demonstrates how knowledge is produced both of and by the individual's relation with the world. Secondly, all Ideas for Deleuze are ontologically determined according to the non-totalising structure of their differential relations (Voss 2013a: 29). As such, Deleuze accounts for the contingency of knowledge necessary for philosophy since Kant's Copernican revolution; Deleuze welcomes the possibility of thought becoming other, and his philosophy has neither a mandate nor the authority to determine what constitutes legitimate knowledge. Indeed, as highlighted by Althusser's work on regional theories, individuals in fact require other modes of thought to live in the world and, in the next chapter, this argument will be developed in terms of Deleuze's idea of mediators. Deleuze's philosophy, contra to the arguments made by Meillassoux and Badiou, fulfils a pragmatic, functional role; rather than delimiting the extent to which thought can think the world, Deleuze invites individuals to be free through posing and solving problems they find interesting or useful (Deleuze [1988] 1991: 15, Deleuze and Guattari [1991] 1994: 16, Porter 2009: 57).

Chambers's work on Althusser's social theory is particularly important with regard to Deleuze's practical philosophy because it accentuates the differential nature of ideas, practices and discourses. Whilst Deleuze's discussion of differential calculus in *Difference and Repetition* focuses on the ontological scale of infinitesimals, Chambers locates the same structural argument in Althusser's social theory. Therefore, whilst Deleuze does, of course, expand into more obviously socio-political themes in his work with Guattari, the conjunction of Althusser, Chambers and Deleuze at this stage foregrounds the importance of relationality at all scales – both micro, macro and those in between.[48] Important to the discussion regarding idealism and scale is the understanding that, for Deleuze, Ideas are ordinal, meaning that they can be grouped and related. Yet counter to Badiou's account of them, these ordinal groups (or, in Badiou's terms, 'sets'), according to Deleuze's ontology, are not Ideal. Ideas are grouped by differential, rather than formal, relations in what Althusser calls regional theories, or what Deleuze and Guattari call in *A Thousand Plateaus* assemblages, which allow the activist to understand the social in institutional terms, as well as through political practice (Williams 2013: 161–2).[49] Developed in the next chapter, this is what Patton refers to as 'formal normativity' and it allows for individuals to pose and solve problems at all levels, the institutional and not just the personal.

In particular, Althusser's emphasis on political practice (i.e. the general theory), as opposed to simply knowledge or theory, is important in reminding the activist that it is not simply enough to know the 'best' way of understanding the world if the point is to change it. Practice, for Althusser, is that which unifies the regional theories and accounts for their constitution. Whilst Badiou's more overtly political works go to lengths to emphasise the importance of practice at the expense of their conceptual precision, as has been discussed, his meta-political theory subordinates practice under his rationalist conceptualisation of politics. In the next chapter, this subordination will be shown to prohibit Badiou's ability to explain how individuals' actions are ethical, even if he provides a theory of how they *might* be ethical in his *Ethics* (2001). As both Althusser's and Deleuze's philosophies conceptualise Ideas and relations according to a univocal ontology, thus allowing them to explain the affective relationships between them, both can account for how practices are always-already co-constitutive with Ideas. If then, as will be argued in the next chapter, ethics (or ethology) is the study of what is good or bad for the individual, then processes of individuation are always-already ethical. Therefore, the suture of Althusser's social theory to Deleuze's philosophy provides the non-idealist structure by which to think the ethics of individuation in relation to different discourses and social structures. Removed of any dogmatic conception of politics, it is this theory that constitutes the grounds of a non-dogmatic theory of resistance.

Notes

1. It would be more accurate to argue that Hume's subject is the persistence of thought through time. The word 'provide' is, however, used to account for a function in Hume's philosophy that is otherwise lacking in Althusser's philosophy.
2. Meillassoux has been discussed predominantly (although not exclusively) in blogs by authors interested in 'object orientated ontology'. See Brassier (2016), Bryant (2016), Harman (2016), and Morton (2016), as well as a new journal, *O-Zone*, dedicated to object orientated ontology. See also Zalloua (2015: esp. 393–4).
3. An extended discussion of abstraction in Deleuze's philosophy is not possible here, but it is worth mentioning that both May and Patton have noted how Deleuze and Guattari's concepts such as 'war machine' and 'State' 'are not specific historical entities but abstractions that are realised to a greater or lesser degree, and always in mixture, in concrete situations' (Patton 1984, May 1991: 27).
4. It is this clarification that casts doubt over both Brassier's and Meillassoux's all-encompassing charge that most philosophers both during and after the Enlightenment constitute either weak or strong correlationists (Brassier 2007: 50, Meillassoux 2008: 35–42, 46). Brassier equates the 'the reigning *doxa* of post-metaphysical philosophy' with the 'idea of a world-in-itself, of a realm of phenomena subsisting independently of our relation to it', which is termed

'difference' (Brassier 2007: 50). Deleuze, however (to mention only one example), never argued that 'reality must be transcendentally guaranteed, whether by pure consciousness, intersubjective consensus, or a community of rational agents' (2007: 50). Moreover, as he develops in *Bergsonism* (though put in terms that he may not have been comfortable with), his transcendental 'guarantee' is the world-in-itself, or pure difference. 'We perceive things where they are' argues Deleuze; 'perception puts us at once *into* matter, is impersonal, and *coincides with the perceived object*' (Deleuze [1988] 1991: 25, emphasis added). The charge of correlationism is no doubt an effective polemic tool, but is undermined by a lack of detailed, referenced reading in both their works. Golumbia makes a similar criticism, although his claim that Meillassoux 'fails to respect most of the methods of that practice: to state clearly its contentions, to define its terms, to distinguish between philosophical issues (particularly epistemology and metaphysics), or to demonstrate textually its historical-philosophical assessments' appreciates neither the scientific or political claims in Meillassoux's sights, nor his criticism of philosophy as a *practice* (Meillassoux 2008: 45–8, Johnston 2011: 109, Golumbia 2016: 3, 12).
5. A historical contextualisation of *After Finitude* with regard to Lenin's disagreement with Kant and Hume can be found in Johnston (2011: 93–6). See also Brassier (2007: 246).
6. Golumbia pulls Meillassoux up on his reading of Kant by showing that 'Kant goes out of his way to account for and even to embrace human *thinking* about the noumena even as he is careful to restrict *knowledge* to that of which we humans have experience' (Golumbia 2016: 9). As Golumbia explains, Meillassoux conflates the act of thinking the in-itself for Kant with having knowledge of it, and still argues that humans cannot think the in-itself. This leads to the position where Meillassoux needs 'to insist that human beings can *know with certainty* objects of *experience* [. . .] *of which they have no experience whatever* [. . .], and that this knowledge is somehow *more* scientific than what current philosophy allows' (2016: 9). This conflation is indeed not made by Kant and it is easy to see why Golumbia plainly says that 'the idea that Kant would write so often about the thing-in-itself while denying that he or his readers could *think* about it is plainly non-sensical' (2016: 10).
7. Drawing on the distinction made by Locke, for Meillassoux, the sensation of pain is not a property of a flame but a result of a subjective relation with it. As such, pain is a secondary quality of the flame. A primary property would be a property of flame irrespective of the subject's (non-)relation to it. See Meillassoux (2008: 1–2).
8. Althusser uses the term 'denegate' to 'designate an unconscious denial masked by a conscious acceptance'. In other words, a process

is denegated when it is used to furnish a result, but when one does not appreciate that this product was a result of said process. For further explanation, see its note in Althusser and Balibar (1970: 312).

9. See Hume ([1748] 1993: 35–7, 70–2). Hume's advocation of a 'non-dogmatic openness' in individuals' understanding of reality influenced the pragmatic theorists of truth. For Misak, pragmatism 'abandons the kind of metaphysics which is currently in so much disrepute – it abandons concepts which pretend to transcend experience. Truth and objectivity are matters of what is best for the community of inquirers to believe, "best" here amounting to that which best fits with the evidence and argument' (2002: 1). Thus Pierce takes up Hume's mantle when he states that 'the whole function of thought is to produce habits of action' (Pierce 2004: 47).

10. Chambers's use of the term 'real' is not without its problems, although it should not be understood as in opposition to something illusory or fake. As developed in note 52 to the first chapter, the real is understood as matter in relation to thought, the relations of which are understood, for Althusser, by the Marxist discourse of science and the 'imaginary' discourse of ideology (Williams 2002).

11. Macherey confirms Butler's debt to Freud and Lacan in her understanding of how the ego recognises itself within her account of ideological interpellation (Macherey 2004: 13–16). For Macherey, Butler's version of the story in which the hailed individual turns around allows the now-subject to exclaim 'I exist!', having performatively affirmed itself in the act of interpellation (2004: 13–14). According to Macherey's Butler, then, an individual becomes a subject through the necessary act of performing in the political, although the entrance to the political is contingent upon their participation first within the social. As will be shown, however, Althusser presumed no such topology. Instead, for Althusser, the individual is always-already a subject within the discourse of ideology, and the interpellative act simply changes the subject's relations. Fruitful research could be undertaken, however, based upon Macherey's distinction between Althusser's and Foucault's ideas of subjectification. Whilst Althusser conceptualised subjectification as the process of placing within the reproduction of ideology, Macherey states that Foucault 'related it to a diffuse disciplinary power that was neither ideological nor dependent on central agencies of decision' (2004: 11). What is to be made of the distinction between power in Althusser's idea of ideology and the non-ideological power of Foucault?

12. Meillassoux develops the implications of the principle of facticity particularly clearly with regard to Hume's billiard ball problem in his second monograph, *Science Fiction and Extro-Science Fiction* (2013: 8–32).

13. See note 30 in Chapter 2, as well as Meillassoux (2008: 104, 105).

14. Although Meillassoux has yet to publish anything explicitly political, Graham Harman's book on Meillassoux, *Philosophy in the Making*, contains an interview, passages of which support this supposition (2011: 163, 173).
15. Specifically, building on Cantor's diagonalisation, Meillassoux's principle of factiality states that 'what is mathematically conceivable is absolutely possible' (Meillassoux 2008: 126).
16. Golumbia agrees, but puts it slightly differently when he claims that 'unlike most proponents of realism in Anglo-American philosophy, Meillassoux refuses even to acknowledge the possibility that human perception might not provide perfect access to objective reality' (Golumbia 2016: 58).
17. DeLanda makes the useful observation that Deleuze's use of the term 'individual' is at least idiosyncratic. According to him, for 'Deleuze the term "individual" refers to an entity *in the process of actualisation*, that is, before it acquires its final qualities and extensities' (DeLanda [2002] 2005: 83–4). Whilst this definition provides a useful reference to processes, thus distinguishing Deleuze's concept of the individual from those of, for example, the liberal tradition, Clisby provides an important rectification of DeLanda's understanding of the virtual/intensive/actual tripartite. For DeLanda, there are distinctly 'three spheres of reality, with virtual multiplicities constraining and guiding intensive processes which in turn would yield specific actual entities' (DeLanda 2005: 86). The implication of DeLanda's definition of the individual then is that there are two kinds of individual: a post-individual entity in the sphere of the actual that is different in kind from non-actual entity that he calls 'individual' above. As Clisby clarifies, however, individuation and actualisation are in themselves different in kind, and there is a metaphysical priority of individuation over actualisation (Clisby 2015: 142). Clisby quotes Deleuze explicitly warning of the dangers of conflating the two: 'any reduction of individuation to a limit or complication of differenciation, compromises the whole philosophy of difference. This would be an error, this time in the actual, analogous to that made in confusing the virtual with the possible' (Deleuze [1994] 2011: 308–9, Clisby 2015: 145). According to Clisby's clarification, DeLanda's definition of the individual is misleading. It would be more correct to say that, for Deleuze, the term 'individual' refers to an entity in the process of *individuation*, where this process is '*part of the actual*', but not reducible to it (Clisby 2015: 146, original emphasis).
18. This chapter will work with the definition of the 'social formation' that is used by Chambers: 'the social formation is itself a political form, a politicised structure, whereas "the social" may well be a sphere separate from "the political" domain' (Chambers 2014: 55). For Chambers, the social formation is distinct from 'the social' in the

sense that the latter is only a particularly demarcated region of the former. The social formation exceeds the social, taking into account the political and aesthetic, as well as the structures and practices that constitute their formation and reproduction.

19. Althusser's appropriation of Spinoza's ontology means that his politics can be seen in the same light. Referencing Althusser's attempts to synthesise Marx's scientific methodology and his initial humanism with Spinoza, he argues the the benefit of this is that 'Spinoza's immanentism can finally liberate us from all forms of dialectics, from all teleology; that his materialism is not narrow, but aleatory and open to the virtualise of being; that through the avowed articulation between immanentism and materialism, knowledge will henceforth rely on resistance, and happiness on the rational passion of the multitude' (Negri 2013: 20). Althusser's politics are therefore, alongside Spinoza's, not dialectic but *subversive* (2013: 5).

20. Against Hyppolite's Hegelian criticism of Deleuze, Nathan Widder develops Deleuze's constructive ontology, invoking what he calls the 'Event of sense that brings together Ideas and bodies' (2003: 452).

21. In an article called 'Origin of the Structure' in the journal *Cahiers pour l'Analyse*, Jean-Jacques Miller defined overdetermination as 'the structuring determination which, by being exercised through the biases of the imaginary, becomes indirect, unequal and eccentric in relation to its effects' (Hallward and Peden 2013: Ch. 2).

22. Although a full discussion of Mill's thought will be left for the next chapter, it is worth noting that, in the *Considerations*, he makes a similar claim: 'there can be no separate Science of Government [. . .] All questions respecting the tendencies of forms of government must stand part of the general science of society, not of any separate branch of it' (Mill 1977: 906).

23. Chambers uses the idea of the social formation, alternating with the 'more generic term' 'social order' in effort to avoid 'limiting [himself] to the Althusserian terminology or theoretical framework' (Chambers 2014: 21, ff. 18). The two conceptualisations used by Chambers are similar to the conceptualisation of class struggle as the motor of history found in Althusser's *Essays in Self-Criticism* (Althusser 1976: 35–77), however Chambers is at pains not to build any form of theory *per se* (Chambers 2014: 20). Chambers provides an, albeit less ambitious, nonetheless equally compelling account of social formation from a composite of different 'perspectives', that emphasises the openness to revision and modification of his work, 'much like the social formation itself' (2014: 20).

24. Drawing out the influence of Spinoza on both Althusser and Deleuze, Diefenbach argues that both 'converge at the question of how a structure differentiates through its distances' (Diefenbach 2013: 169). As Massumi has argued, highlighting the Spinozist influence that

underpins both authors' philosophies, '[t]he relationship between the levels of intensity and qualification is not one of conformity or correspondence, but of resonance or interference, amplification or dampening' (Massumi 1995: 86).
25. La Caze and Lloyd show that theoretical practice and material practice are both affective in the sense inherited from Spinoza's conception of thought and extension (La Caze and Lloyd 2011: 1).
26. Deleuze's theory of time is possibly the most difficult and nuanced component of his philosophy, and spans his texts on Kant ([1963] 2008), Bergson ([1988] 1991), *Difference and Repetition* ([1994] 2011), *The Logic of Sense* ([1969] 2004), through to both volumes of his work on Cinema (2005a and 2005b). Nevertheless, as Lundy explains in his review of Williams's *Gilles Deleuze's Philosophy of Time*, 'Deleuze's books on Cinema, which clearly have much to do with time, add nothing to Deleuze's philosophy of time, and indeed detract from it' (Lundy 2014: 126). By taking cinema as the object of their studies, the *Cinema* books use time functionally more than they develop a philosophy of time itself, which is what is important for the argument in this chapter. As such, and following Williams's claim that Deleuze's philosophy of time is 'expounded in its "most consistent and extensive form"' in *Difference and Repetition*, and whilst not denying the potential importance of the variety of its forms across Deleuze's works, it is this form which is used for the purposes of this chapter (Williams 2011: 161). There has been a large amount of literature that appropriates Deleuze's conceptualisation of time: see Ansell-Pearson (1999), Crocker (2001), Al-Saji (2004), Deamer (2011), Pisters (2011, 2012), Somers-Hall (2011) and Smith (2013). As Williams acknowledges in his detailed study of Deleuze's theory, however, whilst scholarship on Deleuze's work often uses his theory of time in order to underpin claims which are tangentially related to it, there are fewer texts that concentrate specifically on time *per se* (Williams 2011: 2). Williams's *Gilles Deleuze's Philosophy of Time* was written with the clear explication of Deleuze's theory in mind and is indeed an excellent reference point for understanding the topic, whilst his critical introduction and guide for *Difference and Repetition* (Deleuze [1994] 2011) develops his work on the three syntheses in relation to Deleuze's book more generally (Williams 2013). Two other book-length texts to note are Ansell-Pearson's *Germinal Life* (1999), which reads Deleuze's philosophy of time in contrast to, though having developed from, Bergson's concept of duration, and Bryant's *Difference and Givenness* (2008). Whilst not playing down the detail and accuracy of Williams's and Ansell-Pearson's work, Bryant's *Difference and Givenness* will be used predominantly in what follows as it foregrounds the importance and contribution that Deleuze's

theory of time gives to metaphysics. Bryant's text emphasises, as indeed Deleuze does himself, the necessity to conceptualise time in-itself (i.e. as a differential relation that pre-supposes its elements) that accommodates the non-dogmatic persistence of the past into the present. It is this persistence which is the key to removing the idealism latent within Althusser's idea of philosophical practice.

27. One such critic of Deleuze is Peter Hallward, who argues that Deleuze's philosophy comes from *Out of This World* (2006). Although he appreciates the lack of an actual God in Deleuze's thought, Hallward argues that Deleuze falls in line with 'theophanic' conceptions of the world, where every object, process, or idea is an expression of a God (or its equivalent) (2006: 4). Hallward claims that Deleuze's trademark ontological condition of 'becoming' applies writ large across Deleuze's entire philosophy so that 'rather than reserved for that which exceeds creation or orients it towards its limit, an immanent conception of creativity will assign the task of self-transcendence to its every creature (2006: 6). In other words, Hallward's Deleuze makes everything sacred – everything emerges from the one sovereign power of becoming – which, of course, only serves to also make everything profane. However, Deleuze does in fact talk of moving towards a limit in passages that Hallward either misses or ignores. For example, when discussing how the present passes to allow the empirical to be sensed, Deleuze argues that the 'sign of the present is a *passage* to the limit' (Deleuze [1994] 2011: 105, original emphasis). Put (too) simply: for Deleuze, the present is presented to the past *by* the past as a multiplicity of signs that can be 'chosen', a process which Deleuze simply refers to as 'life' ([1994] 2011: 105). The past is constituted by actualised phenomena, the 'empirical' in Deleuze's transcendental empiricism. In other words, for Deleuze, every creature (and object, process and idea) is transcendental, but only having first become empirical. Having become empirical, the creature presents the individual with an encounter, which is the proper condition for becoming (Bryant 2008: 88, 99–100). Thus, both the empirical and the transcendental are needed for Deleuze's philosophy, and the term 'reality' used here is intended to highlight the importance of both. Deleuze's development of the transcendental (virtual) conditions for the empirical (actual) is drawn from his work on Bergson and, in *Bergsonism*, he reminds the reader that 'the virtual is opposed [not to the real, but] to the actual' ([1988] 1991: 96). As such, Hallward is as mistaken in missing or ignoring the actual, as other readers would be in ignoring the virtual.

28. The syntheses of time can be traced to Deleuze's reading of Kant, and his argument that time is 'no longer related to the movement which it measures, but [that] movement is related to the time which conditions it' (Deleuze [1963] 2008: vii).

29. The third synthesis is not developed as much as the previous two in order to maintain this chapter's focus on ideas and matter, the relation of which are best understood by focusing on the first, second and active syntheses. For detailed studies of the third synthesis, see Williams (2011) and Voss (2013b).
30. Deleuze's idea of pure difference as his ontological condition is in stark contrast with Badiou's conceptualisation, for whom Being (in) consists of undifferentiated multiplicity (it is interesting to note that Badiou uses the past participle form of indifference, implying that this has been the result of a process of undifferentiation, although he does not develop this anywhere in his work). *Difference and Repetition* begins with a brief repudiation of the primacy of indifference. For Deleuze, it makes no sense to talk in terms of indifference because, whether this indifference is one of pure void-nothingness (i.e. Badiou's void), or pure totality-indifference, it is only with the concept of difference that one can 'speak of determination *as such*' ([1994] 2011: 36). This is not to say that one must talk of the difference *between* the void and totality (or, for Badiou, the 'One') as already given, because – as with empiricism – this presupposes their differences in the first place (for a development of this argument, see also Morejón 2015: 1–3). Rather, difference for Deleuze is primary, and *a priori* of both identity and representation. According to the principle of difference, then, the mathematical ontology of Badiou is, in Deleuze's terms, an exercise of reason, 'a harmonious organism' which relates 'determination to other determinations within a form' and has four properties (identity, analogy, opposition and resemblance) ([1994] 2011: 37). Importantly, as Williams points out, Deleuze 'does not seek to deny scientific evidence and theories, but instead seeks to complement them with an account of the role of difference' (Williams 2011: 42). Accordingly, Deleuze has no wish to reject reason *per se*, but to explain it as conditioned by difference and, in doing so, remove reason from its idealised place in the clouds. Due to its reliance on *a priori* reason, then, mathematics (including the mathematics of Badiou's 'grand style') is not 'pure' and cannot form an ontological position ([1994] 2011: 44). But this does not necessarily relegate the use of mathematics more generally; Deleuze highlights the expression 'make the difference', inviting the reader to *use* maths in conjunction with all the *other* modalities that are made to express Being (Bryant 2008: 98).
31. Deleuze's correction of this philosophical atomism stems from his reading of Scotus, and Widder argues that an appreciation of Deleuze's reading of Scotus is essential to avoid characterising Deleuze's univocal ontology as a 'closet Platonism' (Widder 2009: 27). Deleuze names Spinoza and Nietzsche as successors to Scotus's ontology even if, as Widder notes, they do not use the same terminology (2009: 27).

According to Scotus then, ontology is not comprised of (Epicurean) atoms in a void, neither is it 'divided into parts, into species and genera, but is difference itself ' (Deleuze [1994] 2011: 44, Diefenbach 2013: 169). Instances cannot be explained in terms of the difference between them because, as Deleuze argues, this is only an empirical explanation, and 'the corresponding determinations are only extrinsic' (Deleuze [1994] 2011: 36). Deleuze has the same criticism of empiricist explanations as Althusser: by explaining the instances in terms of the differences between them, instances are not thought by themselves, and instead are thought *according to* a separate principle which *re*presents the instances in another light (see Althusser and Balibar 1970: 19–37). Drawing on Nietzsche's *On the Genealogy of Morality*, Deleuze uses the example of lightning to show that difference makes itself, and is nothing other than itself (Deleuze [1994] 2011: 36). It is absurd, as Nietzsche demonstrates, that lightning could do anything other than flash because lightning is nothing other than the flash. Lightning is not distinguished as the difference between two like instances, but against that which is not lightning (Deleuze [1994] 2011: 36, Nietzsche 2014: 236). The similarity between flashes of lightning is therefore not a property of the flashes themselves, i.e. it is determined neither by the three syntheses of time nor the lightning flashes themselves, but is a property of the mind's representation of the flashes and is thought by the active syntheses.

32. The somewhat awkward use of the terms 'individual' and 'subject' here is purposeful. As demonstrated above, the concept of the subject, for Althusser, is the individual as interpellated by social relations. The individual is not reducible to the subject, because the concept of the subject is a knowledge effect of the relation between the individual and social relations; there are always also scientific, aesthetic and philosophical questions to be asked of the individual. Deleuze is not as specific about his use of the term 'subject' as Althusser is, and so the term is used here to highlight the regional limits that Deleuze argues constitute the empirical method *vis-à-vis* the idea of the subject.

33. Mullarkey takes issue with Crocker's description of Bergson's conception of the present with regard to the Past in General. Whereas Crocker thinks that the Past in General is the virtual ground of which actual things are expressions in the present, Mullarkey argues that Bergson in fact does away with singular presents altogether. Rather, as Mullarkey explains, 'present actuality, *qua* perspective, is a force, an affect, that virtualises other presents and actualities' (Mullarkey 2004: 477). The present, for Mullarkey, has much more in common with what Massumi has termed the 'autonomy of affect', or a non-sensible dimension that affects change in differential relation

to elements within the virtual (Massumi 1995). Bergson's lack of consistency in this regard between *Time and Free Will* and *Matter and Memory* is conceded by Mullarkey. However, it is clear, contra to criticisms by Badiou and Hallward, that Deleuze's concept of the virtual/intensive/actual tripartite falls more in line with Mullarkey's depiction. See also Clisby (2015).

34. This description does not do either the concept of the virtual or the actual justice, for the description – and perhaps more crucially the priority – of the virtual and actual are highly contested in the secondary literature on Deleuze and Bergson. To do justice to each of the concepts alone would require a large number of words and would take this chapter away from what it is intended to argue. Sauvagnargues, Ansell-Pearson, Williams, Buchanan and Connolly have all contributed to the debate, but two excellent contributions/reviews of the discussion are Mullarkey (2004) and Clisby (2015).

35. This dualism between a creative '*élan vital*' and quantitative extension gives Bergson a source for developing *The Two Sources of Morality and Religion* (1935). For Bergson, the shared nature that humans have as open, aspirational beings with a shared creative nature gives them one source of morality which binds them together. Their second source results from their joint obligations under a society which attempts to close lives off from one another. For an interesting comparison of Bergson's moral theory with another French naturalist, Marie Guyau, see Ansell-Pearson (2014b).

36. It is for this reason that whilst Paul Patton's translation of the title of Chapter 4 in *Difference and Repetition* is 'Ideas and the Synthesis of Difference', others have translated this to 'The Ideal Synthesis of Difference' (Morejón 2015: 11). For Deleuze, syntheses are indeed idea(l)s, but remain open to actualisation within the virtual. Syntheses are not dogmatic ideas *qua* Badiou, formally determining the constitution of difference as a transcendental principle within the actual, but synthesise only in relation to other virtual ideas.

37. Deleuze also notes how Kant attempted to hide what he calls this 'psychologism', i.e. the derivation of the transcendental structures from the empirical psychological acts of consciousness, by removing text from the second version of the first *Critique* (Deleuze [1994] 2011: 171).

38. Originary relationality is what is later defined by Deleuze and Guattari as the non-philosophical foundations of philosophy. See MacKenzie (1997: 10–11).

39. Deleuze uses the idea of function in two contexts. The first is within *Difference and Repetition* when he expands his reading of calculus, whilst the second is in *What is Philosophy?*, where he and Guattari argue that functions are objects of science (Deleuze

and Guattari [1991] 1994: 117). How then did Deleuze understand science at the time he wrote both *Difference and Repetition*, as well as his book on Leibniz and calculus (Deleuze [1988] 1993)? Given the emphasis placed on ontology in *Difference and Repetition*, but also the fact that discussions of ideas, concepts and functions occur, the question is only complicated by Durie's claim that Deleuze's idea of mathematics is the 'field which has enabled various "functions" to displace a series of traditional philosophical concepts, and, more importantly, the philosophical field from which they emerged' (Durie 2006: 182). According to this reading, Deleuze conceptualises mathematical practice as a gradual replacement of philosophical concepts. However, this reading goes against the grain of Deleuze's clarification that mathematics is not a form of the Platonic ideal (Deleuze [1994] 2011: 226). Further research might be done in order to distinguish the relationship between Deleuze's conceptualisations of philosophy, science and mathematics, beyond the distinctions they are given in *What is Philosophy?*, with regard to the idea of function in the calculus of ideas. For the purposes of the argument in this book, the idea of function is understood as it is used in *Difference and Repetition*.

40. Deleuze develops his understanding of calculus in *Difference and Repetition* in reference to Salomon Maimon (Deleuze [1994] 2011: 220); however, this builds upon his work on Leibniz in *The Fold: Leibniz and the Baroque* (Deleuze and Strauss 1991: esp. Ch. 2).

41. Lawlor summarises the importance of singularities for Deleuze, stating that 'singularities are that which is expressed in an expression or that which is perceived in a perception' (Lawlor 1998: 19). Non-actualised, in the sense that they are the pre-conditions for relations, singularities are not sensible but rather constitute what Deleuze calls the 'transcendental field' of sense in *The Logic of Sense*, where they are also known as 'ideal events' and 'surface effects' (Deleuze [1969] 2004: 22, 99, Deleuze [1994] 2011: 240).

42. Deleuze's concept of potential thus involves the metaphysical claims that all relations partly consist of the conditions to be in relation to any other relation, but that this relation must be made, and this leads to the famous pronouncement at the beginning of *A Thousand Plateaus* that 'the multiple *must be made*' (Deleuze and Guattari 2004b: 7).

43. In the chapter on 'The Image of Thought', Deleuze puts it differently, saying that the name Ideas are 'for those instances which go from sensibility to thought and from thought to order, the limit-or transcendent-object of each faculty' (Deleuze [1994] 2011: 183). Here, Deleuze maintains the importance of time in mentioning 'instances', whilst also emphasising the spatial nature of Ideas. For a discussion of the relation between the two, and the infinite speed of Deleuze and Guattari's virtual as opposed to Kant, see Bell (2015: 28–32).

44. Examples of secondary literature that suggests there is a priority of the virtual over the actual are Badiou 2000, Hallward 2006, Reynolds 2008 and Žižek 2012. Mullarkey's article 'Forget the virtual' (Mullarkey 2004) contains a full discussion of what is at stake in prioritisation of either 'virtualism' or 'actualism'.
45. Meillassoux confirms this in his essay 'Subtraction and Contraction: Deleuze, Immanence, and *Matter and Memory*', wherein he argues that, for Deleuze, there are not so much atoms in the void but, following his Spinozist affirmationism and Leibnizian continuism, 'atoms of void' (Meillassoux 2007b: 92). In terming them such, Meillassoux refers to Deleuze's claim that ideas, when not in relation to others, are at once singularly undetermined but determinable (Deleuze [1994] 2011: 216). Mackay summarises Meillassoux's portrayal of the Deleuzian event then by characterising it as not a 'cut in the fabric of being' (as is the case for Badiou), but 'revealed as a stitch in time' of atoms (or, otherwise, a suture) (Mackay 2007: 14).
46. Patton has noted that, throughout his career, Deleuze aligned himself with certain parts of Epicurean naturalism, and not just in his appreciation of Althusser (Patton 2016: 349). Epicurus studied atomism with Nausiphanes, who had been a student of Democritus, one of the founders of atomist thinking, whose thinking was later summarised and developed by Lucretius in *On the Nature of Things* (Lucretius Carus and Johnson 1963).
47. A theory of what here has been called the social formation was later developed by Deleuze, in conjunction with Guattari, in both volumes of *Capitalism and Schizophrenia*. Here, according to Sibertin-Blanc and in a project that resonates with Althusser's idea of differentially related discourses, the authors argue that 'every geohistorical field articulates relationships of coexistence of *all* of the machinic processes (polarisation, anticipation-warding-off, envelopment, among others) at degrees of intensity and in relationships of subordination that are all the more varied' (Sibertin-Blanc 2016: 122). Sibertin-Blanc's *State and Politics* (2016) is important in drawing out from Deleuze and Guattari's work both the ideas state and politics in a manner that can be thought both transcendentally, empirically and as expressed by a number of different manifestations of the state. As he argues, such a task is important as describing the state is complicated by the difference of each actual state from any ideal definition (2016: 47–9). Sibertin-Blanc highlights how Deleuze and Guattari use essays by both Althusser and Balibar in *Reading Capital* (1970) to inform their project. For example, Althusser's 'The Object of Capital' (1970: 71–198) shows how the relationship between labour and surplus labour includes a number of differently related non-economic social practices which thereby determine the dominance of juridical and political relations in the feudal period. Deleuze and Guattari appropriate this claim in their axiomatic

portrayal of capitalism. According to this, capitalism is the decoding of the value of social practices and their recoding as abstract value which exists as an independent substance, which functions in the manner of Althusser's concept of interpellation (Althusser 1971a, Deleuze and Guattari 2004a: 247–8).

48. Protevi's *Political Affect* uses inspiration from Deleuze and Guattari's philosophy in combination with complexity theory and social physiology to develop a social theory that goes 'above, below and alongside the subject' (Protevi 2009: 4). In doing so, he develops a conceptualisation of a naturalised politics as the product of the 'sense-making of bodies politic', rather than the traditional rational, cognitive subject (2009: 185).

49. Buchanan (2015) provides a discussion of Deleuze and Guattari's concept of assemblage in its various permutations across the secondary literature. It is unclear why Buchanan emphasises the importance of intentional beneficence in assemblages against DeLanda's assemblage theory, but what is at stake in the discussion is otherwise clearly explained.

Chapter 4

Genius and Ethology

Deleuze, morality and ethics

The suture of Deleuze's ontology of structures to Althusser's structural social theory in the previous chapter lays the groundwork for thinking a non-idealist and therefore non-dogmatic practice of resistance. In this chapter, the theory of ethics latent within Deleuze's ontology, as presented in *Difference and Repetition*, will, first, be shown to resonate with the more fully developed ethical theory of J. S. Mill. Whilst there are issues with Mill's philosophy, such as the elitist tone of some of his work, as well as the focus on the individual as opposed to practice (these issues are outlined in more detail below), reading it alongside Deleuze's ontology and Althusser's social theory provides an important contribution to a non-dogmatic practice of resistance. Secondly, and more controversially for Deleuze scholars, Mill's idea of genius will be dramatised alongside Deleuze's idea of ethology as the guiding concept of practices of resistance. Whilst any turn towards Mill's work will no doubt put off some readers of Deleuze, the argument in this chapter does not embrace Mill wholeheartedly, and no claim is made regarding the compatibility of Deleuze's and Mill's philosophies *tout court*. However, Mill's work offers an important aid in thinking tangibly about social situations, something that is notoriously difficult to do with Deleuze's philosophy. Furthermore, the development of Althusser's theory of differentially related social discourses is well supplemented by the ethical components of Mill's work. The idea of genius provides the ethical imperative for individuals navigating the social practices, such as psychoanalysis and ideological interpellation, as described by Althusser. To be clear then, this chapter develops Mill's idea of genius specifically as the function of individuation that best guides practices of resistance, and does not draw upon his moral philosophy to any greater extent.

Continuing from the previous chapter, this chapter will continue the predominant focus upon Deleuze's ontological work, as found in *Difference and Repetition*. Whilst the tone of the dual volume *Capitalism and Schizophrenia* is more overtly political, and hence a theory of ethics can more easily be read into it, a focus on *Difference and Repetition* is necessary for establishing the ontological nature of this ethics.[1] Deleuze himself understands *Difference and Repetition* as an ontological project to develop 'difference' as his primary ideal postulate, and a number of commentators have argued that it is the main source in his oeuvre for outlining his ontological stance (Bryant 2008: 113, Hughes 2009: 52–3, Deleuze [1994] 2011: 365). Further work could be done to establish how the ethically ontological bedrock established in *Difference and Repetition* (as well as its development in *The Logic of Sense*) is expanded upon in Deleuze's later work with Guattari, but that is not the purpose of this chapter. This is not to say that there is no continuity in Deleuze's texts, nor that the contribution he makes to the collaborative work does not import the ideas developed in his solo work. Indeed the secondary literature (as outlined below) predominantly focuses and expands upon Deleuze's work with Guattari, augmenting and branching out concepts found within it such as 'becoming', 'de/reterritorialising', 'war machine', and the 'nomad'. To reiterate the introduction, then, the contribution to the secondary literature that this book makes is a return to considering the ontological nature of Deleuze's ideas and, in particular, how a theory of ethics can be developed from his ontological work.

Even if they are wary of it, that there may be an ethical component to Deleuze's work will be of no surprise to many Deleuze scholars. Bogue, for example, in his book on Deleuze's ethical theory, argues that although 'Deleuze does not develop a formal ethics as a discrete component of his philosophy, there is a sense in which the ethical permeates all his work' (Bogue 2007: 3). A collection of essays suggesting various ethical programmes suitable to Deleuze (and Guattari's) philosophy has been published under *Deleuze and Ethics* (Jun and Smith 2011). Nathan Widder has written on Deleuze and Guattari's theory of ethics as developed according to their concept of the 'body without organs' ('BwO') (Deleuze and Guattari 2004b: 165–85). Where Deleuze and Guattari define the

BwO as the '*field of immanence* of desire' (Deleuze and Guattari 2004b: 170, original emphasis), and thus the ground necessary for the constitution of the individual (or 'desiring machine' in the terminology of A Thousand Plateaus), Widder concludes that 'the construction of a BwO is a matter of pragmatism and strategy in relation to the obstacles we encounter and the relays we establish, and so is dependent on context and contingencies' (Widder 2012: 146). The manner in which, for Deleuze, ethics involves the setting of problems by which the individual approaches the world is brought out by Widder who emphasises the necessity of pragmatism and strategy in ethical thought. Craig Lundy has also argued that Deleuze's philosophy advocates a certain strategical approach, going so far as to say that it also advocates a prudential, precautionary, even a conservative attitude to activism (Lundy 2013: 232, 246).

Furthermore, the secondary literature argues that Deleuze's philosophy does indeed contain the germs of an ethical theory, undeveloped in his writing though it may be, and it is accepted that this theory is ontological (Colebrook 2008: 127). Patton, for example, writes that Deleuze and Guattari's 'ontology of assemblages is also an ethics or an ethology' (Patton 2011: 118). Bogue writes that 'for Deleuze, as well as for Spinoza, ethics is ontology, [and] for this reason his ethics is best conceived of as an immanent ethics' (Bogue 2007: 7). In line with the secondary literature, and the previous chapter's discussion of the ontology of social structures, this chapter assumes the position that Deleuze's theory of ethics is ontological (yet does not make the assumption that this necessitates Deleuze having *an* ontology *per se*).[2]

However, despite the general consensus on the existence of an ontological theory of ethics in Deleuze's work, it is clear that he offers no standard 'normative theory of the basis of [. . .] rights nor of the kinds and degrees of equality or regional autonomy that should prevail' either in his work or in his work with Guattari (Patton 2011: 117). Bergson, for example, who, as was noted above, was a significant influence on Deleuze's theory of life, collaborated with Woodrow Wilson to establish the League of Nations, chaired its International Committee on Intellectual Cooperation, and went on to profoundly influence John Humphrey (the principal drafter of the Universal Declaration of Human Rights) (Lefebvre 2011: V, Lefebvre 2013). As such, Bergson was clearly comfortable working with norms, morality for him being a necessary result of individuals' immersion in society (see Bergson 1935, Ansell-Pearson

2014b). Deleuze, however, made no such foray into what he called 'macropolitics', i.e. the realm of political institutions and social classes, preferring to emphasise the importance of a 'micropolitics' 'that involves subterranean movements of sensibility, affect, and allegiance' (Patton 2011: 116). Rather than a normative political philosophy, then, Patton classifies Deleuze and Guattari's political philosophy as 'formally normative' (2011: 117). For Patton, political institutions are not conceptualised by Deleuze and Guattari individually, or as part of a separate realm of 'the political', but instead 'treated as continuous with the coordination and control of flows of matter and desire in non-state societies governed by the Territorial machine with its systems of alliance and filiation' (2011: 117). It makes no sense, for Deleuze and Guattari, to conceptualise political institutions as metaphysically separate to the realm of either individuals or practices, as that would rely upon the dogmatic use of axioms to uphold the distinction. Instead, Deleuze and Guattari's use of norms are, for Patton, formal, i.e. more akin to components in a structure that also contains ideas and relations of individuals, practices and other institutions. Given the use of the term formal within the context of this book so far might imply a dangerous slide into the dualities characteristic of Badiou's formalist system, it is better to call Deleuze and Guattari's theory a 'structural normativity'.[3]

Nevertheless, the point is clear: ontologically, Deleuze and Guattari conceptualise institutions in the same structuralist terms that they do individuals, classes and other social entities. There is no ideal treaty, social contract or political theology that might render an institution, set of practices or individual sacred or hierarchical in their social ontology. Instead, for Deleuze and Guattari, politics concerns a differentially related multiplicity of elements within different regimes of affect, capture, coordination and control (Deleuze and Guattari 2004a: 240–5, Deleuze and Guattari 2004b: 372, Patton 2011: 118). Having therefore demonstrated the non-ideal nature of Deleuze's philosophy in the preceding chapter, this chapter will develop a non-dogmatic, structurally normative theory of ethics using the social theory of Althusser, Deleuze's ontology, and the ethical work of J. S. Mill.

Yet why limit the remit of argument to ethics, and not to morality more generally? Facing the challenges by those who think poststructuralism incapable of advocating morality more generally, Todd May (1995) has developed just such a theory. Whilst his book (which follows on from his work on the political philosophy of poststructuralist anarchism (May 1994)) is an important gesture in the face of those who claim poststructuralism is unable to think morality, understanding its overriding problem is important for appreciating why a theory of ethics is, conversely, so important.

In his introduction, May notes the criticism faced by poststructuralists (a term he uses to refer predominantly to Foucault, Lyotard and Deleuze) from critical theorists in particular. This criticism follows the recognition that, for poststructuralists, 'power is both creative and pervasive', such that it 'not only represses pre-given objects but also creates objects' (May 1995: 6). Given this observation, May outlines two problems that are generally raised against poststructuralism. Firstly, if objects (as well as social practices and institutions) are all the products of power relations, then 'what is it about the social practice of moral discourse that renders [poststructuralism] capable of passing judgement on other practices?' (1995: 8). Secondly, 'if power is everywhere, then is the result of all resistance not just another set of power relations?' (1995: 8). This is a variation of Hegel's criticism of Hölderlin and Schelling: if differentiation and determination are only graspable via intuition – i.e. there is no differentiation in the world itself – then the world is plunged into 'a night in which, as the saying goes, all cows are black' (Hegel 1998: 9); without recourse to some logic that determines the place of things in the world, there is for Hegel, no ability to distinguish objects as actually differentiating from one another (Badiou [1982] 2013: 1–11).

According to the variation outlined by May, the critics of poststructuralism claim that there must be some position by which critical gestures can be made. Crucially, this position must not itself be susceptible to the power relations that would otherwise seek to incorporate and blunt their critical edge (see Habermas 2015: esp. 282–4). In his answer to this challenge, May is right to argue that the famous Deleuzian maxim – 'we must experiment' (May 1995: 11) – is a necessary prerequisite for resistance but, left simply as that, the maxim is ultimately unsatisfactory. Whilst in keeping with Deleuze's emphasis on creativity and his rejection of macropolitics, such a maxim is not capable of distinguishing between what, following Spinoza, Deleuze calls life-affirming and life-denying forces (May 1991: 29–30, May 1995: 11, Ruddick 2010).[4] In the face of a restrictive, unhealthy or disempowering situation or set of practices, a solution that points simply at alterity might result in even worse conditions: more is needed to guide practices of resistance than simply the command to do otherwise.

The validity of May's theory – a 'multivalue consequentialism' (May 1995: 81) – rests on his assertion that it 'allows for guidance and evaluation of acts, evaluation of situations, and a relative weighing of moral goods' (May 1995: 93). May gives a convincing argument as to why multivalve consequentialism, a form of moral theory that focuses on the judgement of the predictable consequences of acts, is concomitant with the anti-representationalism of poststructural philosophies. What undermines his theory is his distinction between public morality and what he calls the 'aestheticism of individuals'. For May, articulating a position shared by the utilitarian Jeremy Bentham, morals should *only* be public, based around a shared use of language, and not private (May 1995: 43, 94, 137–46). The individual is private, morally neutral, and subject only to an aesthetics of living, i.e. the judgement of whether or not their life is beautiful (May 1995: 140–1). Yet the preference for a public morality opens moral claims up to the uncriticised influence of the dogmatic claims so far discussed in this book. What is to stop dominant social orders and practices determining moral imperatives? It is for precisely this danger that poststructuralist thought has traditionally eschewed moral philosophy in favour of ethics.

Specifically, the reason for preferring a theory of ethics over moral theory is because the latter concerns 'laws, principles, and norms which prescribe how human beings ought and ought not to act', rather than the former which is the study of what is good in particular situations and contexts (Korsgaard and O'Neill 1996: 8–9, Jun 2011: 91). The pre-modern concern for the ethical good life was gradually replaced during the Christian Middle Ages by the moral question 'How should one act?', when the 'classical concept of virtue [was] at first eclipsed but ultimately fused by with the Hebraic concept of *law*' (Jun 2011: 91). Foregrounding a hierarchical Christian order subjugated man under a theocratic regime of the sacred, where 'the good' was practised by the individual but decreed by the church (Foucault 2014: 163–98). Whilst, as Jun shows, modern moral philosophers moved away from theological sources of moral authority towards the secular, this was nevertheless only to constitute and codify moral precedence in the form of profane law: 'an exteriorised and transcendent concept, estranged from ordinary human life' (Jun 2011: 92). Put simply, Christian scholars and the moral philosophers of the modern period prioritised the right over the good. However, Nietzsche's attack on

Christian morality in *On the Genealogy of Morality* and *Beyond Good and Evil* (Nietzsche 2014) divested the idea of God of any rarefied authority from which the good life could be determined and, in doing so, threw the very notion of transcendent normativity into question. With such a history attached to moral thought then, it is hard to see how poststructuralist philosophy (and Deleuzian thought in particular) could have anything to do with it.

Certainly, bearing in mind the discussion of the problematic nature of ideas in the previous chapter, any moral postulate must, for Deleuze, be thought of as located both in the virtual and the actual. Given that the virtual plane forms the transcendental conditions for processes of individuation, and not just one singular idea within it, moral ideas that are simply subtracted from the virtual fall foul of Deleuze's criticism of 'good sense'. Good sense, outlined as one part of the dogmatic image of thought in *Difference and Repetition*, is to attribute normative value to particular empirical objects which are then taken as transcendental conditions for thought (Deleuze [1994] 2011: 169). In order to function within Deleuze's philosophy, however, and avoid the charge of dogmatism, any normative concepts must be open to counter-actualisation. In other words, they must only be actualised from their place in the virtual plane. In terms of the calculus developed in the previous chapter, norms (i.e. normative ideas) are variables that lack a relation to anything else; they are singular and, by themselves, have no function in both senses of the term. However, putting a norm into a series with another variable, the idea of a political practice for example, adds a function to the variable. In this case, it determines a series that might guide the practice of an activist. The point, however, is that this series is potentially differential, contains an infinite number of singularities, and each singularity is capable of determining a series with another relation. Thus, norms are not fixed *a priori* of their articulation within situations, for each situation (or variable) will articulate the norm with a different function, thus determining a new, different series.[5]

According to Deleuze's philosophy of ideas, then, normative ideas are problematic and are not ontologically dogmatic. This is to say that ideas can only be *used*; Williams describes Deleuze's concept of life as 'like a structure of identifiable shapes and concepts, given significance by the sensations, intensities and Ideas that flow through and determine individuals' (Williams 2005: 27).

Therefore, whilst one criteria for structural norms according to a Deleuzian ontology is precisely that ideas must always be conceptualised as part of the virtual structure, the second, fitting with the esteem Deleuze held for Spinoza's work, is that concepts must be practical. Ansell-Pearson puts this succinctly when he argues that, for Deleuze, 'if philosophy has a use it is to be found in the doctrine of the Epicureans, as well as in later thinkers such as Spinoza and Nietzsche, namely, the creation of the free human being and an empirical education in the art of living well' (Ansell-Pearson 2014a: 122). Ansell-Pearson's interest in Bergson's moral philosophy creeps into his reading of Deleuze, and it is not clear that concepts such as 'freedom' (or indeed any particular emphasis on the human being) are as compatible with Deleuze's work as they might be with Bergson's. What is clear, however, in an argument that is borne out in *Proust and Signs* ([1964] 2008), is that the very fact that there is both philosophy and life creates the imperative to think what might be good for life.

Deleuze calls this imperative and the resultant practice both an 'apprenticeship to signs' and, elsewhere, simply 'learning' (Deleuze [1964] 2008: 4), whilst Massumi describes it as an 'ethics of engagement' (Massumi 2015: n.p.). Philosophy, contra Kant's system of the categorical imperative, cannot rely upon a set of concepts designated *a priori* of any given situation because each and every given situation (and its elements) is necessarily different to those before it. Instead, as MacKenzie puts it well, 'Deleuze and Guattari see philosophy as an activity co-extensive with activity in the world itself' (Mackenzie 2004: 68). Situations determine problems which impel individuals (whether collective or singular) to solve them. And yet, as series are counter-actualised to form new series, which contain the persistence of prior series within them, it is clear that solutions to these prior problems will not be sufficient for problems to come. Each situation, comprised of a multiplicity of practices and different even from its repetition of similar previous situations, forms new problems which must be overcome in a never-ending apprenticeship. The good is not defined by the right, a rule, or substance, neither of which would be sufficient to determine what is good in new situations. Rather, the good is defined by the relation of the individual to their situation in series – it is good in practice: 'a practice of concepts, and it must be judged in the light of the other practices with which it interferes' (Deleuze 2005b: 268).

Ethical mediation

Deleuze's mention of judgement hints at his persistent interest in Kant and provides the key to showing the compatibility between Deleuze's ontological theory of ethics and Althusser's social theory.[6] As argued in Chapter 1, for Kant, judgement played a central role in his transcendental idealism. According to him, judgement is performed by the faculty of judgement, a primary component of the rational mind. Whilst judgement is given no fewer than four definitions in the *Critique of Pure Reason* (Kant [1787] 1996: A68/B93; A69/B94; B141; A130–2/B170–2), for the purposes of this discussion it can be defined as the synthesis of either transcendental or pure logic with intuition in order to provide a unified understanding of objects. However, whilst Deleuze's emphatic disagreement with Kant's unified subject has already been shown, as has his emphasis on the process of individuation and a vitalist conceptualisation of life, the question remains: how and why does Deleuze still use the language of judgement?[7]

The most famous discussion of the idea of judgement in Deleuze's work is his essay 'To Have Done with Judgement' (Deleuze 1997: 126–35). Here, Deleuze opposes judgement to combat, whilst reiterating Nietzsche's argument that the condition of judgement is one's debt to a judge (1997: 126, 132). For Deleuze, judgement presupposes a 'coherent moral order' (Uhlmann 1996: 110, Deleuze 1997: 127), under which the individual is eternally subjected and to whom they owe their finitude. The result of judgement, for Deleuze, is the subordination of life to an abstract categorical authority that imposes limits over processes of individuation (Deleuze 1997: 129). In contrast, Deleuze's idea of combat is the practice of 'being done' with judgement (and potentially everything else at the same time) (1997: 132). In being done with everything, combat is 'the process through which a force enriches itself by seizing hold of other forces and joining itself to them in a new ensemble: a becoming' (1997: 132). Becomings resonate more powerfully as a result, not of the cancelling out of contradictory forces, but of the necessity to engage with, circumvent, undermine and subvert them. Whereas the prefix 'counter' is suitable for the practice of opposing a force through judgement, acting 'contra' to force is proper and more productive for combat.

Given Deleuze's criticism of Kant's doctrine of the unified faculties, then, it is perhaps easy to agree with his argument in the essay that the subordination of the individual under authority is necessarily to be resisted. However, Deleuze's opposition between practices of judgement and combat hides the necessary presumption that, in order for judgement to operate, the individual must accept their place under an authority. In other words, the debtor must accept their place in the relationship with a judge. It is not clear, however, why an individual should conceptualise themselves as subservient to a *unified* moral authority, and not, as has been argued, act in relation to a system of structural norms. If Deleuze's development of the conditions of real experience (as opposed to possible experience) shows, not that there aren't conditions, but that these conditions cannot be presupposed (Deleuze [1994] 2011: 81), it also follows that there is authority by which the individual is judged, but that this authority cannot be defined *a priori*. With no coherent, Kantian moral order, the violence done to the individual by the encounter with an event forces the individual to select which norms to prioritise in the knowledge that different norms hold judgement in different situations. Once selected (by the active syntheses), it is these norms which then impose limits upon the individual. In this light, practices of resistance involve combat with ethically selected norms from the virtual structure of ideas to guide processes of individuation. Therefore, if Deleuze's call to have done with judgement is to be consistent with his ontology of ideas, it must be seen as a socio-historical argument rather than an ontological dogma. The relation of his socio-historical claims to his ontology in this regard can be developed by drawing on Deleuze's idea of the mediator.

In his 1985 interview *Mediators*, Deleuze gives three examples where mathematical, scientific and literary concepts are placed in relation with each other. Riemannian spaces (a concept used in differential geometry to measure vectors in three-dimensional space) are placed next to the baker's transformation (a practice in physics that is used to model deterministic chaos), which is in turn placed next to Resnais's film *Je t'aime, je t'aime*. Deleuze points to what he describes as the practical and temporal similarity of the three examples, and claims both that all three are like 'layers that are constantly shifted around' and that 'there are remarkable similarities between scientific creators of functions and cinematic creators of images. And the same goes for philosophical concepts, since there are also concepts of these spaces' (Deleuze 1995: 124–5). Whilst Deleuze is not arguing that each example is doing the same thing, *per se*, Deleuze is making the argument that 'philosophy, art, and science come into relations of mutual resonance and exchange' (Deleuze 1995: 125, Williams 2005: 9). In doing so, he makes a similar claim to that made by Althusser in the first Note, where he argued that regional theories are in differential relation with each other. As was shown in Chapter 2, Althusser's claim was that, whilst each relatively autonomous theory has its own set of practices and functionality that distinguishes itself from the others, each theory produces a lieutenant that articulates the effect of itself in the others (Althusser and Matheron 2003: 49). It is in this manner that regional theories are unified by political practice, as political practice for Althusser involves the movement of an individual through various discourses, the effects engendered on these discourses and the change in the individual as a result of their immersion in them. Deleuze and Althusser are therefore allied in their attempts to think not just the determination of social structures, but the differentiation and relationship between the structures' constitutive discourses.[8]

However, as was argued in Chapter 2, Althusser's philosophy relies on the logic of aleatory reasoning that, without Deleuze's correction, presupposes the void at every moment of philosophical practice to idealise away any persistence of concepts with which an individual might articulate change. Furthermore, under Althusser's articulation of aleatory materialism (as opposed to Deleuze's portrayal) the void removes any means to articulate any kind of agency whatsoever: creativity is subordinated to the void, which resets the clinamen, and abdicates the relation of the new to the randomness of the atoms' fall. As Deleuze puts it, any 'discipline that set out to follow a creative movement coming from outside would itself relinquish any creative role' (Deleuze 1995: 125) and, in order to account for a creative moment from *within* the differentially related layers, Deleuze advocates the idea of the mediator.[9] According to him,

> Mediators are fundamental. Creation's all about mediators. Without them nothing happens. They can be people – for a philosopher, artists or scientists; for a scientist, philosophers or artists – but things too, event plants or animals. [. . .] It's a series. (Deleuze 1995: 125)

Whilst Deleuze does not expand upon his idea of the mediator much beyond this short explanation, further insight into what he means can be gained from the beginning of the interview. Here, Deleuze observes a tendency within philosophy to return to modernist abstractions ('origins, all that sort of thing' (Deleuze 1995: 121), despite the fact that philosophy had already divested itself of such concepts. Thus, Deleuze finds it necessary to develop an idea that accounts for the movement between different practices, and the individual's position within them, without needing to identify when a given practice originated. The idea of the mediator is just this: an idea of how 'to "get into something" instead of being the origin of an effort' (1995: 121) or, put differently, how to understand an individual's differential relation within a given set of practices and structural norms.

However, doesn't the term 'mediator' imply precisely the sort of person who takes a problem and creates solutions in line with the set of given assumptions of, for example, conflict resolution and negotiation? The danger of such a mediator would the assumption that their *a priori* theories would necessarily benefit all within a given situation, rather than a specific group of predominant actors. For an ethical practice of resistance, emphasis must be placed upon critique adopted generally towards any and all hypotheses and suggested courses of action, rather than the hopeful adoption of received wisdom. MacKenzie addresses just such a concern and, in developing what he terms the 'idea of pure critique', distinguishes between the ideas of the critic as creator and the pure critic (MacKenzie 2004: 67). In line with his Deleuzian criticism of transcendental logic, the idea of critique can only be pure, for MacKenzie, if it does not imply the use of other ideas as its transcendental condition – and this includes the idea of the critic itself.

The idea of a critic as creator implies the identity of a creator as the one who criticises, thus generating 'a safe-haven for indifference within the idea of pure critique itself' (2004: 67). In other words, there is a danger that the mediator conceived as such, i.e. as a rational subject, creates change from their judgement of a set of actual, i.e. pre-given, solutions. Given the propensity for philosophical concepts to be associated with 'dangerous fundamentalisms, be they philosophical, political, economic, religious, cultural or whatever' (MacKenzie 2004: XI), it is clear that such a concept of creation might simply be a tool for the reproduction of the dominant mode of production. It is not uncommon, for example, to hear the term 'wealth-creator' used not for workers, but for the share- and stake-holders of companies who benefit from the profits generated by labour power. There seems to be a tension therefore between MacKenzie's Deleuzian argument, Deleuze's implication here that there are in fact creative roles, and indeed his emphatic statement that 'Philosopher's Aren't Reflective, but Creative' (Deleuze 1995: 122).

MacKenzie is, however, well aware of Deleuze's use of the idea of creation, and is not saying that there is no such thing as novelty. Instead, he uses the term to avoid specifically thinking of mediators as those 'forces that reconcile actual oppositions' in order to 'avoid presupposing that the actual is a pre-conceptual given beyond the reach of pure critique' (MacKenzie 2004: 70). Putting this in terms of the syntheses of time explored in the previous chapter, the first idea of mediator as creator would not take into account the first passive synthesis of the living present, where memory is contracted along with elements of sense. Rather, it would imply that individuation could take place with the active syntheses selecting from a formally transcendental memory and that there was nothing new to learn and think. MacKenzie thus suggests another definition of a mediator, that of the 'forces and processes whereby the virtual possibility of always becoming-other is transformed into actually existing otherness' (2004: 70). This second definition opens up the possibility for change to occur that is not pre-figured by any fidelity to the actual. Here, the first passive synthesis is taken seriously in accordance with active syntheses, highlighting the importance that Deleuze places on experimentation. If one knows that s/he cannot simply choose from a range of fixed options, then the emphasis is placed on a revised understanding of creativity.[10] This revised understanding looks to the resonance and exchange that different discourses express when they are brought into encounter with one another. Individuals must, according to Deleuze's idea of the mediator, look for mediators as potential solutions for their problems, always in the knowledge that things might not turn out as they planned. By engaging with mediators, the forces and processes in different social forms and practices, individuals experiment creatively to find the right tools to benefit their cause. This what Deleuze means when he writes in the *Postscript on the Societies of Control*, '[i]t's not a question of worrying or of hoping for the best, but of finding new weapons' (Deleuze 1995: 175).

It is here that Deleuze's use of the idea of judgement can be seen in a new light from that of Kant's. Whereas, for Kant, the faculty of judgement relied upon *a priori* logic to determine the conditions for possible knowledge, and thus determine what is morally right (see Kant 1997), Deleuze's idea of judgement is even more complicated. On the one hand, Deleuze's metaphysical (rather than transcendental) account of memory (i.e. the second passive synthesis) means that his 'transcendental empiricism is that philosophical position which determines the conditions of real rather than possible experience' (Deleuze [1988] 1991: 27, Bryant 2008: 3). Because the conditions of real experience (i.e. ideas and their relations) are virtually determined, and are not a set of principles plucked from the actual, judgement must look elsewhere than the subject, or Kant's transcendental idealism, for the norms by which to judge. On the other hand, Deleuze does not hide these norms away: they are to be found within the beguiling simplicity of Deleuze's virtual/intensive/actual tripartite system.

The structural normativity of Deleuze's philosophy means that all the norms by which to judge are found, not within an actual set of principles, but within the virtual realm of ideas, or the second synthesis of time. However, because, for Deleuze, all practices, ideas and institutions exist as relations within the virtual structure, when the first synthesis relates elements of the second syntheses to actualise, it extends, modifies and changes existing series, as well as determining new ones. Of course, these series may be either the reciprocally determined series that constitute differentially related social practices and discourses, or the directly determined series of opposition, etc. Either way, the individual's place within the differential virtual structure means that the ideas of the latter are those to be used in ethical practices: for the virtual determines the practices, discourses and institutions which mediate processes of individuation in the actual. Whilst it is important to note that the individual, for Deleuze, is only a singular expression belonging to an overdetermining process of individuation, it is nevertheless possible (and necessary for a theory of ethics) to frame a theory of ethics according to it. According to Deleuze's philosophy, then, the individual is judged according to the difference that it makes – for better or for worse – to whichever series is extended, modified or determined. In other words, it is judged by the effect that it has on social relations, practices and institutions, and this judgement takes the form of the reciprocal relationship that changes accordingly. This is what Deleuze and Guattari mean when, in *What is Philosophy?*, they emphasise the importance of being 'worthy of the event' (Deleuze and Guattari [1991] 1994: 160, Kirkeby 2004: 308).

The necessity of ethics

The rest of this chapter will make one claim: when removed of its Enlightenment baggage (i.e. the assumption of a unified subject), Mill's idea of 'genius' is the idea necessary to furnish Deleuze's metaphysical and ethical account of individuation with an imperative. This ethical imperative, when understood as part of Althusser's social theory, can inform a non-dogmatic practice of resistance and this will be outlined in the conclusion. The ethical imperative to be attached to Deleuze's philosophy is Mill's concept of genius.[11] Before substantiating this claim, however, a brief synopsis of the discussion so far is necessary to determine what is needed to make and support this claim. Chapters 1 and 2 discussed the dangers of, first, formally distinguishing between the world and the way of understanding it and, secondly, the necessity to understand thought in relation to the world. It was argued that such dyadic philosophies were unable to account for the relation between the formal and the empirical and thus could not construct adequately conceptualisations of either politics or ethics. In answer to the previous chapters, Chapter 3 demonstrated how Deleuze's philosophy does account for the relation between the formal and the empirical or, in Deleuze's terms, the transcendental and the empirical. The chapter then demonstrated that, for Deleuze, ideas were in differential relation to the relations that (mutually or directly) determined them. One benefit of a relational account of philosophy is that the constitution of the ideas used within the philosophy itself is accounted for; Deleuze's metaphysics are not idealist for the fact that Deleuze can account for the constitution of the ideas, including those that constitute his philosophy. Rather than simply assuming the adequacy of one particular form of expression (such as mathematics) to understand or articulate being, Deleuze shows that the ideas and concepts by which the world is known are constituted immanently with the world as it becomes new (Flaxman 2015: 67).[12] This also applies to the ideas that constitute his philosophy, and there is nothing to say that philosophy might become other than that which Deleuze writes. Rather than this contingency being a reason to avoid Deleuzian philosophy for one that professes more socio-historical permanence (such as Meillassoux's speculative realism), however, it is in fact the opposite. Given that Deleuzian philosophy is one of contingency (even if not necessarily so), it must rely on being practically useful if it is to be anything at all.[13] Thereby, Deleuze provides a philosophy which demonstrates the contingency that is denegated within other philosophical approaches. At the same time, it accounts for its superiority by taking to heart its own contingency and facilitating processes of individuation precisely because of it.

A second benefit is that the three syntheses of time, alongside his reading of Simondon, furnish Deleuze's philosophy with a theory of individuation necessary for an account of ethics (see Deleuze [1994] 2011: 307–9). The philosophies of both Badiou and Deleuze are hesitant to define a programmatic set of moral codes, due to their emphasis on the event. However, Deleuze's philosophy is more suited to articulating an ethical theory, and the reasons for this are twofold. First, Deleuze's philosophy accounts for the relation between ideas and practices, whereas neither Badiou's nor Meillassoux's does.[14] Therefore, ethical acts, according to Deleuze's philosophy, are capable of being judged according to their effects, rather than simply by virtue of their principles. This puts Deleuze broadly in line with consequentialist and utilitarian ethicists such as Bentham, James and John Stuart Mill, although there are important differences between Deleuze's position and Bentham's. Deleuze's philosophy is particularly sympathetic to J. S. Mill's ethics because unlike Bentham, who rejected the consideration of individuals' ideas in moral reasoning in favour of evaluating their practices, Mill argues that actions and character were indissolubly linked (Halliday 1976: 58). It is not simply by 'public' standards that the individual is to be judged for Deleuze and Mill, but by a more complicated relationship between thought and practice that takes ethics into account via what Mill called 'self-regarding conduct'.[15] Secondly, and whilst Badiou does emphasise the specificity of considering different situations in ethical thought, his reliance on an ontological conception of politics reduces this specificity to a situational veneration of a kind of secular onto-theology. This is a translation of the Kantian imperative into the ontological register: Badiou has replaced the categorical imperative with truth procedures, and judgement with forcing. Deleuze, on the other hand, conceptualises the individuals as differentially related with their situation, and their norms are determined by this intensive relation. Judgement then, according to Deleuze, is the effects that new or modified relations have on processes of individuation, that are themselves a result of their participation in situations.

A further clarification can be made to contrast the ethical positions of Deleuze and Badiou: whilst Badiou explicitly emphasises the limited scope of ethics as pertinent only to the consistent individual, the theory to be drawn out from Deleuze's philosophy is not so limited. Contra to the emphasis in this discussion so far placed upon the individual, Bryant, in *The Ethics of the Event*, at first seems to foreground the collective nature of social groups as often discussed by Deleuze (Bryant 2011: 34). This might imply that Deleuze had in mind categorical determinations similar to those in Kant – groups with pre-fixed dynamics would act according to categorical rules that governed the consistency, and hence behaviour, of the groups. Deleuze's philosophy, however, makes no such distinctions and, as Bryant puts it, is 'indifferent' to them, and thus 'able to move fluidly among these determinations in drawing together acts or elements in a collective' (2011: 34). It is important to highlight this 'transversal' nature of Deleuze's philosophy here in order to prepare the way for discussion of Mill.[16] Mill's talk of rational individuals must be read in light of the syntheses of time discussed in the previous chapter as, for Deleuze, processes of individuation apply just as much to people as they do social institutions. One extension of this conclusion that foregrounds the importance of the encounter is that, unlike Badiou, neither Deleuze nor Mill needs to account for why the ethical imperative should be adhered to – or the reason to be ethical in the first place – because of their recognition that processes of individuation are always-already ethical. As processes of individuation actualise their virtual conditions of ideas and their relations, all individuals are necessarily determined in accordance with the selection of ideas in the encounter by the first passive and active syntheses. Therefore, first, *any* practice of resistance that is undertaken – even if one undertakes to do nothing – is necessarily ethical (O'Sullivan 2008: 91, 99).[17] Secondly, *all* processes of individuation, whether this be of the individual or of a social group/institution, are ethical. Deleuze's position in relation to Badiou's theory of ethics will be outlined further below. For now, to clarify the argument within this book against what might be assumed given the position of Mill's *On Liberty* within the liberal tradition of political philosophy: the actualisation of ideas by processes of individuation is not a process particular to individuals any more than it is institutions, or social groups. As an ethical concept, genius applies just as much to individuals, institutions and social groups, and there is no social form that is not implicated in the necessity to act ethically. But what is Mill's idea of genius?

Genius and the art of life

Mill defines the idea of genius in his essay *On Genius* as 'the discovery of new truth' (1977: 330). Put like this, Mill could be mistaken for a simple Enlightenment moralist who advocates triumphs of intellectual virtue as a primary social good above all else. However, this was precisely the theory of knowledge that Mill took issue with, in particularly with regard to the positivist Auguste Comte's 'law of three stages', despite the two authors' friendship (Mill 1977: 851, Rosen 2013: 83, 98–110). Comte argued that the final stage in the evolution of rationality was that of empirical positivism, a stage in which natural laws could be discovered through the use of reason and observation (Comte [1853] 2009: 1–4). Contra Comte, Mill does not define genius as a property of a rarefied class of elite thinkers, historicised as the high point of intellectual thinking. Rather, genius is for Mill something which anyone could acquire, in greater or lesser amounts (Mill 1977: 332) and, in this sense, was more akin to a metaphysical property of individuals.[18] Furthermore, it is an idea within a particular branch of science: Mill's idea of genius is the idea to which the science of ethology should aim at, where ethology is defined as 'the science which corresponds to the art of education; in the widest sense of the term, including the formation of national or collective character as well as the individual' (Mill 1977: 869).

Rosen's example of ethology's particular relationship with education is useful in understanding the idea of genius in context (Rosen 2013: 75). Whereas education is, for Mill, an art, he nevertheless specifies that 'the grounds, then, of every rule of art, are to be found in the theorems of science' (Mill 1977: 947). Whilst this was reflective of philosophers and scientists in various disciplines during the Enlightenment (Rosen 2013: 77), scientific practice – i.e. the development of knowledge by which to function in the world – should not be confused with the dominant mode of doing so: empiricism. Whilst the empirical methodology has been criticised throughout this book (where it has not been wedded to Deleuze's concern for the transcendental), the role of science as a methodology to facilitate living in the world should not be underemphasised.[19] Indeed, both Althusser and Deleuze advocate the necessity for scientific practice, as has already been shown.[20] Mill is also critical, albeit not to the same extent as Deleuze and Althusser, of the empirical method and is more interested in processes that determine contingent empirical laws. As he puts it in the *Logic*, 'the really scientific truths, then, are not these empirical laws, but the causal laws which explain them' (Mill 1977: 862).

Ethology, for Mill, was thus an extension of the critique of Bentham's limited psychology to social theory and 'stood logically between psychology and social science, preventing empirically based psychological principles from forming the basis of social science' (Rosen 2013: 74). Disagreeing with the thesis that humans shared universal psychological principles (an argument that developed from Aristotelian logic and was expressed at the time most prominently by Locke's 1841 *Essay Concerning Human Understanding*), Mill's science of ethology was to develop an (ever-changing) set of concepts with which to understand how individuals and societies might maximise their ability to better themselves. The crucial distinction between Mill and the assumption that in order to better oneself one must be able to imagine their *best* self is that, for Mill, the norms according to which the individual lives are determined by the situation one is in, and not a teleological conception of the self. This understanding resonates closely with that of Deleuze, who identifies ethology as the group of studies which define 'bodies, animals, or humans by the affects they are capable of' (Deleuze 1988b: 125). Because Mill recognised that both individuals and their social circumstances were more mutable than predictably stable, Mill's emphasis on science was that it provided the grounds by which individuals could discover how they could be the happiest.

This science is summed up in Mill's Greatest Happiness Principle (GHP), as presented in *Utilitarianism*, which 'holds that actions are right in proportion as they tend to promote happiness, wrong as they tend to produce the reverse of happiness. By happiness is intended pleasure, and the absence of pain; by unhappiness, pain, and the privation of pleasure' (Mill 1977: 210). This principle could be read as if it advocated happiness as an end in itself, thus placing Mill in line with Benthamite utilitarianism in advocating moral judgement based upon an individual's public or social conduct (Halliday 1976: 58).[21] However, Mill saw Bentham's version of utilitarianism as needlessly judgemental, being suitable only for the philosophical guidance of legislative policy development, or legal reform at best (1976: 61). Mill's concept of happiness, by contrast, is not an evaluative concept by which to judge the individual, and he did not subscribe to the Benthamite hedonic calculus (Quinton 1989: 63).[22]

Instead, Mill was concerned more with 'mental and emotional culture, on the ability to pursue virtue for its own sake and on the disinterested growth of concern for others' (1989: 63). It makes no sense, as Mill argues in *On Genius*, for individuals to be judged on outcomes of one's actions if those same individuals have not been allowed to develop their ability to make ethical decisions for themselves: how can one be judged morally for dutifully following moral laws by the same people that instruct them to do so? As Haddock clarifies, it was important for Mill 'that an active citizenry should emerge, rather than a passive but contented populace' (Haddock 2008: 184). Happiness and pain then do not indicate individuals' universal *telos* for Mill, but rather two guiding principles by which individuals can judge the best course of action in any one situation, as that situation pertains to them.[23] The GHP should be seen, not as a judgement upon individuals' actions, but as a functional maxim for practical reason. Individuals, as Mill elaborates in *Utilitarianism*, have an ethical duty to cultivate themselves, not as an end in itself *qua* Bentham's moralistic philosophy, but in order to be the best that they can be in any given situation according to what is best for them in that situation. Thus, contra to the traditional view of Mill as an overbearing moralist, the emphasis upon individual self-improvement in Mill's utilitarianism leads Halliday to conclude that 'Mill was both a romantic and a utilitarian, and he remains so throughout his life' (Halliday 1976: 64). Mill's romanticism lies in his belief that individuals can better themselves, not according to transcendental moral categories (*qua* Kant or Bentham), but according to their ability to develop themselves beyond their immediate means, situation and (perhaps most importantly) ability to think the truth of their current situation. In light of Mill's romantic utilitarianism, contrasted against Bentham's more austere theory, genius, as the ability to discover a new truth, loses its moralistic undertones and takes on an important ethical pragmatism. First, in not using the term as a status symbol often considered to belong to ivory tower philosophers, by 'genius' Mill means 'nothing but a mind with capacity to know' (Mill 1977: 334). There is no sense that genius is, for Mill, a level which the individual can claim to have reached and thus compare themselves to others. Secondly, neither is there a discipline that might *necessarily* afford an individual a higher level of genius than another. Thirdly, genius, for Mill, cannot arrive from the discovery of truths already known passed on 'vicariously', through instruction or from mimicry (Mill 1977: 331). Mill makes a point to single out mathematics as an axiom from which discoveries can be deduced but not discovered; mathematicians cannot, for Mill, be geniuses unless they develop a new function/concept aside from the dominant axiomatic. Mill does accept that genius can be involved in learning from man-made objects, stating that genius is involved in the comprehension, without which a great work can only be 'felt' (1977: 333).[24]

The point of Mill's idea of genius, however, is that it is a function that all individuals can express, which facilitates individuals developing both themselves to the best of their ability and an awareness sensitive to social challenges that might occur (Mill 1977: 339, Mill [1859] 2002: 28, 47–9). If individuals are to be the best that they can be within any given situation, it follows for Mill that they must expand their knowledge of the available courses of action to the maximum possible extent. For this reason, genius is not a regulative dogma by which to comparatively appraise an individual's course of action. Rather, genius is an *impetus*, a necessary corollary to ethical action that demands of individuals that their actions are oriented to actively develop themselves. Whilst judgement only manifests as the mutually reciprocal relation between processes of individual and mediators, nevertheless it is essential for mediators to be chosen. Thus, genius is the ethical imperative responsible for ensuring that the individual's thought is not dulled or stultified, as Mill and Deleuze are keen to guard against.

Returning to the art of education, then, the foundation of art upon science is not, for Mill, motivated by a necessity to revive a mechanical theory of the passions, such as that found in Hobbes (see Hobbes [1651] 1996: Ch. 1). In order to guide individual (i.e. persons' or social institutions') progress, Mill does not attempt to secure an understanding of the subject which could then function as a transcendental guarantor for correct moral practice; there is no idea of the universal or generic human in Mill's thought that would underpin a judgement of the right over the good. De Beauvoir describes this form of morality in *The Ethics of Ambiguity*, stating that,

> [w]e may call this attitude aesthetic because the one who adopts it claims to have no other relation with the world than that of detached contemplation; outside of time and far from men, he faces history, which he thinks he does not belong to, like a pure beholding; this impersonal version equalises all situations; it apprehends them only in the indifference of their differences; it excludes any preference. (De Beauvoir 2011: 68)

For de Beauvoir, the aesthetic attitude constitutes a 'withdrawal' from the present and a 'pure contemplation' (de Beauvoir 2011: 69–70). Rather than considering the effects of their action in relation to a definite situation, aesthetes simply act on what they perceive is 'correct'. Deleuze describes this phenomenon as either the 'dogmatic, orthodox or moral image' of thought, characterising it as the philosophical position whereby 'thought has an affinity with the true; it formally possesses the true and materially wants the true' (Deleuze [1994] 2011: 167).[25] Mill maintained a differentiation in thought, recognising that science was the classification of causes, whereas art was the classification of effects (Halliday 1976: 86). Whilst, for Mill, the rules of art presuppose the truths of science, nevertheless science cannot give the individual a rulebook for practice because it lacks the ability to think the effects of action (1976: 77). It is only through artistic practice that individuals can develop themselves, not through passive aesthetic contemplation, but by active engagement in situations. Whether this be the art of education, or otherwise in the 'Art of Life' as Mill developed in the *Logic* (1976: 60–1), ethology develops rules for action that are based upon laws developed by science, and which are then applied to the social. As Mill wrote in the *Logic*:

> The art proposes to itself an end to be attained, defines the end, and hands it over to the science. The science receives it, considers it as a phenomenon or effect to be studied, and having investigated its causes and conditions, sends it back to art with a theorem of the combinations of circumstances by which it could be produced. Art then examines these combinations of circumstances, and according as any of them are or are not in human power, pronounces the end attainable or not. The only one of the premises, therefore, which Art supplies, is the original major premise, which asserts that the attainment of the given end is desirable. Science then lends to Art the proposition (obtained by a series of inductions or of deductions) that the performance of certain actions will attain the end. From these premises Art concludes that the performance of these actions is desirable, and finding it also practicable, converts the theorem into a rule or precept. (Mill 1977: 944–5)

The repetition of genius

Deleuze, whilst not subordinating art under science, shares with Mill an understanding of art that means artistic practice is needed to break through otherwise homogenising social practices. Whilst

Mill talks of the 'collective mediocrity' of men (meaning groups of people without the ability to value things – such as their own development – who therefore conform to authority) (Mill [1859] 2002: 55), Deleuze writes that the 'more our daily life appears standardised, stereotyped and subject to an accelerated reproduction of objects of consumption, the more art must be injected into it in order to extract from it that little difference which plays simultaneously between other levels of repetition' (Deleuze [1994] 2011: 365). Indeed, throughout Deleuze's oeuvre, he is concerned that thought is subject to pressures that enforce its constancy and mute its affective potential (May 1991: 30). In *Proust and Signs*, Deleuze introduces the concept of 'profundity' to signify the richness of a practices' signs, and as a term by which to understand the affectivity of various practices on the individual. Deleuze lists five types of signs that make up 'different worlds, worldly signs, empty signs, deceptive signs of love, sensuous material signs, and lastly the essential signs of art (which transform others)' (Deleuze [1964] 2008: 14).[26] It seems clear, then, that both Mill and Deleuze are concerned with exploring how practices of individuation are related to other individuals and practices that can either intensify their own process of individuation or abate them.[27] The idea of genius provides, as a response to technologies and practices that attempt to stifle creativity – and thus the ability of the individual to individuate themselves as profoundly as they otherwise might – the imperative by which to guard against such efforts.

This can be made clear by contrast with Badiou's theory of ethics: Mill's idea of genius is the impetus necessary for overcoming Badiou's radical differentiation between thought and extension. As discussed in Chapter 1, Badiou appropriates Spinoza's concept of 'perseverance in Being', in order to claim that the individual claims fidelity to the truth event in order to become a militant of the truth procedure. However, Žižek shows the circularity of Badiou's argument, in that it is only by virtue of an already subjectively engaged individual (i.e. some-one who is already a militant) that an individual can pay fidelity to a truth procedure. The radical disjunction between truth and *doxa* within Badiou's meta-ontology prohibits Badiou from explaining adequately how and why individuals might pay fidelity, or indeed be impelled to become a militant in the first place. Mill's ethology, however, and the idea of genius, provide the key to understanding what motivates the individual to pay fidelity to a particular truth procedure, but only through making the idea of the truth procedure profane. Through investigating and synthesising the best available courses of action in a presented situation, ethology provides a range of possible options for the individual to actualise as their art of life. Of course, for Badiou, the 'true' course of action is not a cognitively determined pathway *per se*, but is determined by a militant's fidelity to a truth event that is forced through subsequent situations. This might seem to cause a problem for ethology because it requires ethology to conceptualise ethical practices that do not involve rational/subjective decision-making. However, ethology, or the science of the causes of individual practice, does not limit what determines the options that individuals have to choose from for their artistic practice; there is no reason as to why fidelity to an event *should not* be a preferable course of action, provided that there is no necessary rarefication of this one event to a higher level, or expression, of Being than any other event.

In fact, it might just be that fidelity to an event is precisely what is in the individual's best interest – i.e. it is ethically good for the individual – if that fidelity also affords the individual the possibility of knowing how to maximise their ability to positively individuate in the future to come. Furthermore, under some conditions, it might be the case that it is appropriate to force the consequences of an event through subsequent circumstances. And yet, given Deleuze's repudiation of dogmatic concepts and the image of thought, neither fidelity nor forcing can be thought of as goods in themselves, *a priori* of the process of individuation. Deleuze explicitly warns against the dangers of such 'aristocratic' thought, stating that 'it is not a question of saying what few think and knowing what it means to think' (Deleuze [1994] 2011: 165). If ethics is a necessary function within the process of individuation – i.e. the first passive and active syntheses select ideas and relations from the second syntheses to individuate, and this implies the necessity of choosing what is best in a given situation – then ideas must be selected ethically according to the principle of genius. This is what Deleuze means when, from his criticism of aristocratic thought, he calls for 'someone – if only one – with the necessary modesty not managing to know what everybody knows, and modestly denying what everybody is supposed to recognise' ([1994] 2011: 165). That said, it is possible, yet perhaps unlikely, that a particular set of ideas to be forced fulfils the imperative to experiment that Deleuze implores. Whilst neither the principle of genius, nor Deleuze's encouragement to experiment, necessarily implies that a certain position shouldn't be pursued through changing circumstances, the ramification that, for Deleuze, each new situation is a different variation does imply that the militant should reconsider the ethical course of action.

Mediated genius

If there is one thing necessary to shore up an account of genius as the ethical imperative in Deleuze's thought, it is to account for the relation between genius and mediation in terms of the ontology of individuation as developed in the previous chapter. In particular, there is a danger in discussing Mill's philosophy that one lapses back into subject-orientated concepts and the idealism of rational choice theory. This would be to fall back into the problem whereby 'mediators [become] surreptitious creators' (MacKenzie 2004: 69). Secondly, there is a danger when discussing the importance of genius that it leads the individual to develop knowledge for the sake of knowledge, or to do things for the sake of being active. This second concern can be dealt with simply: there is indeed a danger of the knowledge developed by ethology being useless, but only if use is measured by what is practised by the individual. To put this in terms of the syntheses of time discussed in the previous chapter: the second synthesis of time constitutes memory as the pure past, and thus forms the transcendental conditions for individuation (Hughes 2009: 106–7). Given that, as has been argued, expanding the possibility to learn constitutes the Deleuzian ethical imperative, it might stand to reason that simply learning all that is possible about the world, or exploring all there is to explore, is good for the individual. However, this conclusion would ignore the fact that signs 'force' processes of individuation, as well as the relations that processes of individuation have with the virtual structure. In other words, because individuals are only judged according to Deleuze's consequentialist logic, i.e. based on the effect they have upon themselves, other individuals, practices and institutions, knowledge and activity mean nothing by themselves. It is only when knowledge is used in order to ask and address interesting or useful questions – i.e., when it makes a difference (MacKenzie 2004: 91) – that it becomes good. Braidotti confirms this when she writes elaborately that 'the point of fusion between the self and his/her habitat, the cosmos as a whole [. . .] marks the point of evanescence of the self and its replacement by a living nexus of multiple interconnections that empower not the self, but the collective; not identity, but affirmative subjectivity; not consciousness, but affir mative interconnections' (Braidotti 2006: 154). In short, ethology necessitates a form of the multi-value consequentialism that May develops in *The Moral Theory of Poststructuralism* (1995), but one that does not raise normative judgement to the moral level. Individuals undertake ethical practices based upon their affective embodiment in a situation and their prioritisation of the multiple effects they may have upon themselves and their surroundings.[28]

The first concern requires a more elaborate response, and one that will prove unsatisfactory when looking for quick and easy practices of resistance. MacKenzie warns of the danger that the idea of mediators brings, i.e. the notion of creativity whereby a mediator chooses the most preferable from an actually-existing set of options. Of course, this is not really creation at all, because it implies creation has already happened. As MacKenzie puts it, once a 'difference is *made* the logic of pure difference is surpassed by a logic of identity-in-difference' (MacKenzie 2004: 71). In other words, possibilities do not *actually* exist because, in order for them to do so, they would have to already have been subject to a process of individuation. The possibility would be actual, not possible, and would in fact be identifiable as the course of action *having already been* taken. All this implies that there is a danger in presuming that the best course of action is the one that is already available to the individual or, as MacKenzie puts it, if 'the real is given as that which has occurred in the past, then the possible is that which merely confirms the real as a given totality' (MacKenzie 2004: 75).

Yet there is nothing in either Mill's or Deleuze's ideas of ethology that would hint at an underlying presumption that all that could be done is set out in memory. Rather, Mill's idea of genius acknowledges that there is a constant necessity to learn new ways to understand and act in a world in which every new situation presents different challenges to preconceived knowledge. Hence Mill's emphasis on originality: '[t]he man of the greatest philosophic genius does no more than this, evinces no higher faculty; whoever thinks at all, thinks to that extent, originally' (Mill 1977: 332), whilst Deleuze refutes such a presumption in various different ways across *Difference and Repetition*. MacKenzie's account of a pure critique draws on Deleuze's refutation of the problem, and renders it as follows:

> The problem with this understanding of creativity is that it is self-contradictory. If the real is given as that which has occurred in the past, then the possible is that which merely confirms the real as a given totality. In short, there would be no possibility of true novelty or creativity, as these would be reduced to mere repetitions of the same reality that is already assumed as historically given for all time. (MacKenzie 2004: 75)[29]

It is clear that, whilst the the past has to be taken as history – indeed this is the task of the second synthesis – nevertheless this history must be understood as the real, virtual *conditions* of individuation and not possibility. As Deleuze enigmatically puts it, '[t]he possible has no reality (although it may have an actuality); conversely, the virtual is not actual, but *as such possesses a reality*' (Deleuze [1988] 1991: 96). Differential calculus, as discussed in the previous chapter, can be returned to in order to address the temptation to revert back to the idea of a creator.

The virtual, for Deleuze, is the differential structure of singular Ideas in a relation of potentiality to one another. Processes of individuation are expressed following the reciprocal determination of differential relations (dx/dy), where a series is individuated according to a functional variation in a relation, $y = f(x)$. As explained in the previous chapter, the abscissa dx is populated by an infinite number of singular points which are the as-yet undetermined, yet perfectly determinable, points for new series.[30] So, whilst some series will be determined and individuated passively, forming what Deleuze calls in another register the second, passive synthesis of time, there are also singular points within this synthesis which determine the further potential for individuation (Deleuze [1994] 2011: 130). These points are what Deleuze calls the extensive differences of identity (as opposed to intensive differences) and are defined as such by the active syntheses which use them to determine linear relations (Bell 2015: 32). This explains the reality of the virtual: the infinite number of singular points upon the abscissa – whether it is differential or directly determined – are not actualised, but do nevertheless form the conditions of determination.[31] Both directly determined and differentially determined points – anywhere along the axis – are available for individuation, thus explaining the importance of experimentation for Deleuze. Put simply, whilst Ideas can always be looked to in order to provide guidance for future action, Deleuze shows how Ideas are contingent upon relations that happened in a past present, a present that has itself been synthesised in the past (Deleuze [1988] 1991: 98).

There are therefore three possibilities for resistance in the face of a real situation: hold on to an idea and actualise it in the new situation (always in the understanding that no course of action will repeat identically the next time); throw caution to the wind and create a new series by ignoring (to the best of one's ability) the lessons that the past can teach; or tactically experiment with what one already knows. The principle of genius impels the individual to expand the range of Ideas that they may experiment with, on the understanding that this knowledge comes about from original, creative practice in the world (Mill 1977: 336). This does not mean that, by reading enough books or doing enough things, an individual could simply know everything there is to know, because this presumes that nothing else in the world would change but them. However, ethology does teach the individual to cautiously and pragmatically experiment in the face of different situations, tactically choosing options that supplement and liberate the individual from that which attempts to homogenise and confine them.[32]

Notes

1. Deleuze himself said that *Anti-Oedipus* was 'from beginning to end a book of political philosophy' (Deleuze 1995: 170). This is not to say that *Difference and Repetition* is not also explicitly political in parts, and that the received wisdom arguing that Deleuze's pre-Guattari works were not political (see for example Žižek (2012b: 18)) is 'patently untrue' (Buchanan and Thoburn 2008: 1). See Deleuze ([1994] 2011: 64, 337, 382) for textual examples.
2. Contra to claims made by authors within the current ontological turn in anthropology, for whom there are many ontologies that are specific to different regions and cultures, the argument in this book makes no such determining claims (see for example Harris and Robb 2012, Descola 2013, Swenson 2015). Instead, and in line with the argumentation regarding dyads throughout Chapter 2, to posit an ontology would thus also posit that there is also that which ontology could not account for. Instead, it is more fitting to refer to ethics as ontological, pertaining to one or more ontologies which are always-already being constructed or, in Althusser's terms, ontological practice. It is often necessary to talk of an author's ontology for the sake of argument, and for lack of better terminology, but the term is used herein with this understanding.
3. As is the case with Badiou's mathematical ontology, Deleuze defines formal differences as those grounded 'in the object' and able to be referred back to an originary principle or subject (Deleuze [1994] 2011: 49). In accordance with the ontology developed within this book, the term 'structural normativity' is preferred because it does not imply an originary ground or point of reference. Structures are comprised by different modes of individuation that are themselves series of singularities, and difference is prioritised over identity

([1994] 2011: 49). The idea of structure opens the path to disparate and divergent processes of individuation, in differentially related modes, without presuming a determinant, totalising authority.

4. See also Ansell-Pearson (2014) for a discussion of Deleuze's reading of Epicurean naturalism. According to Ansell-Pearson, Deleuze was heavily influenced by Epicurus, who defined 'philosophy as a "rule of life"' (Lucretius Carus and Johnson 1963: V: 10, Ansell-Pearson 2014a: 122), demonstrating the latter's commitment to developing a therapeutic treatment of life. Ansell-Pearson accounts for Deleuze's ethics in terms of how individuals' decisions affect their own health and happiness. The theory of ethics in this chapter is not intended to run counter to Ansell-Pearson's, but simply to develop connections with the ontological aspect of Deleuze's philosophy.
5. See Smith (2008) for further discussion on how Deleuze uses calculus as a model for thought and, in particular, detail on Deleuze's use of the terms 'new' and 'possible'.
6. MacKenzie argues that it is not that Deleuze (or Deleuze and Guattari's work) is specifically Kantian, merely that all three authors are situated within the same critical terrain. This is to say that all four authors (MacKenzie included) share the task of solving the problem, 'how can we critique without this idea of criticism being susceptible to itself?' (MacKenzie 2004: XVIII). Hughes however, in his reader of *Difference and Repetition*, places great emphasis on Deleuze's fascination with Kant, going so far as to say that *Difference and Repetition* is formally modelled after the first *Critique* (Hughes 2009: 3).
7. In *Negotiations*, Deleuze states that '[e]verything I've written is vitalistic, at least I hope it is . . .' (Deleuze 1995: 143).
8. A 2012 conference in London entitled 'Deleuze, Philosophy, Transdisciplinarity' was organised, and a special issue of *Deleuze Studies* published, in order to discuss the ramifications of Deleuze's claim on the blurb of the French edition of *Difference and Repetition* that '[p]hilosophy is not interdisciplinary' (Collett *et al.* 2013: 157). The organisers point to Deleuze and Guattari's *What is Philosophy?* ([1991] 1994) because it 'puts forth a unique take on transdisciplinarity, [and] because it advocates a relation between disciplines that is more than a simple separation' (Collett *et al.* 2013: 160).
9. Massumi translates the original French into 'intercessor' (Massumi 2002: 255), but this definition is not used here on account of the implication that an intercessor might intervene on someone else's behalf. The English term 'mediator' does not necessarily imply working for another.
10. Deleuze does of course warn against the assumption that mediators are only necessarily humans, and the emphasis placed upon people here is made to bring discussion in line with the book's discussion of political resistance more generally. This does not imply that plants,

animals, buildings or institutions cannot also be mediators but, for the purposes of this discussion of resistance, it is necessary to foreground the socio-political primacy of individuals.

11. The growing number of texts now written on Deleuze's conceptualisation of ethics in relation to his work on both Spinoza and Nietzsche begs the question: why develop his theory of ethics in relation to Mill, as opposed to Spinoza or Nietzsche? There are (at least) three reasons for doing so. First, the argument in this chapter is not intended to run counter to the existing literature and, rather, it is hoped that it may resonate with existing work to create new, productive lines of flight with existing arguments. Secondly, in line with Deleuze's distaste for the dogmatic adherence to tradition within the history of ideas, Deleuze's philosophy welcomes the dramatisation of diverse concepts in order to address problems. The dramatisation of the idea of genius outside the confines of its Enlightenment context is wholly in line with how Deleuze argued one should practice philosophy. Thirdly, more importantly, and as was argued in the introduction, an encounter with Mill's philosophy supplements Deleuze's ontology with a register with which to think social structures. Whilst the two volumes of *Capitalism and Schizophrenia* are explicitly works of political philosophy, their relations to ontology are neither as explicit, nor clear. The encounter with Mill's idea of genius therefore has the aim of furnishing Deleuze's ontological work within *Difference and Repetition* with an explicitly political register to inform practices of resistance.

12. The importance of novelty in thought runs through all of Deleuze's texts, including those he co-authored with Guattari. A clear example of this theme is in Deleuze and Guattari's portrayal of discussion in *What is Philosophy?* where they state that '[t]he best one can say about discussions is that they take things no farther, since the participants never talk about the same thing. Of what concern is it to philosophy that someone has such a view, and thinks this or that, if the problems at stake are not stated?' ([1991] 1994: 28). Here, Deleuze and Guattari highlight the importance of addressing a well-stated problem (i.e. not either type of false problem – 'nonexistent' or 'badly stated' – that Deleuze sees highlighted in Bergson (Deleuze [1988] 1991: 17–21), rather than simply discussing an issue. Rather than simply setting 'empty generalisations against one another' (Deleuze and Guattari [1991] 1994: 29), they argue that concepts must be created in order to solve problems, always in the knowledge that each concept is inherently problematic and will determine new problems to be addressed. See also Deleuze's discussion with Foucault, *Intellectuals and Power*, where the two describe philosophy as a 'relay race' with practice (Foucault and Deleuze 1980).

13. In emphasising the disruptive effect of the sign upon thought – their 'violence' in Deleuze's terms (Deleuze [1964] 2008: 16) – Deleuze follows Dewey to show that one significant task of philosophy is to account for a changing world in a 'pragmatic approach to learning' (Williams 2015: 47). Although ontologies and categories (i.e. concepts) can be adequate for good, healthy individuation, new concepts must be created in order to accommodate new signs and metaphysically precarious situations. If there is a theory of truth in Deleuze's philosophy, then, it would not be one to designate something as true, in the manner of traditional accounts of truth. Rather, it 'might be thought of as a functional component of the sense that understands the world, which appropriates and creates different structures as necessary' (Henry 2016: 12).
14. Badiou introduces the concept of 'forcing' in Being and Event to account for the relation, and develops this in *Logics of Worlds* (2009). Nevertheless, as has already been established, Badiou only succeeds in naming the relation, and not accounting for how it determines either the empirical from the formal, or vice versa. Deleuze's philosophy is of benefit over Badiou's because it can account for the determination of both via their relation.
15. Haddock is correct to doubt whether the distinction between self-regarding and other-regarding actions can be maintained given 'our complex involvement with other people' (Haddock 2008: 179). However, the analytic distinction between the two seems beside the point for Mill, who, as Haddock himself recognises, thinks that 'if we want to do the best we can for ourselves, then we have to retain an open mind. And we should extend the same thought to anyone we may encounter in our society' (Haddock 2008: 180). In other words, Mill's distinction between self- and other-regarding conduct can be read not as a dogmatic distinction, used to engender a programmatic moral theory, but as an argumentative tool used to problematise government intervention that is justified by a reductive measure of public utility (2008: 179). Mill's point is that neither self- nor other-regarding conduct can be objectively measured, nor judged independently of the other, and doing so delegitimises authorities who claim to do so. See also Ten (1980: 10–49) for a literature review and full discussion of the idea of self-regarding conduct.
16. For a full discussion on the transversal nature of Deleuze's thought, see Williams (2005: esp. Ch. 2).
17. This is not to say that all ethical practices necessitate practices of resistance, and there is no argument in this chapter that implies the moral superiority of practices of resistance over other practices. Whilst it might be unethical for one person not to resist, this does not imply that somebody *else* can be disparaged for not resisting.

Indeed it might be the case that resistance is, in some situations, unethical itself. What is ethical for one individual is not necessarily the case for another, and no argument is being made to justify comparison between two people's moral standing.

18. Mill was openly hostile to metaphysics, praising Bentham for his 'systematic opposition to the explanation of phenomena by ridiculous metaphysical entities', and preferred instead to talk of a deductive form of psychology (Mill 1977: 489, Grover 1992: 102, 108–9). Nevertheless, in order to make deductive arguments from psychology (the methodology of which is predominantly inductive), Mill had to make some ontological claims about the properties of individuals that were not subject to the empirical method. As Robson clarifies, he 'seldom ventures into the hazy land between ontology and physiology, but when he does, it is clear that he sees the desire for liberty as a basic element in the human constitution' (Robson 1968: 128, ff. 132).

19. Heidegger's term 'being-in-the-world', or 'Dasein' is an idea, inherited from Hegel, that describes the condition by which an individual can take up a 'relationship' with the world (Heidegger [1953] 2010: 12: 84). Deleuze, on the other hand, does not conceptualise such a duality between Being (*Dasein*) and its phenomenological presentation (*es gibt*), but emphasises the role of vitalist processes of individuation both in and with life.

20. See Stengers (2011) for a discussion of the importance of science in the history of materialist philosophy.

21. Bentham's priority is shown in his statement that '[t]he greatest happiness of all those whose interest is in question is the right and proper, and the only right and proper and universally desirable, end of human action' (Bentham [1823] 1948: 125). For Bentham, law should be primarily concerned with the restriction of harmful acts and the development of happiness is a private matter (Quinton 1989: 29).

22. This was a sevenfold list of dimensions that Bentham developed to allow the measurement and comparison of pleasures and pains. The dimensions are intensity, duration, certainty, propinquity, fecundity, purity and extent. See Quinton (1989: 33–4) for an overview of the calculus and its place in Bentham's moral philosophy.

23. With perhaps too personal a list, Quinton clarifies the nature of pleasure in Mill's philosophy as primary to the objects which gratify it: '[w]hat is desired is always some specific thing: a glass of wine, a good-looking woman, a peerage. The achievement of these objects is no doubt attended with pleasure, but it is the objects and not the pleasure that is desired' (Quinton 1989: 61). Mill's concept of desire therefore is directly in line with Deleuze's conceptualisation, as Quinton confirms by summarising that '[p]leasure, one might say,

is not a stuff but a relation' (1989: 61). Mill remains an Enlightenment thinker of the rational individual, yet identifies desire as a primary *drive* of rationality. Deleuze and Guattari begin *Anti-Oedipus* by defining desire as the primary productive force of social (and therefore also singular, if not individual) 'machines' (Deleuze and Guattari 2004a: 1–57). Despite the different registers in which they argue, Mill and Deleuze are nevertheless similar in this respect, given Deleuze's insistence that individuals' drives 'never exist in a free and unbound state, [and that] nor are they ever merely individual; they are always arranged and assembled by the social formation in which we find ourselves' (Smith 2007: 71). Smith's article 'Deleuze and the Question of Desire' (2007) has an excellent account of the role that desire plays in an immanent theory of ethics.
24. Mill makes an offhand remark which creates a strange and entirely undeveloped distinction in suggesting that '*conceptive*' genius is sometimes a 'higher faculty than *creative*' (Mill 1977: 333).
25. Mill draws on a similar point when he praises the German astronomer Herschel for doing the contrary, and appreciating the necessity of understanding the individual's practice within a given situation. For Mill, Herschel demonstrates 'the superiority of science over empiricism under the name of common sense – the advantage of systematic investigation, and higher general cultivation of the intellect' (Mill 1831: 179).
26. In *Difference and Repetition*, the most profound signs of *Proust and Signs*, those of art, are known as intensity. See Massumi (1995) for a description of how intensity, also known as affect, is tempered by its differential relationship with other signs or, as Massumi puts it, structure. As he puts it in one example, '[l]anguage, though headstrong, is not simply in opposition to intensity. It would seem to function differentially in relation to it' (1995: 86). Deleuze does not wish to set up any opposition of one sign to another because 'each type of sign has its particular line, it participates in the other lines as well, encroaches on them as it develops' (Deleuze [1964] 2008: 56). Instead, Deleuze is more interested in explaining their differential relations and asking which, in a given situation, is the most affective.
27. Expressing Deleuze's philosophy of life, Braidotti puts it differently, claiming that 'our fundamental drive (*conatus*) is to express the potency of life (*potentia*), by joining forces with other flows of becoming' (Braidotti 2006: 153). In contrast, Boltanski and Chiapello in *The New Spirit of Capitalism* (2005, 2007) analyse corporate management texts in order to demonstrate the change from Fordist corporate work structures towards more fluid business practices, at the cost of material and psychological security. Far from celebrating the emphasis on creativity and expression in poststructuralist texts, the authors criticise poststructuralism for, at the very

least, not providing sufficient resistance to capitalism or, at worst, being actively complicit in its dominance. See also Raunig (2013), who encounters Deleuze and Guattari critically with the authors of the Frankfurt School to create a philosophy of 'resistance and solidarity in the common' (Majewska 2015).
28. John Protevi has conceptualised the affective relations involved in processes of individuation and cognitive science (2010), as well as those that relate the subject to its social relations and the processes that constitute it (2009). The 4EA (embodied, embedded, enacted, extended, and affective) group is particularly interesting for its development of a non-reductive and non-idealist form of cognitive science. Chemero (2009) is excellent for its clear exposition of the benefits that 4EA conceptualisation has over traditional theories of mind. Research in the field of affective cognition has also been undertaken by Connolly (2002, 2013) and Bennett (2004). Kleinherenbrink (2014) is particularly interesting in foregrounding the importance of thinking gender dynamics in cognitive science.
29. MacKenzie uses the term 'real' in a different manner than Chambers, for whom imaginary ideology is the set of relations that affixes the social relations of real individuals to other individuals and social institutions. MacKenzie elsewhere discusses the relationship between the real and ideology in Deleuze and Ricœur, pointing out Deleuze and Guattari's declaration in *A Thousand Plateaus* that 'there is no ideology and never has been' (Deleuze and Guattari 2004b: 5, MacKenzie 2012). Deleuze and Guattari go on to state that, in fact, 'all that consists is Real' (Deleuze and Guattari 2004b: 77). As MacKenzie suggests, more work must be done on Deleuze's relationship with ideology (see also Porter 2006), but it is safe to say that MacKenzie uses the term here only to mean what, in *Negotiations*, Deleuze refers to as 'history': 'just the set of more or less negative preconditions that make it possible to experiment with something beyond history' (Deleuze 1995: 170).
30. Bell (2015) provides an excellent commentary on the concept of infinity in Deleuze's use of calculus and philosophy more generally.
31. When Deleuze argues that 'the possible is that which is realised' (Deleuze [1988] 1991: 96–7), he is referring to the active synthesis of resemblance having compared an actual development to its virtual idea and creating a series from this comparison.
32. In arguing for ethical, as opposed to moral, practices of resistance, individuation has been foregrounded in favour of the discussion of collective practice. Both these focuses call for further work to be carried out with regard to the more explicitly normative thought of authors inspired by Deleuze, such as Patton, as well as those who are not, such as Arendt, Butler and members of the Frankfurt School. This work might investigate these thinkers' emphasis on space (as opposed to both space and time) from the perspective

of the ethically oriented ontology developed in this book. Further work could also expand the focus on individuation to that of the collective and, with this in mind, developing the work of Haraway and Lloyd's concept of 'inessential collectives' (Lloyd 2005) could prove particularly important in the light of contemporary politics' 'dividuating' practices (see Deleuze 1992b). A third strand of research might investigate whether or not Deleuze departed from his interest in metaphysics when he started working with Guattari for *Capitalism and Schizophrenia*. What are the stakes at play in the change of tenor from the ontology of ideas in *Difference and Repetition* to the political philosophy of machinic ideas such as the 'rhizome', 'plateaus', 'de/reterritorialisation' and 'sexuality'? What are the implications of any changes for practices of resistance, given the discussion of their ontological fundaments in this book?

Conclusion: The Art of Practical Resistance

No doubt resistance involves the drafting of battle plans, tactics and goals. It involves negotiating the complex power relations, intertwining structures of desire and vested interests that overdetermine the social formation at the same time as they are produced by it. The goal of practices of resistance is a projection of what Badiou terms a 'hypothesis' (Badiou 2013) that pushes into the future a synthesis of what is known of the real and the acknowledgement that this knowledge is insufficient. The activist knows that the outcome of efforts to resist is unknowable, but that one nevertheless must, as Marx affirmed to a reporter on the Dover cliffs, struggle (Hamad 2015: 142). When faced with a situation that compels one to ask with Engels 'what is to be done?', how might the individual act well? How, also, might one avoid his prediction that '"[d]ogmatism, doctrinairism" [is] the inevitable retribution that follows the violent strait-lacing of thought' (Lenin [1902] 1961: pt. 1D)?

The problem is, as has been shown, not as simple as even the most careful reading of situations might present. Badiou's analysis shows that the apparent reality of a situation often misleads the individual into political action that is against their true nature. The state of the situation is such that, for Badiou, the individual can only reproduce the structures of power in which they are immersed without a certain moment that breaks their pattern of thought. Everything must be ignored to the benefit of the enlightenment bestowed upon the individual by this event, for how can one act upon knowledge that he or she knows is misleading? In this, Badiou could not be a clearer advocate of ideological interpolation, but on his own terms. Whilst Badiou accounts for the nature of Being that emerges from the event as unknowable, fidelity to it is the subject's acknowledgement that events count for more than what individuals are otherwise; the subject becomes the militant, Badiou's account of what it is to be 'worthy of the event' (Deleuze [1969] 2004: 149) and truthfully a participant of politics (Boundas 2006). A quasi-religious summons to bear out its consequences, the political event at once asks and answers Engels' question, elevating belief from the status of *doxa* to truth.

Much is at stake, however, when so much faith is placed in the event, and particularly if that event's truth is affirmed by negation. How might one read a situation if nothing is subtracted from it to reveal the clarity of truth? Both Althusser and Deleuze, to differing conclusions, argue that it is necessary to *make* sense of a situation, rather than find truth hidden within it (Althusser and Balibar 1970: 52, Deleuze [1956–7] 2015: 24). For Althusser, a sense of a situation depends on what type of situation one is in, or at least what questions are being asked of it. Althusser's *Reading Capital* anticipates Deleuze's argument in *Difference and Repetition* in which he claims that, '[t]he formulation of a *problem* is merely the theoretical expression of the conditions which allow a *solution* already produced outside the process of knowledge' (Deleuze [1994] 2011: 198, cf. Althusser and Balibar 1970: 52). The sense of a situation when confronted by a policeman will, of course, differ in kind from an encounter with a work of art. The importance of Althusser's work to the argument herein then is that he encourages the individual to ask questions of their relations to different social practices. He forms the grounds of an immanent political sociology in which the effects of social practices of the individual (and vice versa) are understood as separate, yet in affective, differential relation with each other. Further work might be done to draw out the importance of his promissory Notes, the differential relation of discourses and the relations between science, philosophy and art as developed in the works of Deleuze, Brassier and Meillassoux.

The importance of the encounter with(in) a situation is also important for Deleuze, who argues that encounters do violence to the individual's understanding of the world, a violence that challenges memory to account for this new difference presented to it (Bryant 2008: 77, Deleuze [1964] 2008: 16). Following an encounter with(in) a situation, individuals struggle to account for their relation to it, and what they should do next. The aim of this struggle, however, again, depends on the affective characteristics of the situation: against Badiou's claim that commitment to the event determines the true course of action regardless of the situation (but only for the militant), both Althusser and Deleuze argue that all life matters, and that the goals that individuals set are not prefigured by their status as one particular actor. As has been argued, there is no rarefied social position to ally oneself with, and Badiou's idea of militant practice is simply one amongst many practices of resistance that are possible according to Althusser's and Deleuze's philosophies.

However, if Althusser's work conceptualises the differential relations between typologies of social practices then, in his haste to remove all forms of idealism and 'absolute historicism' from his philosophy (Althusser and Balibar 1970: 119), Althusser reintroduces it with the idea of the void. Breaking the persistence of ideas through time in the social formation, Althusser's structuralism becomes a series of static ruptures, disconnected from each other. Deleuze's structuralism, however, inheriting the modified ideas of relations from Hume and time from Bergson, accounts for the passing of time and both the determination and constitution of structures. Through demonstrating the passive and active relations of ideas, both with themselves and with time itself, Deleuze accounts for how ideas persist both through and in time. Thus, in developing this reading of Deleuze and Althusser, this book has fabricated an ontology proper to structuralism, and accounts for how processes of individuation reciprocally constitute the persistence and variation of structures in the social formation. So what does this mean for what and how the individual might resist?

In practices of resistance, the individual takes stock of their situation and what they know of how they have come to be there. Having been forced to make sense of a situation, in the engaged, embodied and active sense of a process, ethics is an ontological property of individuation, which is therefore always-already ethical.[1] Whether they like it or not, individuals are always-already enmeshed in the social dynamics and relations of power, and the concept of ethology in both Mill's and Deleuze's work testifies to the challenges that this immersion brings with it. It is not simply that the individual can refuse to make ethical decisions: as de Beauvoir argued, '[t]here is no way for a man to escape from this world', and solipsism belies the fact that an individual's choice to avoid decision-making is an ethical decision itself (de Beauvoir 2011: 67–70). Likewise, dogmatic appeal to idealist principles denegates the grounds upon which these principles are built in the presupposition that they are benevolent. In line with Deleuze's criticism of both good and common sense, there is nothing necessarily benevolent about the world and the way in which individuals exist in it, and individuals should not assume that either ideas or ideals work for their benefit. Instead, the practice of ethology and the idea of genius can guide individuals in understanding how to better themselves within different situations.

The idea of genius is, then, the function of ethical individuation that impels individuals to distinguish themselves from within situations, which would otherwise dampen their potential. However, this is not to encourage solipsism under another name, and the individual is not conceptualised as counter to the other. Furthermore, individuals' practices of resistance do not have to occur *against* the other, but can be understood as functioning *with* it, harnessing the potential contained within situations to the benefit of the former. As Nietzsche argued, there is no suggestion that Nietzsche's bird of prey is morally superior to the lamb, and indeed there is no comparison of one against the other (*The Genealogy of Morals* in Nietzsche 2014: 1: §13). Rather, Nietzsche's point, which is echoed by Deleuze's ethics, is simply that the bird of prey will be itself, as the lamb will be a lamb: '[t]o demand of strength that it not express itself as strength, that it not be a will to overwhelm, a will to topple, a will to become master, a thirst for enemies and obstacles and triumphs, is just as absurd as demanding of weakness, that it express itself as strength' (2014: 1: §13). Practices of resistance are conceptualised *contra* the other, taking the other into account and amplifying, multiplying and transforming its potential within a situation. The question that activists might ask of themselves then, when posing a question devoid of dogma is, 'given the situation in which I am, with the potential futures I both know and don't know, what is to be done?'. The idea of genius reminds the individual that there will always be more to learn, more relations to create and enrich, and more problems to face. In this light, individuals learn to encounter the world, in a cautious, yet pragmatic and productive, struggle.

Note

1. In a seminar he gave in 1980, Deleuze asked why Spinoza titled his book on ontology *Ethics* (Deleuze 1980), before explaining that ethics is an unfolding of ontology itself.

Bibliography

Adams, D. (1979), *The Hitchhiker's Guide to the Galaxy*, Basingstoke and London: Macmillan.
Agamben, G. (1998), *Homo Sacer: Sovereign Power and Bare Life*, Stanford: Stanford University Press.
Al-Saji, A. (2004), 'The Memory of Another Past: Bergson, Deleuze and a New Theory of Time', *Continental Philosophy Review* 37:2, 203–39.
Althusser, L. (1971a), 'Ideology and Ideological State Apparatuses (Notes Towards an Investigation)', in *Lenin and Philosophy and Other Essays*, London and New York: Monthly Review Press, pp. 127–86.
Althusser, L. (1971b), *Lenin and Philosophy and Other Essays*, New York: Monthly Review Press.
Althusser, L. (1976), *Essays in Self-Criticism*, London and Paris: NLB.
Althusser, L. (1978), 'What Must Change in the Party', *New Left Review* 1:178, 19–45.
Althusser, L. (1984), *Essays on Ideology*, London and New York: Verso.
Althusser, L. (1997), 'The Only Materialist Tradition', in W. Montag and T. Stolze (eds), *The New Spinoza*, Minneapolis: University of Minnesota Press.
Althusser, L. ([1965] 2005), *For Marx*, London and New York: Verso.
Althusser, L. (2006), *Philosophy of the Encounter: Later Writings, 1978–87*, London: Verso.
Althusser, L. and É. Balibar (1970), *Reading Capital*, London: NLB.
Althusser, L., O. Corpet and F. Matheron (1996), *Writings on Psychoanalysis: Freud and Lacan*, New York and Chichester: Columbia University Press.
Althusser, L., O. Corpet and Y. Moulier Boutang (1993), *The Future Lasts Forever: A Memoir*, New York: New Press.
Althusser, L. and F. Matheron (2003), *The Humanist Controversy and Other Writings (1966–67)*, London and New York: Verso.

Ansell-Pearson, K. (1999), *Germinal Life: The Difference and Repetition of Deleuze*, London: Routledge.
Ansell-Pearson, K. (2014a), 'Affirmative Naturalism: Deleuze and Epicureanism', *Cosmos and History: The Journal of Natural and Social Philosophy* 10:2, 121–37.
Ansell-Pearson, K. (2014b), 'Morality and the Philosophy of Life in Guyau and Bergson', *Continental Philosophy Review* 47:1, 59–85.
Ardal, P. S. (1966), *Passion and Value in Hume's Treatise. 18*, Edinburgh: Edinburgh University Press.
Badiou, A. (1992), *Manifesto for Philosophy*, New York: State University of New York Press.
Badiou, A. (1997), *Saint Paul: The Foundation of Universalism*, Stanford: Stanford University Press.
Badiou, A. (1998), *Briefings on Existence: A Short Treatise on Transitory Ontology*, Albany: State University of New York Press.
Badiou, A. (2000), *The Clamor of Being*, Minneapolis: University of Minnesota Press.
Badiou, A. (2001), *Ethics: An Essay on the Understanding of Evil*, London and New York: Verso.
Badiou, A. (2003), 'Beyond Formalism: An Interview with P. Hallward and B. Bosteels', *Angelaki: Journal of the Theoretical Humanities* 8:2, 11–36.
Badiou, A. (2004), *Theoretical Writings*, London and New York: Continuum.
Badiou, A. (2005a), 'The Adventure of French Philosophy', *New Left Review* 35: 67–77.
Badiou, A. (2005b), *Handbook of Inaesthetics*, Stanford: Stanford University Press.
Badiou, A. (2005c), *Infinite Thought*, London and New York: Continuum.
Badiou, A. (2005d), *Metapolitics*, London and New York: Verso.
Badiou, A. ([1997] 2006), 'Philosophy as Creative Repetition', *The Symptom*, <http://www.lacan.com/badrepeat.html> (last accessed 18 October 2018).
Badiou, A. ([1966] 2007), *The Concept of Model: An Introduction to the Materialist Epistemology of Mathematics*, Melbourne: re.press.
Badiou, A. (2008), '"We Need a Popular Discipline": Contemporary Politics and the Crisis of the Negative', *Critical Inquiry* 34.
Badiou, A. ([1992] 2008), *Conditions*, London and New York: Continuum.
Badiou, A. (2009), *Logics of Worlds*, London and New York: Continuum.
Badiou, A. (2010a), *The Communist Hypothesis*, London and New York: Verso.

Badiou, A. (2010b), 'The Idea of Communism', in C. Douzinas and S. Žižek (eds), *The Idea of Communism*, London and New York: Verso.
Badiou, A. (2010c), *Theoretical Writings*, London and New York: Bloomsbury.
Badiou, A. (2011), *Being and Event*, London: Continuum.
Badiou, A. (2013a), 'Affirmative Dialectics: From Logic to Anthropology', *Badiou Studies* 2:1, 1–13.
Badiou, A. (2013b), 'The Althusserian Definition of "Theory"', lecture at *Reading Capital, 1965–2013* conference, Princeton University.
Badiou, A. ([1982] 2013), *Theory of the Subject*, London and New York: Bloomsbury.
Badiou, A. (2014), *Mathematics of the Transcendental*, London, New Delhi, New York and Sydney: Bloomsbury.
Badiou, A., D. Macey and S. Corcoran (2010), *The Communist Hypothesis*, London: Verso.
Badiou, A. and A. Toscano (2006), 'Plato, Our Dear Plato!', *Angelaki: Journal of the Theoretical Humanities* 11:3, 39–41.
Badiou, A. and N. Truong (2012), *In Praise of Love*, London: Serpent's Tail.
Balibar, É. (1993), 'The Non-Contemporaneity of Althusser', in E. A. Kaplan and M. Sprinker (eds), *The Althusserian Legacy*, London: Verso.
Barker, J. (2002), *Alain Badiou: A Critical Introduction*, London and Sterling, VA: Pluto Press.
Barlett, A. J., J. Clemens and J. Roffe (2014), *Lacan Deleuze Badiou*, Edinburgh: Edinburgh University Press.
Bell, J. (2006), 'Charting the Road of Inquiry: Deleuze's Humean Pragmatics and the Challenge of Badiou', *The Southern Journal of Philosophy* 44:3, 399–425.
Bell, J. (2008), *Deleuze's Hume: Philosophy, Culture and the Scottish Enlightenment*, Edinburgh: Edinburgh University Press.
Bell, J. (2009), 'Of the Rise and Progress of Philosophical Concepts: Deleuze's Humean Historiography', in J. Bell and C. Colebrook (eds), *Deleuze and History*, Edinburgh: Edinburgh University Press, pp. 54–71.
Bell, J. A. (2015), 'Infinite Pragmatics: Deleuze, Pierce, and the Habits of Things', in S. Bowden, S. Bignall and P. Patton (eds), *Deleuze and Pragmatism*, Abingdon and New York: Routledge, pp. 21–35.
Bennett, J. (2004), 'The Force of Things: Steps toward an Ecology of Matter', *Political Theory* 32:3, 347–72.
Bentham, J. ([1823] 1948), *A Fragment on Government and An Introduction to the Principles of Morals and Legislation*, Oxford: Clarendon Press.

Bergson, H. (1911), *Creative Evolution*, New York: Henry Holt.
Bergson, H. (1935), *The Two Sources of Religion and Morality*, New York: Henry Holt.
Bergson, H. ([1960] 1989), *Time and Free Will: An Essay on the Immediate Data of Consciousness*, London and New York: George Allen & Unwin.
Bergson, H. ([1908] 1991), *Matter and Memory*, New York: Zone Books.
Bogue, R. (2007), *Deleuze's Way: Essays in Transverse Ethics*, Aldershot and Burlington, VT: Ashcroft.
Boltanski, L. and E. Chiapello (2005), 'The New Spirit of Capitalism', *International Journal of Politics, Culture, and Society* 18:3–4, 161–88.
Boltanski, L. and E. Chiapello (2007), *The New Spirit of Capitalism*, London: Verso.
Bosteels, B. (2001), 'Alain Badiou's Theory of the Subject: Part 1. The Recommencement of Dialectical Materialism?', *Pli* 12: 200–29.
Bosteels, B. (2005), 'Post-Maoism: Badiou and Politics', *Positions: East Asia Cultures Critique* 13:3, 575–634.
Bosteels, B. (2011), *Badiou and Politics*, Durham, NC and London: Duke University Press.
Boundas, C. V. (2006), 'What Difference Does Deleuze's Difference Make?', in C. V. Boundas (ed.), *Deleuze and Philosophy*, Edinburgh: Edinburgh University Press.
Boutang, P.-A. (1988), *L'Abécédaire de Gilles Deleuze*, Paris: Éditions Montparnasse.
Bowden, S. (2011), *The Priority of Events: Deleuze's Logic of Sense*, Edinburgh: Edinburgh University Press.
Braidotti, R. (2006), 'The Ethics of Becoming-Imperceptible', in C. V. Boundas (ed.), *Deleuze and Philosophy*, Edinburgh: Edinburgh University Press.
Brassier, R. (2005), 'Badiou's Materialist Epistemology of Mathematics', *Angelaki* 10:2, 135–50.
Brassier, R. (2007), *Nihil Unbound: Enlightenment and Extinction*, Basingstoke: Palgrave Macmillan.
Brassier, R. (2016), *Speculative Heresy*, <https://speculativeheresy.wordpress.com> (last accessed 18 October 2018).
Brown, N. (2009), *Rationalist Empiricism/Dialectical Materialism: From Althusser to Meillassoux*, CRMEP Research Seminar Paper, Middlesex University, London.
Brown, N. (2011), 'Specular and the Specific: On Hallward and Meillassoux', in L. R. Bryant, N. Srnicek and G. Harman (eds), *The Speculative Turn: Continental Materialism and Realism*, Melbourne: re.press.

Bryant, L. R. (2007), 'Thoughts of Immanence', *Larval Subjects*, <https://larvalsubjects.wordpress.com/2007/08/27/thoughts-of-immanence/> (last accessed 18 October 2018).

Bryant, L. R. (2008), *Difference and Givenness: Deleuze's Transcendental Empiricism and the Ontology of Immanence*, Evanston, IL: Northwestern University Press.

Bryant, L. R. (2011), 'The Ethics of the Event', in N. J. Jun and D. W. Smith (eds), *Deleuze and Ethics*, Deleuze Connections, Edinburgh: Edinburgh University Press, pp. 21–43.

Bryant, L. R. (2016), *Larval Subjects*, <https://larvalsubjects.wordpress.com> (last accessed 18 October 2018).

Buchanan, I. (2015), 'Assemblage Theory and Its Discontents', *Deleuze Studies* 9:3, 382–92.

Buchanan, I. and N. Thoburn (eds) (2008), *Deleuze and Politics*, Deleuze Connections, Edinburgh: Edinburgh University Press.

Buckle, S. (2007), 'Hume's Sceptical Materialism', *Philosophy* 82:4, 553–78.

Butler, J. (1997), *The Psychic Life of Power: Theories in Subjection*, Stanford: Stanford University Press.

Chambers, S. A. (2010), 'Untimely Politics avant la lettre: The Temporality of Social Formations', 2010 Annual Meeting of the American Political Science Association, Washington, DC.

Chambers, S. A. (2014), *Bearing Society in Mind: Theories and Politics of the Social Formation*, London and New York: Rowman and Littlefield International.

Chemero, A. (2009), *Radical Embodied Cognitive Science*, Cambridge, MA and London: MIT Press.

Choat, S. (2010), *Marx Through Post-Structuralism: Lyotard, Derrida, Foucault, Deleuze*, London and New York: Continuum.

Chomsky, N. and M. Foucault (1971), 'Human Nature: Justice versus Power', <https://chomsky.info/1971xxxx/> (last accessed 18 October 2018).

Clisby, D. (2015), 'Deleuze's Secret Dualism? Competing Accounts of the Relationship between the Virtual and the Actual', *Parrhesia* 24, 127–49.

Colebrook, C. (2008), 'Bourgeois Thermodynamics', in I. Buchanan and N. Thoburn (eds), *Deleuze and Politics*, Deleuze Connections, Edinburgh: Edinburgh University Press.

Collett, G., M. Kosugi and C. Sdrolia (2013), 'Editorial Introduction: For a Transdisciplinary Practice of Thought', *Deleuze Studies* 7:2, 157–68.

Comte, A. ([1853] 2009), *The Positive Philosophy of Auguste Comte. 1*, Cambridge: Cambridge University Press.

Connolly, W. (2002), *Neuropolitics: Thinking, Culture, Speed. Out of Bounds*, Minneapolis: University of Minnesota Press.
Connolly, W. E. (2013), 'Biology, Politics, Creativity', *Perspectives on Politics* 11:02, 508–11.
Cordero, N.-L. (2004), *By Being, It Is: The Thesis of Parmenides*, Las Vegas: Parmenides Publishing.
Critchley, S. (2012), 'Why Badiou is a Rousseauist', *Badiou Studies* 1:1, 1–8.
Crocker, S. (2001), 'Into the Interval: On Deleuze's Reversal of Time and Movement', *Continental Philosophy Review* 34:1, 45–67.
Dahl, R. A. (1973), *Polyarchy: Participation and Opposition*, New Haven and London: Yale University Press.
Dahl, R. A. (1989), *Democracy and Its Critics*, New Haven and London: Yale University Press.
De Beauvoir, S. (2011), *The Ethics of Ambiguity*, trans. B. Frechtman, Newburyport, MA: Philosophical Library/Open Road.
De Vaus, D. A. (2001), *Research Design in Social Research*, London, California, New Delhi and Singapore: SAGE.
Deamer, D. (2011), 'A Deleuzian Cineosis: Cinematic Semiosis and Syntheses of Time', *Deleuze Studies* 5:3, 358–82.
Debord, G. (2002), *The Society of the Spectacle*, Canberra: Hobgoblin Press.
DeLanda, M. (2005), 'Space: Extensive and Intensive, Actual and Virtual', in I. Buchanan and G. Lambert (eds), *Deleuze and Space*, Deleuze Connections, Edinburgh: Edinburgh University Press.
DeLanda, M. ([2002] 2005), *Intensive Science and Virtual Philosophy*, London and New York: Bloomsbury.
Deleuze, G. (1956), 'Bergson's Conception of Difference', *Les Études Bergsoniennes* 4, 77–113.
Deleuze, G. (1980, 9 December), 'Cours Vincennes sur Spinoza', <http://www2.univ-paris8.fr/deleuze/article.php3?id_article=137> (last accessed 18 October 2016).
Deleuze, G. (1981, 17 February), 'Sur Spinoza', <https://www.webdeleuze.com/textes/38> (last accessed 18 October 2018).
Deleuze, G. (1988a), *Foucault*, Minneapolis: University of Minnesota Press.
Deleuze, G. (1988b), *Spinoza: Practical Philosophy*, San Francisco: City Lights Books.
Deleuze, G. (1991), *Empiricism and Subjectivity: An Essay on Hume's Theory of Human Nature*, New York: Columbia University Press.
Deleuze, G. ([1988] 1991), *Bergsonism*, New York: Zone Books.
Deleuze, G. (1992a), *Expressionism in Philosophy; Spinoza*, London and New York: Zone Books.

Deleuze, G. (1992b), 'Postscript on the Societies of Control', *October* 59, 3–7.
Deleuze, G. ([1988] 1993), *The Fold: Leibniz and the Baroque*, London: The Athlone Press.
Deleuze, G. (1995), *Negotiations*, London and New York: Columbia University Press.
Deleuze, G. (1997), *Essays Critical and Clinical*, Minneapolis: University of Minnesota Press.
Deleuze, G. (2001), *Pure Immanence*, New York: Zone Books.
Deleuze, G. (2004a), *Desert Islands: And Other Texts, 1953–1974*, Los Angeles and New York: Semiotext(e).
Deleuze, G. (2004b), *Difference and Repetition*, London and New York: Continuum.
Deleuze, G. (2004c), 'How Do We Recognize Structuralism?', in *Desert Islands: And Other Texts, 1953–1974*, Los Angeles and New York: Semiotext(e).
Deleuze, G. ([1969] 2004), *The Logic of Sense*, London: Continuum.
Deleuze, G. (2005a), *Cinema 1: The Movement Image*, London: Continuum.
Deleuze, G. (2005b), *Cinema 2: The Time Image*, London: Continuum.
Deleuze, G. ([1963] 2008), *Kant's Critical Philosophy: The Doctrine of the Faculties*, London and New York: Bloomsbury.
Deleuze, G. ([1964] 2008), *Proust and Signs*, London and New York: Continuum.
Deleuze, G. ([1994] 2011), *Difference and Repetition*, London and New York: Continuum.
Deleuze, G. ([1956–7] 2015), *What Is Grounding?* Grand Rapids, &&& Publishing.
Deleuze, G. and F. Guattari (1986), *Kafka: Toward a Minor Literature*, Minneapolis and London: University of Minnesota Press.
Deleuze, G. and F. Guattari ([1991] 1994), *What is Philosophy?*, New York: Columbia University Press.
Deleuze, G. and F. Guattari (2004a), *Anti-Oedipus*, London and New York: Continuum.
Deleuze, G. and F. Guattari (2004b), *A Thousand Plateaus*, New York and London: Continuum.
Deleuze, G. and J. Strauss (1991), 'The Fold', *Yale French Studies* 80, 227–47.
Descola, P. (2013), *Beyond Nature and Culture*, Chicago, University of Chicago Press.
Dewey, J. (1958), *Experience and Nature*, New York: Dover Publications.
Diefenbach, K. (2013), 'Althusser with Deleuze: How to Think Spinoza's Immanent Cause', in K. Diefenbach, S. R. Farris, G. Kirn and P. D.

Thomas (eds), *Encountering Althusser: Politics and Materialism in Contemporary Radical Thought*, London: Bloomsbury.
Diefenbach, K., S. R. Farris, G. Kirn and P. D. Thomas (eds) (2013), *Encountering Althusser: Politics and Materialism in Contemporary Radical Thought*, London: Bloomsbury.
Duffy, S. B. (2006), 'The Mathematics of Deleuze's Differential Logic and Metaphysics', in S. B. Duffy (ed.), *Virtual Mathematics: The Logic of Difference*, Bolton: Clinamen.
Durie, R. (2006), 'Problems in the Relation between Maths and Philosophy', in S. B. Duffy (ed.), *Virtual Mathematics: The Logic of Difference*, Bolton: Clinamen.
Egyed, B. (2006), 'Counter-Actualisation and the Method of Intuition', in C. V. Boundas (ed.), *Deleuze and Philosophy*, Deleuze Connections, Edinburgh: Edinburgh University Press, pp. 74–83.
Elliott, G. (1993), 'Althusser's Solitude', in E. A. Kaplan and M. Sprinker (eds), *The Althusserian Legacy*, London: Verso.
Elliott, G. (2006), *Althusser: The Detour of History*, Leiden and London: Brill.
Engels, F. (1893), *Engels to Franz Mehring*, New York: International Publishers.
Epicurus (1925), 'The Letter of Epicurus to Herodotus', in Diogenes Laertius, *Lives of Eminent Philosophers* 10, London: William Heinemann and New York: G. P. Putnam's Sons.
Evans, A. (2006), 'The Surd', in S. B. Duffy (ed.), *Virtual Mathematics: The Logic of Difference*, Bolton: Clinamen.
Flaxman, G. (2015), 'A More Radical Empiricism', in S. Bowden, S. Bignall and P. Patton (eds), *Deleuze and Pragmatism*, Deleuze Connections, Abingdon and New York: Routledge.
Foucault, M. (2014), *Wrong-Doing, Truth-Telling*, Chicago and London: University of Chicago Press.
Foucault, M., M. Bertani, A. Fontana, F. Ewald and D. Macey (2003), '"Society Must Be Defended": Lectures at the Collège de France, 1975–1976', Basingstoke: Macmillan.
Foucault, M. and G. Deleuze (1980), 'Intellectuals and Power: A Conversation between Michel Foucault and Gilles Deleuze', in M. Foucault and D. F. Bouchard (eds), *Language, Counter-Memory, Practice: Selected Essays and Interviews*, Ithaca and London: Cornell University Press.
Fourtounis, G. (2005), 'On Althusser's Immanentist Structuralism: Reading Montag Reading Althusser Reading Spinoza', *Rethinking Marxism* 17:1, 101–18.
Frederiek, D. (2009), *Badiou and Theology*, London and New York: T&T Clark.

Freud, S. ([1930] 2015), *Civilization and Its Discontents*, Ontario: Broadview Press.
Gabriel, M. (2013), 'Why the World Does Not Exist', lecture, TEDxMunich.
Gabriel, M. (2015), *Fields of Sense: A New Realist Ontology*, Edinburgh: Edinburgh University Press.
Gabriel, M. and G. S. Moss (2015), *Why the World Does Not Exist*, Cambridge and Malden, MA: Polity Press.
Garo, I. (2011), *Foucault, Deleuze, Althusser et Marx*, Paris: Éditions Demopolis.
Gerring, J. (2008), *Social Science Methodology: A Critical Framework*, New York: Cambridge University Press.
Gironi, F. (2014), *Naturalising Badiou: Mathematical Ontology and Structural Realism*, Basingstoke: Palgrave Macmillan.
Gödel, K. (1931), *On Formally Undecidable Propositions of Principia Mathematica and Related Systems* trans. Bernard Meltzer, Edinburgh: Edinburgh University Press.
Golumbia, D. (2016), '"Correlationism": The Dogma that Never Was', *boundary 2* 43:2, 1–25.
Gordy, M. (1983), 'Reading Althusser: Time and the Social Whole', *History and Theory* 22:1, 1–21.
Grover, D. (1992), *A Prosentential Theory of Truth*, Princeton: Princeton University Press.
Habermas, J. (2015), *The Philosophical Discourse of Modernity: Twelve Lectures*, Cambridge and Malden, MA: Polity.
Haddock, B. A. (2008), *A History of Political Thought: From Antiquity to the Present*, Cambridge, MA: Polity.
Halliday, R. J. (1976), *John Stuart Mill*, London: Allen & Unwin.
Hallward, P. (2003), *Badiou: A Subject to Truth*, Minneapolis and London: University of Minnesota Press.
Hallward, P. (2005), 'The Politics of Prescription', *South Atlantic Quarterly* 104:4, 769–89.
Hallward, P. (2006), *Out of this World: Deleuze and the Philosophy of Creation*, London and New York: Verso.
Hallward, P. (2009), 'Communism of the Intellect, Communism of the Will', in C. Douzinas and S. Žižek (eds), *The Idea of Communism*, London and New York: Verso.
Hallward, P. (2011), 'Anything is Possible: A Reading of Quentin Meillassoux's After Finitude', in L. R. Bryant, N. Srnicek and G. Harman (eds), *The Speculative Turn: Continental Materialism and Realism*, Melbourne: re.press.
Hallward, P. and K. Peden (eds) (2013), *Concept and Form*, 1, London and New York: Verso.

Hamad, Y. Y. (2015), 'Reclaiming Marx: Principles of Justice as a Critical Foundation in Moral Realism', in M. J. Thompson (ed.), *Constructing Marxist Ethics: Critique, Normativity, Praxis*, Leiden and Boston: Brill.

Hamilton, W. (1860), *Lectures on Metaphysics and Logic*, 2, Edinburgh and London: William Blackwood and Sons.

Harman, G. (2011), *Quentin Meillassoux: Philosophy in the Making*, Edinburgh: Edinburgh University Press.

Harman, G. (2016), *Object-Orientated Philosophy*, <https://doctorzamalek2.wordpress.com> (last accessed 18 October 2018).

Harris, O. J. and J. Robb (2012), 'Multiple Ontologies and the Problem of the Body in History', *American Anthropologist* 114:4, 668–79.

Hegel, G. W. F. (1969), *Science of Logic*, London and New York: G. Allen & Unwin.

Hegel, G. W. F. ([1830] 1991), *The Encyclopedia Logic: Part 1 of the Encyclopaedia of Philosophical Sciences*, Indianapolis: Hackett.

Hegel, G. W. F. (1998), *Phenomenology of Spirit*, Delhi: Motilal Banarsidass.

Heidegger, M. (1977), *Basic Writings: From Being and Time (1927) to The Task of Thinking (1964)*, New York: Harper and Row.

Heidegger, M. (1997), *Kant and the Problem of Metaphysics*, trans. Richard Taft, Bloomington and Indianapolis: Indiana University Press.

Heidegger, M. ([1953] 2010), *Being and Time*, Albany: State University of New York Press.

Henry, C. (2016), 'On Truth and Instrumentalisation', *London Journal of Critical Thought* 1, 5–15.

Hewlett, N. (2010), *Badiou, Balibar, Rancière: Re-thinking Emancipation*, London and New York: Continuum.

Heywood, A. (2007), *Politics*, Basingstoke: Palgrave Macmillan.

Hobbes, T. ([1651] 1996), *Leviathan*, Oxford: Oxford University Press.

Hughes, J. (2009), *Deleuze's 'Difference and Repetition': A Reader's Guide*, London: Bloomsbury.

Hume, D. ([1757] 1777), *Four Dissertations*, London: Andrew Millar.

Hume, D. ([1888] 1967), *A Treatise of Human Nature*, Oxford: Clarendon Press.

Hume, D. ([1748] 1993), *An Enquiry Concerning Human Understanding*, Indianapolis: Hackett.

Immerwahr, J. (1994), 'Hume's Dissertation on the Passions', *Journal of the History of Philosophy* 32:2, 225–40.

Jameson, F. (1981), *The Political Unconscious: Narrative as a Socially Symbolic Act*, Ithaca: Cornell University Press.

Johnston, A. (2011), 'Hume's Revenge: À Dieu, Meillassoux?', in L. R. Bryant, N. Srnicek and G. Harman (eds), *The Speculative Turn: Continental Materialism and Realism*, Melbourne: re.press.

Jones, B. and A. Gray (2010), *Politics UK*, Harlow and New York: Pearson Education.

Jun, N. (2011), 'Deleuze, Values, and Normativity', in N. Jun and D. W. Smith (eds), *Deleuze and Ethics*, Deleuze Connections, Edinburgh: Edinburgh University Press, pp. 89–107.

Jun, N. J. and D. W. Smith (eds) (2011), *Deleuze and Ethics*, Deleuze Connections, Edinburgh: Edinburgh University Press.

Kant, I. ([1787] 1996), *Critique of Pure Reason*, Indianapolis: Hackett.

Kant, I. (1997), *Groundwork for the Metaphysics of Morals*, Cambridge: Cambridge University Press.

Kaplan, E. A. and M. Sprinker (eds) (1993), *The Althusserian Legacy*, London: Verso.

Kirkeby, O. F. (2004), 'Eventum Tantum: To Make the World Worthy of What Could Happen to It', *ephemera* 4:3, 290–308.

Kleinherenbrink, A. (2014), 'Mapping Plasticity: Sex/Gender and the Changing Brain', *Tijdschrift voor Genderstudies* 17:4, 305–26.

Korsgaard, C. M. and O. O'Neill (1996), *The Sources of Normativity*, Cambridge: Cambridge University Press.

Kropotkin, P. A. (1989), *Memoirs of a Revolutionist*, Montreal: Black Rose.

Kuehn, M. (1983), 'Kant's Conception of "Hume's Problem"', *Journal of the History of Philosophy* 21:2, 175–93.

La Caze, M. and H. M. Lloyd (2011), 'Editors' Introduction: Philosophy and the "Affective Turn"', *Parrhesia* 13, 1–13.

Lacan, J. (1956), 'Fetishism: The Symbolic, The Real and The Imaginary', in S. Lorand and M. Balint (eds), *Perversions: Psychodynamics and Therapy*, New York: Random House.

Lacan, J. ([1949] 1977), 'The Mirror-Stage as Formative of the I as Revealed in Psychoanalytic Experience', in J. Lacan, *Écrits: A Selection*, New York: Norton.

Lacan, J. ([1973] 1999), 'On Feminine Sexuality: The Limits of Love and Knowledge 1972–73', in J.-A. Miller (ed.), *Encore: The Seminar of Jacques Lacan, Book XX*, New York: Norton.

Lampert, M. (2015), 'Resisting Ideology: On Butler's Critique of Althusser', *diacritics* 43:2, 124–47.

Laruelle, F. (2013), *Anti-Badiou: The Introduction of Maoism into Philosophy*, London and New York: Bloomsbury.

Lawlor, L. (1998), 'The End of Phenomenology: Expressionism in Deleuze and Merleau-Ponty', *Continental Philosophy Review* 31:1, 15–34.

Lefebvre, A. (2011), 'Human Rights in Deleuze and Bergson's Later Philosophy', *Theory & Event* 14:3.
Lefebvre, A. (2013), *Human Rights as a Way of Life: On Bergson's Political Philosophy*, Stanford: Stanford University Press.
Lenin, V. I. ([1902] 1961), 'What Is to Be Done?'. *Collected Works 5*, Institute of Marxism-Leninism, Moscow: Progress, pp. 347–530.
Lichbach, M. I. and A. S. Zuckerman (1997), *Comparative Politics: Rationality, Culture, and Structure*, Cambridge: Cambridge University Press.
Livingston, P. (2008), 'Review of Being and Event', *Inquiry* 51:2, 217–38.
Livingston, P. M. (2011), *The Politics of Logic: Badiou, Wittgenstein, and the Consequences of Formalism*, London and New York: Routledge.
Lloyd, M. (2005), *Beyond Identity Politics: Feminism, Power & Politics*, London: Sage.
Locke, J. (1841), *An Essay Concerning Human Understanding*, London, Glasgow, Dublin and Sydney: Thomas Tegg.
Locke, J. ([1690] 1988), *Two Treatises of Government and A Letter Concerning Toleration*, New Haven and London: Yale University Press.
Lucretius Carus, T. and L. L. Johnson (1963), *On the Nature of Things*, Fontwell, Sussex: Centaur Press.
Lukács, G. (1966), 'What is Orthodox Marxism?', *International Socialism* 24, 10–14.
Lundy, C. (2013), 'Who Are Our Nomads Today?: Deleuze's Political Ontology and the Revolutionary Problematic', *Deleuze Studies* 7:2, 231–49.
Lundy, C. (2014), 'James Williams, Gilles Deleuze's Philosophy of Time: A Critical Introduction and Guide', *Time & Society* 23:1, 124–7.
Macherey, P. (2004), 'Out of Melancholia: Notes on Judith Butler's *The Psychic Life of Power: Theories in Subjection*', *Rethinking Marxism* 16:1, 7–17.
McIntyre, J. (2000), 'Hume's Passions: Direct and Indirect', *Hume Studies* XXVI:1, 77–96.
Mackay, R. (ed.) (2007), *Collapse*, III, Falmouth: Urbanomic.
MacKenzie, I. (1997), 'Creativity as Criticism: The Philosophical Constructivism of Deleuze and Guattari', *Radical Philosophy* 88, 7–18.
MacKenzie, I. M. (2004), *The Idea of Pure Critique*, New York and London: Continuum.
MacKenzie, I. (2012), 'Events and the Critique of Ideology', *Études Ricoeuriennes/Ricoeur Studies* 3:1, 102–13.

Majewska, E. (2015), 'The Common in the Time of Creative Reproductions: On Gerald Raunig's Factories of Knowledge, Industries of Creativity', *e-flux* 62, unpaginated.
Marx, K. ([1845] 1969), 'Thesis on Feuerbach', in K. Marx and F. Engels, *Marx/Engels Selected Works*, Moscow: Progress, pp. 13–15.
Marx, K. ([1867] 1976), *Capital: A Critique of Political Economy*, Harmondsworth and New York: Penguin.
Massumi, B. (1995), 'The Autonomy of Affect', *Cultural Critique* 31:22, 83–109.
Massumi, B. (2002), *Parables for the Virtual: Movement, Affect, Sensation*, Durham, NC and London: Duke University Press.
Massumi, B. (2015), 'Undigesting Deleuze', *Los Angeles Review of Books*, <https://lareviewofbooks.org/article/undigesting-deleuze/#!> (last accessed 18 October 2018).
Matheron, F. and E. A. Post (1998), 'The Recurrence of the Void in Louis Althusser', *Rethinking Marxism* 10:3, 22–37.
May, T. G. (1991), 'The Politics of Life in the Thought of Gilles Deleuze', *SubStance* 20:3, 24–35.
May, T. (1994), *The Political Philosophy of Poststructuralist Anarchism*, University Park, PA: Pennsylvania State University Press.
May, T. G. (1995), *The Moral Theory of Poststructuralism*, University Park, PA: Pennsylvania State University Press.
Meiborg, C. and S. v. Tuinen (eds) (2016), *Deleuze and the Passions*, New York: Punctum Books.
Meillassoux, Q. (2007a), 'Potentiality and Virtuality', *Collapse* II, Falmouth: Urbanomic, pp. 55–81.
Meillassoux, Q. (2007b), 'Subtraction and Contraction: Deleuze, Immanence, and *Matter and Memory*', in R. Mackay (ed.), *Collapse* III, Falmouth: Urbanomic, pp. 63–107.
Meillassoux, Q. (2008), *After Finitude: An Essay on the Necessity of Contingency*, London and New York: Continuum.
Meillassoux, Q. (2013), *Science Fiction and Extro-Science Fiction*, Minneapolis: Univocal Publishing.
Mill, J. S. (1831), Review of Herschel, *A Preliminary Discourse. Examiner*, 179–80.
Mill, J. S. (1977), *Collected Works of John Stuart Mill*, vols I, VIII and X, London and Toronto: Routledge.
Mill, J. S. ([1859] 2002), *On Liberty*, Dover, MA: Dover Publications.
Misak, C. (2002), *Truth, Politics, Morality: Pragmatism and Deliberation*, London and New York: Routledge.
Montag, W. (2003), *Louis Althusser*, Basingstoke and New York: Palgrave Macmillan.

Montag, W. (2010), 'The Late Althusser: Materialism of the Encounter or Philosophy of Nothing?', *Culture, Theory and Critique* 51:2, 157–70.
Montag, W. (2013a), *Althusser and His Contemporaries: Philosophy's Perpetual War*, Durham, NC and London: Duke University Press.
Montag, W. (2013b), 'Rancière's Lost Object', *Cultural Critique* 83, 139–55.
Montag, W. and T. Stolze (1997), *The New Spinoza*, 11, Minneapolis: University of Minnesota Press.
Morejón, G. (2015), *Differentiation and Distinction: On the Problem of Individuation from Scotus to Deleuze*, Chicago: DePaul University.
Morfino, V. (2005), 'An Althusserian Lexicon', *borderlands e-journal* 4:2.
Morgan, D. (2011), 'Review: The Communist Hypothesis', *Marx & Philosophy Review of Books*, <https://marxandphilosophy.org.uk/reviews/7620_the-communist-hypothesis-review-by-david-morgan/> (last accessed 18 October 2018).
Morton, T. (2016), *Ecology Without Nature*, <http://ecologywithoutnature.blogspot.co.uk> (last accessed 18 October 2016).
Mullarkey, J. (2004), 'Forget the Virtual: Bergson, Actualism, and the Refraction of Reality', *Continental Philosophy Review* 37:4, 469–93.
Nadler, S. (2006), *Spinoza's Ethics: An Introduction*, Cambridge and New York: Cambridge University Press.
Negri, A. (2013), *Spinoza for Our Time: Politics and Postmodernity*, New York: Columbia University Press.
Nietzsche, F. (2014), *Beyond Good and Evil/On the Genealogy of Morality*, Stanford: Stanford University Press.
Norris, C. (2012), *Derrida, Badiou and the Formal Imperative*, London and New York: Continuum.
Osborne, P. (2013), 'More than Everything Žižek's Badiouian Hegel', *Radical Philosophy* 177, 19–31.
O'Sullivan, S. (2008), 'The Production of the New and the Care of the Self', in S. O'Sullivan and S. Zepke (eds), *Deleuze, Guattari and the Production of the New*, London: Bloomsbury, pp. 91–103.
Parmenides (1920), 'On Nature', in J. Burnet (ed.), *Early Greek Philosophy*, London: A. & C. Black.
Pateman, C. (1970), *Participation and Democratic Theory*, Cambridge: Cambridge University Press.
Patton, P. (1984), 'Conceptual Politics and the War-Machine in "Mille Plateaux"', *SubStance* 13:3/4, 61–80.
Patton, P. (2011), 'What is Deleuzean Political Philosophy?', *Crítica Contemporánea. Revista de Teoría Politica* 1, 115–26.
Patton, P. (2016), 'Deleuze and Naturalism', *International Journal of Philosophical Studies* 24:3, 348–64.

Peden, K. (2008), 'Gilles Deleuze: From Hume to Spinoza (An Attempt to Make Good on a Popkin Request)', in J. D. Popkin (ed.), *The Legacies of Richard Popkin*, Dordrecht: Springer Netherlands, pp. 57–70.

Phelps, H. (2013), *Alain Badiou: Between Theology and Anti-Theology*, Durham: Acumen.

Pierce, C. S. (2004), 'How to Make Our Ideas Clear', in F. F. Schmitt (ed.), *Theories of Truth*, Malden, Oxford and Carlton: Blackwell.

Pisters, P. (2011), 'Synaptic Signals: Time Travelling Through the Brain in the Neuro-Image', *Deleuze Studies* 5:2.

Pisters, P. (2012), *The Neuro-Image: A Deleuzian Film-Philosophy of Digital Screen Culture*, Stanford: Stanford University Press.

Plato (1892), *The Dialogues of Plato* 4, Oxford: Oxford University Press.

Plato (2006), *The Being of the Beautiful: Plato's Theaetetus, Sophist, and Statesman*, Chicago and London: University of Chicago Press.

Pollock, P. H. (2012), *The Essentials of Political Analysis*, Washington, DC: CQ Press.

Porter, R. (2006), *Ideology: Contemporary Social, Political and Cultural Theory*, Cardiff: University of Wales Press.

Porter, R. (2009), *Deleuze and Guattari: Aesthetics and Politics*, Cardiff: University of Wales Press.

Power, N. (2006), 'Towards an Anthropology of Infinitude: Badiou and the Political Subject', in P. Ashton, A. J. Bartlett and J. Clemens (eds), *The Praxis of Alain Badiou*, Melbourne: re. Press.

Protevi, J. (2009), *Political Affect: Connecting the Social and the Somatic*, Minneapolis and London: University of Minnesota Press.

Protevi, J. (2010), 'Adding Deleuze to the Mix', *Phenomenology and the Cognitive Sciences* 9, 417–36.

Quinton, A. (1989), *Utilitarian Ethics*, London: Duckworth.

Rancière, J. ([1974] 2011), *Althusser's Lesson*, London and New York: Continuum.

Raunig, G. (2013), *Factories of Knowledge, Industries of Creativity*, Cambridge, MA: Semiotext(e)/Intervention.

Reed, J. (2005), 'Althusser and Hume: A Materialist Encounter', in S. H. Daniel (ed.), *Current Continental Theory and Modern Philosophy*, Evanston, IL: Northwestern University Press.

Resch, R. P. (1992), *Althusser and the Renewal of Marxist Social Theory*, Berkeley, Los Angeles and Oxford: University of California Press.

Reynolds, J. (2008), 'Transcendental Priority and Deleuzian Normativity: A Reply to James Williams', *Deleuze Studies* 2:1, 101–8.

Ricoeur, P. (1994), 'Althusser's Theory of Ideology', in G. Elliott (ed.), *Althusser: A Critical Reader*, Oxford and Cambridge, MA: Blackwell.

Roberts, B. (2016), 'An "Exemplary Contemporary Technical Object": Thinking Cinema Between Hansen and Stiegler', *New Formations* 88, 88–104.
Robson, J. M. (1968), *The Improvement of Mankind: the Social and Political Thought of John Stuart Mill*, Toronto: University of Toronto Press, and London: Routledge and K. Paul.
Roffe, J. (2017), 'Practising Philosophy', in S. Attiwill, T. Bird, A. Eckersley and J. Roffe (eds), *Practising with Deleuze: Design, Dance, Art, Writing, Philosophy*, Edinburgh: Edinburgh University Press, pp. 183–98.
Rosen, F. (2013), *Mill*, Oxford: Oxford University Press.
Ruddick, S. (2010), 'The Politics of Affect: Spinoza in the Work of Negri and Deleuze', *Theory, Culture & Society* 27:4, 21–45.
Ryder, A. (2013), 'Badiou's Materialist Reinvention of the Kantian Subject', *Badiou Studies* 2:1: 38–59.
Sacilotto, D. (2013), 'Towards a Materialist Rationalism: Plato, Hegel, Badiou', *Badiou Studies* 2:1, 60–98.
Sayers, S. (2003), *Marxism and Human Nature*, London and New York: Routledge.
Schmitt, C. (1996), *The Concept of the Political*, Chicago: University of Chicago Press.
Sibertin-Blanc, G. (2016), *State and Politics: Deleuze and Guattari on Marx*, South Pasadena: Semiotext(e).
Smith, D. W. (2006), 'Axiomatics and Problematics as Two Modes of Formalisation: Deleuze's Epistemology of Mathematics', in S. B. Duffy (ed.), *Virtual Mathematics: The Logic of Difference*, Bolton: Clinamen.
Smith, D. W. (2007), 'Deleuze and the Question of Desire: Toward an Immanent Theory of Ethics', *Parrhesia* 2, 66–78.
Smith, D. W. (2008), 'The Conditions of the New', *Deleuze Studies* 1:1, 1–21.
Smith, D. W. (2013), 'Temporality and Truth', *Deleuze Studies* 7:3, 377–89.
Somers-Hall, H. (2011), 'Time Out of Joint: Hamlet and the Pure Form of Time', *Deleuze Studies* 5: supplement, 56–76.
Spinoza, B. ([1677] 1992), *Ethics: Treatise on The Emendation of the Intellect and Selected Letters*, Indianapolis and Cambridge: Hackett.
Steinberger, P. J. (2002), 'Hobbesian Resistance', *American Journal of Political Science* 46:4, 856–65.
Stengers, I. (2011), 'Wondering about Materialism', in L. R. Bryant, N. Srnicek and G. Harman (eds), *The Speculative Turn: Continental Materialism and Realism*, Melbourne: re.press, pp. 268–380.
Stiegler, B. (1998), *Technics and Time, 1: The Fault of Epimetheus*, Stanford: Stanford University Press.

Stiegler, B. (2010), *For a New Critique of Political Economy*, Cambridge and Malden: Polity.
Stolze, T. (1998), 'Deleuze and Althusser: Flirting with Structuralism', *Rethinking Marxism* 10:3, 51–63.
Swenson, E. (2015), 'The Materialities of Place Making in the Ancient Andes: A Critical Appraisal of the Ontological Turn in Archaeological Interpretation', *Journal of Archaeological Method and Theory* 22:3, 677–712.
Ten, C. L. (1980), *Mill on Liberty*, Oxford: Clarendon Press and New York: Oxford University Press.
Thompson, E. P. (1978), *The Poverty of Theory: And Other Essays*, London: Merlin Press.
Trott, A. (2011), 'The Truth of Politics in Alain Badiou: "There is Only One World"', *Parrhesia* 12, 82–93.
Uhlmann, A. (1996), 'To Have Done with Judgement: Beckett and Deleuze', *SubStance* 25:3, 110–31.
Voss, D. (2013a), *Conditions of Thought: Deleuze and the Transcendental Ideas*, Edinburgh: Edinburgh University Press.
Voss, D. (2013b), 'Deleuze's Third Synthesis of Time', *Deleuze Studies* 7:2, 194–216.
Warren, M. E. (2007), 'Institutionalizing Deliberative Democracy', *Deliberation, Participation and Democracy*, Basingstoke: Palgrave Macmillan, pp. 272–88.
Widder, N. (2003), 'Thought after Dialectics: Deleuze's Ontology of Sense', *The Southern Journal of Philosophy* 41:3, 451–76.
Widder, N. (2009), 'John Duns Scotus', in G. Jones and J. Roffe (eds), *Deleuze's Philosophical Lineage*, Edinburgh: Edinburgh University Press.
Widder, N. (2012), *Political Theory after Deleuze*, London and New York: Bloomsbury.
Williams, C. (2001), *Contemporary French Philosophy: Modernity and the Persistence of the Subject*, London: Continuum.
Williams, C. (2002), 'Ideology and Imaginary: Returning to Althusser', in I. MacKenzie and S. Malesevic (eds), *Ideology after Poststructuralism*, London and Sterling, VA: Pluto Press.
Williams, C. (2013), 'Althusser and Spinoza: the enigma of the subject', in K. Diefenbach, S. R. Farris, G. Kirn and P. Thomas (eds), *Encountering Althusser: Politics and Materialism in Contemporary Radical Thought*, London, New Delhi, New York and Sydney: Bloomsbury.
Williams, J. (2005), *The Transversal Thought of Gilles Deleuze: Encounters and Influences*, Manchester: Clinamen Press.

Williams, J. (2008), 'Correspondence: Why Deleuze Doesn't Blow the Actual on Virtual Priority. A Rejoinder to Jack Reynolds', *Deleuze Studies* 2:1, 97–100.
Williams, J. (2011), *Gilles Deleuze's Philosophy of Time: A Critical Introduction and Guide*, Edinburgh: Edinburgh University Press.
Williams, J. (2013), *Gilles Deleuze's Difference and Repetition: A Critical Introduction and Guide*, Edinburgh: Edinburgh University Press.
Williams, J. (2015), 'Pragmatism in Pursuit of the Sign', in S. Bowden, S. Bignall and P. Patton (eds), *Deleuze and Pragmatism*, Abingdon and New York: Routledge.
Wittgenstein, L. ([1953] 2001), *Philosophical Investigations*, Oxford: Blackwell.
Zalloua, Z. (2015), 'On Meillassoux's "Transparent Cage": Speculative Realism and Its Discontents', *symploke* 23:1–2, 393–409.
Žižek, S. (2000), *The Ticklish Subject*, London and New York: Verso.
Žižek, S. (2012a), *Less Than Nothing: Hegel and the Shadow of Dialectical Materialism*, London: Verso Books.
Žižek, S. (2012b), *Organs without Bodies: On Deleuze and Consequences*, London and New York: Routledge.

Index

Althusser, Louis
  aleatory materialism,
    72–3, 103–6, 119n43
  ancestral statement, 127,
    134–5
  anti-humanism, 68–72,
    95–102
  Badiou, relationship to,
    65–6
  class struggle, 76–9,
    114n20
  Deleuze, relationship to,
    66–7
  denegation, 116n31
  discourse, 97–102, 159
  encounter, 72–3, 81–3
  general/regional theory,
    97–101, 103, 106
  Hegel, criticism of, 74–5
  historical materialism, 78,
    119n43
  Hume, suture to, 91, 101
  ideology, 112n11, 132–3
    ideological interpellation,
      39–42, 115n25, 132
  Institutional State
    Apparatus, 39, 82,
    115n25, 131–3
  philosophy, 76–81, 96,
    144–6
  relations of production,
    reproduction of, 39,
    133
  subject, 100, 105–6;
    see also Spinoza,
    Baruch, perseverance in
    being
  time, 83–6, 104
  various readings of,
    68–72
atomism, 72, 158, 169–70n31
authority, 27–8, 183–4

Badiou, Alain
  being *qua* being,
    16–22, 25
  commitment, 3
  counting operation,
    18–20, 57n34, 60n49;
    see also set theory

Deleuze (disagreement with), 54n22
doxa, 18–22, 42–4, 55n25, 62n60; see also Badiou, sophistry
formalisation, 20, 23, 56, 229; see also ontologies, formalism
human condition, 33
inconsistent multiplicity, 16, 20, 57
mathematics
  grand/little style of, 25–6
  scriptural materiality, 25, 154
  use of, 24–7
Maoism, 11, 46, 65, 122
marks, 25–6; see also Badiou, Alain, mathematics, scriptural materiality
metaontology, 15–16, 20–3, 59n44
Parliamentary government, 11–13, 51n10
rupture, 17–20, 58–9n38
science and mathematics, relationship between, 61n56
sophistry, 11–15, 20–2, 50–1n9; see also Badiou, doxa
subject, 33–4, 144
subtraction, 17–19, 43,
totalisation, 19, 54–5n22, 55n24; see also mathematics, totalisation
truth, 11–12, 15–27, 31–47

Balibar, Étienne, 65–70
Bergson, Henri, 148–53, 171n35, 177

Chambers, Samuel, 130–4, 143–5,
  Butler, criticism of, 131–4, 164n11
  social formation, 141–5, 159, 166n23
chance, 33, 135, 138–40
contradiction, 14, 74, 100, 134
creativity, 92, 185–7, 200–2

Deleuze, Gilles
  Althusser, contrast with, 185
  Badiou, contrast with, 190–1, 197–8
  Bergson, contrast with, 149–52
  calculus, use of, 153–6
  experimentation, 179, 201–2
  individual, 147–9, 152–3, 165n17
  individuation, 188, 190–1, 199–201; see also series
  institutions, 178
  Kant, contrast with, 152–3, 183–4
  learning, 182, 199; see also Mill, John Stuart, ethology
  mediation, 183–8, 199–200

Deleuze, Gilles (*cont.*)
  morality, criticism of, 181
  ontology, 169n30,
    169–70n31, 177–8
  philosophy, idea of, 77–8
  profundity, 197
  time, synthesis of, 146–50,
    154–60, 171n36, 184
Dewey, John, 107–9
dogma, 12–13, 23–4, 51n14,
  102–7, 178–81
Douzinas, Costas, 3, 216,
  222
dyad, 22, 42–5

empiricism, 26, 85–7,
  114n19, 138–9
Epicurus, 46; *see also*
  atomism
epistemology, 130–1,
  142–5
ethics, 38–41, 175–8,
  194–5
  morality, 177–80
  see also Mill, John Stuart,
  ethology
event, 17–19, 34–41,
  46–7, 94
  evental site, 18–20

Foucault, 16–17, 54n20

Hallward, Peter, 42–4, 136–8,
  168n27
Hobbes, Thomas, 12–13,
  51n12

Hume, David, 86–93, 95–6,
  120–1
  association, principle of,
    88–91, 118n39, 121n50
  imagination, 90–1
  institution, 93–4, 117n34
  passions, 116–17n33
  relationality, 88–9, 95, 106

identity, 39–40, 169n30
indifference, 169n30

joy, 109
judgement, 13, 30–2, 183–4,
  187–90

Kant, Immanuel, 28–32,
  151–4
Kropotkin, Peter, 48

Lacan, Jacques, 19–20
Livingston, Paul, 10
Locke, John, 12–13, 51n13

MacKenzie, Iain, 159–60,
  186–7, 199–200
Marx, Karl, 143–4, 210
  revolutionary practice, 2
mathematics
  consistency, 10, 36, 40, 50n7
  differential relation, 98–102,
    152–7, 201
  Russel's Paradox, 50n7
  totalisation, 10, 49n5,
    50n7
  see also set theory

Meillassoux, Quentin, 27–8,
    124–41, 162–3n4
  anhypothetical principle,
    134
  contingency, necessity of,
    76, 128–30, 135–41
  correlationism, 27, 124–9,
    162–3n4
  factiality, principle of,
    137–9, 165
  facticity, principle of,
    134–5, 164n12
  Hume's problem, 127–30,
    140
  resistance, according to,
    137–9
  speculation, 123–6, 129–30,
    134–41
  totalisation of natural
    laws, 135–6;
    see also mathematics,
    totalisation
Mill, John Stuart
  Bentham, contrast with,
    190, 193, 205n18
  ethology, 192–3, 196–200
  genius, 192, 194–200, 213
  happiness, 193
  self-regarding conduct,
    190, 205n15
Montag, Warren, 69–72,
    80–3

ontologies
  formalism, 20, 23–6, 50n7,
    134–9, 178
  idealism, 45, 80–8, 94–5,
    158–62
  naturalism, 61–2n56
  rationalism, 71, 79–80n,
    114n19
  realism see speculation

Parmenides, 15–18, 45,
    52–3n18, 62n60
Plato, 24, 50n9
  laws of thought, 45
  neo-Platonism, 3

relative autonomy, 74–5,
    79–81, 84
resistance, 45–6, 48–9,
    137–9, 201–2
  activist, 142–7, 177, 221
Rousseau, Jean-Jacques,
    117–18n35

Sacilotto, Daniel, 20–3
series, 83–7, 108–9, 155–6,
    181–2; see also Deleuze,
    Gilles, calculus, use of
  persistence, 81–4, 90, 101–4
  reciprocal determination,
    158
set theory, 52n19
  axiom, 24–8, 42–4, 136
  of choice, 57–8n34
  Cantor, 57n34
  Fraenkel, Abraham, 53
  Gödel, Kurt, 10
  incompleteness theorem, 10
  Zermelo, Ernst, 57n34

Spinoza, Baruch, 35–7,
    54–5n22
    perseverance in being, 35–7
Stiegler, Bernard, 117n34

Williams, James, 146–8,
    152–6, 167n26

Žižek, Slavoj, 38–42, 47

EU representative:
Easy Access System Europe
Mustamäe tee 50, 10621 Tallinn, Estonia
Gpsr.requests@easproject.com

www.ingramcontent.com/pod-product-compliance
Lightning Source LLC
Chambersburg PA
CBHW070345240426
43671CB00013BA/2415